Free Expression and Censorship in America

FREE EXPRESSION AND CENSORSHIP IN AMERICA

An Encyclopedia

HERBERT N. FOERSTEL

Ⓖ Ⓟ

Greenwood Press
Westport, Connecticut • London

363.3/09
Foe

Library of Congress Cataloging-in-Publication Data

Foerstel, Herbert N.
　　Free expression and censorship in America : an encyclopedia /
Herbert N. Foerstel.
　　　　p. cm.
　　Includes bibliographical references and index.
　　ISBN 0–313–29231–0 (alk. paper)
　　　1. Censorship—United States—Encyclopedias. 2. Freedom of
speech—United States—Encyclopedias. I. Title.
Z658.U5F644 1997
363.3′1′0973—dc20　　96–42157

British Library Cataloguing in Publication Data is available.

Library of Congress Catalog Card Number: 96–42157
ISBN: 0–313–29231–0

First published in 1997

Greenwood Press, 88 Post Road West, Westport, CT 06881
An imprint of Greenwood Publishing Group, Inc.

Printed in the United States of America

The paper used in this book complies with the
Permanent Paper Standard issued by the National
Information Standards Organization (Z39.48–1984).

10 9 8 7 6 5 4 3 2 1

CONTENTS

INTRODUCTION

American history is replete with spectacular advances in free expression, the most notable being the drafting of the First Amendment to the Constitution, but it has a parallel record of censorship and secrecy. In the continuing struggle over free speech and open access to information, the censors have always represented themselves as the ultimate protectors of constitutional freedoms, claiming that free expression and the "right to know" threaten the very survival of American democracy, making it vulnerable to aggression from without and moral decay from within. Thus will the permissive society lose the very freedoms it cherishes. First Amendment advocates prefer the view of its author, James Madison, who proclaimed, "A popular government without popular information or a means of acquiring it is but a prologue to a farce or a tragedy or perhaps both."

Throughout American history, God and country have been invoked to justify not only America's most glorious adventures, but mindless acts of thought control as well. Zealots in defense of patriotism and "American values" have frequently defined the limits of free expression for all Americans. The broad application of the theory of seditious libel in American colonial history survived even the First Amendment to persecute and prosecute Americans for their political opinions. The patriotic defense of America's liberty from perceived foreign threats generated a national security apparatus that cherished secrecy above all things, and that structure endures today.

Sedition and secularism have long been represented as the twin pillars that threaten America's political and spiritual survival, and during much of the twentieth century, "godless communism" was seen as the source of both dangers. A host of laws against seditious and "un-American" activities were passed and prosecuted during the Red Scare surrounding World War I and the Cold War following World War II. Despite the end of the Cold War, much of the national security state and its secrecy apparatus remains in place, but the permissiveness of liberal society, with its tolerance for sinful thoughts and images, has replaced communism as the primary enemy within.

Government remains the most formidable censor, even in the post–Cold War world. Stamping out indecency has become a congressional imperative as politicians of both parties work at censoring the arts, the broadcast media, and even the Internet. Indecent expression, unlike obscenity, is protected speech, yet it has been successfully banned through extralegal, bureaucratic action by the National Endowment for the Arts (NEA) and the Federal Communications Commission (FCC). Their definition of indecency has been arbitrary and capricious. The NEA has relied on the taxpayers' reluctance to fund controversial art, while the FCC has exploited the fear that unsupervised children might hear something inappropriate on the airwaves. In both cases the result has been a lowest-common-denominator approach to acceptable expression. The sanitizing of the Internet was accomplished by a simplistic extension of the rules governing the broadcast media. In the national security area, military secrets are gradually being replaced by economic secrets as the federal government applies the security classification system or export controls to the entire range of high technology. Most disturbing is the existence of a systematic, coordinated interagency effort to prevent access to unclassified information. This has spawned a variety of "sensitive but unclassified" categories of government-controlled information.

The 1980s celebrated self-interest through a combination of social cynicism and capitalist idealism. The 1990s have brought the harsh light of day back to the political scene, revealing long-ignored budget deficits, lowered expectations, and a general unease with society and its institutions. Politicians offer few convincing explanations for America's plight and see no reliable solutions, but scapegoats abound. The arts and the mass media are increasingly seen as the cause of social instability, rather than a reflection of it. The time is right for thought control.

The challenges to freedom of expression from the political right, including religious fundamentalist organizations, have been so long-standing and persistent that they are simply taken for granted today as a kind of background noise against which the signals of personal and social expression are communicated. The infrequency of censorship from the left has been attributed to the liberal's intolerance for intolerance, an attitude that has ironically produced a new strain of censorship: political correctness.

Because censorship from the left is something of an oddity, it is far more newsworthy than the right wing's routine forays against objectionable speech, and the media have gleefully exploited the current flap over political correctness. Another reason for the popular interest in this phenomenon is the non-partisan nature of the criticism. It is difficult to recall a First Amendment conflict where conservatives led the charge against censorship, followed dutifully by liberals. Let us hope that the future brings broader political cooperation in protecting free expression.

As a First Amendment advocate, I make no pretense of support for secrecy and censorship, but the ideal of an open society has a power and appeal that can be communicated in an honest and direct narrative. My assumption is that whenever the alleged protection of the rights of Americans prevents their exercise, there must be fundamental and principled conflict. This encyclopedia chronicles that conflict, presenting some of its prominent players and analyzing its recurring themes. The scope of coverage is historical, with an emphasis on the twentieth century. The most controversial political topics of the 1990s—abortion, homosexuality, immigration, indecency in the arts and media, the Internet, campaign financing, and others—all have prominent First Amendment aspects and are covered in detail in this work. Articles are heavily researched but readable essays, intended for more than brief reference consultation. Coverage of all topics is current through 1996. The biographies presented are unavoidably selective. Some—for example, Howard Stern, Danny Goldberg, and Frank Zappa—are "pop" figures whose First Amendment struggles shed light on our broader modern culture, but most are traditional heroes of free expression.

When material within the alphabetically arranged articles is quoted or heavily derived from other sources, it is followed by the full source citation, except for legal citations, which give case name and year only. General sources or recommended readings are listed at the end of each article under "References," and a Selected Bibliography on secrecy and censorship follows the main body of the book. A Table of Cases contains full legal citations and page references for all cases discussed or quoted, and a subject index provides detailed topical access.

A

ABORTION The subject of abortion has been a focus of free-speech controversy for many years. In the late nineteenth century, Anthony Comstock made a name for himself and his Society for the Suppression of Vice by confiscating printed material on sex, birth control, and abortion. In the early twentieth century, the Post Office banned the publications of Margaret Sanger from the mails because they spoke of birth control and abortion. Later, as family planning became a respectable part of middle-class American life, abortion became a legitimate aspect of public discussion and legal debate.

The Supreme Court's 1973 *Roe v. Wade* decision legalizing a woman's right to an abortion was followed by *Bigelow v. Virginia* (1976), which ruled unconstitutional a Virginia statute prohibiting any publication, lecture, or advertisement encouraging the procurement of an abortion. These decisions did not end the national debate, but only politicized it. Republican administrations under Presidents Reagan and Bush imposed a gag rule on any abortion counseling in federally supported clinics, a limitation on medical speech that was widely regarded as unconstitutional. Doctors were not even allowed to hand a patient the Yellow Pages, because they included listings of clinics that provide abortions. Nonetheless, in *Rust v. Sullivan* (1991), the Supreme Court voted 5–4 to uphold the regulations that required doctors in federally funded family-planning programs to advise pregnant women about the option of childbirth, to withhold all discussion of the option of abortion, and to provide a one-sided pro-life referral list for prenatal care. The Court majority that upheld these regulations was, with the exception of Justice Byron White, appointed by the Presidents under whose administrations the regulations were formulated.

The First Amendment concerns aroused by *Rust* went beyond the area of abortion. These fears were substantiated when the Bush administration's Justice Department relied on *Rust* to argue that government officials have unlimited discretion to dictate the content of publicly funded art. In 1991, after a Democratic Congress passed legislation removing the abortion gag order from federally funded clinics, President George Bush vetoed the bill. But on November 3, 1992, a federal appeals court in Washington blocked the enforcement of the policy, saying that the Bush administration had failed to seek public comment on it. Finally, in January 1993, on the anniversary of the *Roe v. Wade* decision, President Clinton issued an order rescinding the ban on abortion counseling and four other policies from the Reagan and Bush administrations that discouraged abortions. Family planners and First Amendment groups hailed the action as the end of a five-year effort by federal authorities to censor information offered to low-income clients. The 1995 Contract with America propounded by the new Republican Congress promised to restore the abortion gag order, but the closest the Republicans have come to fulfilling that promise was the inclusion of a provision in the 1996 Telecommunications Act that would prohibit the use of the Internet to communicate information about abortion.

In the meantime, the increasingly violent antiabortion protests around the country raised public and political concern. Between 1985 and 1994, there were almost five hundred attempts to physically block access to abortion clinics, resulting in more than one thousand violent incidents, including the 1993 murder of a doctor outside a Florida clinic. This pattern of organized, violent protest soon produced judicial and legislative initiatives that challenged the First Amendment rights of the antiabortion protesters. The National Organization for Women (NOW) attempted to sue the more extreme protest groups under the Racketeer Influenced and Corrupt Organizations Act (RICO). The case, *National Organization for Women v. Scheidler*, was dismissed in federal court and by the U.S. Court of Appeals for the Seventh Circuit on the grounds that "non-economic" crimes were outside the bounds of RICO. NOW appealed to the Supreme Court, and in January 1994 the Court unanimously ruled that RICO could be used against protesters who conspired to shut down abortion clinics. Writing for the Court, Chief Justice William Rehnquist did not address the First Amendment claims of *Scheidler*, but Justice David Souter, who wrote a concurring opinion, stressed that the Court was not barring First Amendment challenges to RICO's use in particular cases. "I think it prudent to notice that RICO actions could deter protected advocacy and to caution courts applying RICO to bear in mind the First Amendment interests that could be at stake," concluded Souter, joined by Justice Anthony Kennedy.

Within months of its RICO decision, the Supreme Court was faced with another important decision concerning the First Amendment rights of antiabortion protesters. In *Madsen v. Women's Health Center*, the Court addressed a Florida case in which a trial judge had forbidden demonstrations within thirty-six feet of abortion clinic property, had prohibited contact with clients within three hundred feet of clinic property, and had banned "approaching, congregating, picketing, patrolling, [or] demonstrating" within three hundred feet of the home of any clinic personnel. In upholding the restraints on protesters, the Florida Supreme Court had said, "While the First Amendment confers on each citizen a powerful right to express oneself, it gives the picketer no boon to jeopardize the health, safety, and rights of others."

Nonetheless, the U.S. Court of Appeals for the Eleventh Circuit ruled that the injunction was an unconstitutional restriction on speech in a public forum, and the issue was sent to the Supreme Court. Mathew Staver, the lawyer representing Madsen and the other protesters, said, "Clearly the government may not grant the use of a forum [that is, the public streets and sidewalks] to people whose views it finds acceptable but deny use to those wishing to express less favorable or more controversial views." Talbot D'Alemberte, representing the clinic, argued in court papers, "Activities such as inhibiting access to medical facilities, blocking roadways, threatening clinic workers and intentionally frightening clinic patients before and during surgery do not constitute expression protected by the First Amendment" ("Limit on Protests at Abortion Clinic Reaches Top Court," *Washington Post*, April 24, 1994, p. A13).

On June 31, 1994, the Court rendered a judgment that upheld some parts of the injunction while disallowing others. In a 6–3 opinion delivered by Chief Justice Rehnquist, the Court affirmed the right of judges to prevent demonstrators from coming within thirty-six feet of a clinic and to restrain protesters from chanting, shouting, or making other loud noises within earshot of patients during the clinic's morning surgical and recovery hours. On the other hand, the Court said that preventing protesters from approaching patients within three hundred feet of a clinic hampered the First Amendment rights of demonstrators. Rehnquist wrote, "The First Amendment does not demand that patients at a medical facility undertake Herculean efforts to escape the cacophony of political protests." In his dissent, Justice Antonin Scalia said that the Court's decision "ought to give all friends of liberty great concern."

Just one month before the Court's opinion in *Madsen v. Women's Health Center*, President Clinton had signed the Freedom of Access to Clinic Entrances Act, making it a federal crime to physically block access to clinics, damage their property, or injure or intimidate patients and staff. Violators would face a maximum of six months in jail and a $10,000 fine for a first nonviolent offense and up to eighteen months in jail and a $25,000 fine for subsequent physical obstructions. Violent conduct, such as arson or bomb-ings, would face harsher penalties.

Representative Jim Bunning (R-Ky.) said that the Freedom of Access bill was designed to prevent pro-life protest and make pro-life convictions a thought crime. President Clinton said, "This bill is designed to eliminate violence and coercion. It is not a strike against the First Amendment" ("President Signs Clinic Access Law," *Washington Post*, May 27, 1994, p. A10). In March 1996, the Supreme Court announced that it would revisit the question of limiting antiabortion demonstrations in the case of *Pro-Choice Network of Western New York v. Schenck* (N.Y. 1995) to be heard during the 1996–97 term.

REFERENCE: U.S. Senate Subcommittee on the Constitution of the Committee on the Judiciary, *First Amendment Implications of the Rust v. Sullivan Decision: Hearing before the Subcommittee on the Constitution of the Committee on the Judiciary*, 102nd Cong., 1st sess., July 30, 1991.

ABRAMS, FLOYD, 1936–   Floyd Abrams has been widely regarded as America's foremost First Amendment lawyer, but he was not always so. He grew up in Queens, New York, the son of a successful businessman. While studying government at Cornell University, he wrote his senior thesis on the need for stricter control over press coverage of court proceedings. Years later he would argue for virtually unlimited press access to the courts, including television coverage. "A lot of the most important events in our country's life come to court in one form or another," said Abrams. "To strip the public of the benefits of the debate that surrounds those judicial proceedings is to strip them of the knowledge they need to have as citizens" (Jeanie Kasindorf, "The Rights Stuff," *New York*, December 21, 1992, p. 116).

After Cornell, Abrams went on to Yale Law School, then spent two years clerking for a U.S. district court judge before joining large corporate-law firm, Cahill, Gordon, and Reindel. At Cahill he was an obscure junior partner doing corporate litigation until 1968, when he began work on some cases for NBC, including the case of a TV reporter who refused to reveal the name of a source to a grand jury. In 1970, the Supreme Court agreed to hear that case, along with a similar case concerning a *New York Times* reporter. At about that time, President Nixon's Attorney General, John Mitchell, was demanding that the *Times* refrain from publishing the *Pentagon Papers*. The *Times* asked Abrams to come in on the *Pentagon Papers* case, and his life has never been the same since.

Abrams said that the *Pentagon Papers* case radicalized his view of the First Amendment, and in the ensuing years, he filed briefs in more than fifty Supreme Court cases and defended reporters and news organizations in a wide variety of court cases. But Abrams also took his defense of the First Amendment directly to the public through lectures, media appear-ances, and articles. He has been the First Amendment point man in court-room and public debates on the major issues of the day. In 1990, he asked a federal judge to rule that the antiobscenity pledge required by the National Endowment for the Arts was unconstitutional. In 1991, he pushed for TV cameras in all of the nation's courts. In 1992, he represented Nina Totenberg of National Public Radio, who was being pressured to reveal her sources concerning sexual harassment charges by Anita Hill against Supreme Court nominee Clarence Thomas. In 1993, he argued against forced censorship of violence on TV. In 1994, he debated feminist Catharine MacKinnon on the issue of pornography. Whenever a threat to the First Amendment arises, Floyd Abrams does battle.

REFERENCE: *Essential Liberty: First Amendment Battles for a Free Press.* Preface by Joan Kopper; Introduction by Harrison F. Salisbury; Essays by Francis Wilkinson; Afterword by Floyd Abrams. New York, Columbia University Graduate School of Journalism, 1992.

ACCURACY IN MEDIA   Accuracy in Media (AIM) is a conservative organization of business professionals and Republican activists that functions as a news-media watchdog against "liberal bias." Founded in 1969 by Reed Irvine, its executive director, AIM seeks out liberal or antibusiness reporting in the media and presents the opposing viewpoint through media interviews, letters to the editor, or its regular publications and radio shows. AIM airs a daily three-minute radio show, "Media Monitor," on over two hundred stations throughout the nation. It also publishes the semimonthly *AIM Report*, which documents examples of alleged liberal bias or inaccuracy in news stories and then reports these stories from a conservative perspective. AIM is located at 1275 K Street, NW, Suite 1150, Washington, DC 20005.

REFERENCE: John B. Harer, *Intellectual Freedom: A Reference Handbook*, Santa Barbara, ABC-CLIO, 1992.

AGGREGATE THEORY   *See* **MOSAIC THEORY.**

AMERICAN CIVIL LIBERTIES UNION   The American Civil Liberties Union (ACLU) is a nonprofit, nonpartisan public interest organization devoted to protecting the civil liberties of all Americans. Its mission is to preserve the Bill of Rights for each new generation of Americans. It defends the right of people to express their views, not the views that they express.

The ACLU is a fifty–state network of affiliate offices in most major cities, more than three hundred chapters in smaller towns, and regional offices in Denver and Atlanta. Its national office is in New York City, aided by a legislative office in Washington, D.C. It is governed by an eighty-four-member Board of Directors that has one representative from each state affiliate and thirty at-large members elected by all ACLU members within a state. The ACLU has a number of national projects devoted to specific issues: AIDS, arts censorship, capital punishment, children's rights, education reform, lesbian and gay rights, immigrants' rights, national security, privacy and technology, religious freedom, voting rights, women's rights, and workplace rights. The ACLU's more than sixty staff attorneys collaborate with more than two thousand volunteer attorneys in handling almost six thousand cases annually, making it the largest public interest law firm in the nation. Indeed, the ACLU appears before the U.S. Supreme Court more than any other organization except the Department of Justice.

When Roger Baldwin founded the organization in 1920, American citizens were being jailed for expressing antiwar views and the U.S. Attorney General was conducting raids on aliens suspected of holding "unorthodox" beliefs. Racial segregation and violence against blacks were commonplace, and sex discrimination was institutionalized. Constitutional rights were routinely denied to homosexuals, the poor, prisoners, mental patients, and a host of other powerless groups. The U.S. Supreme Court had yet to uphold a single free-speech claim under the First Amendment.

In its first year of existence, the ACLU worked to stop the deportation of aliens for their political beliefs, supported the rights of trade unions to meet and organize, and secured the release of hundreds of prisoners sentenced during World War I for expressing antiwar opinions. Subsequent ACLU highlights included the initiation of the 1925 Scopes case challenging Tennessee's antievolution law, support for the 1933 legal battle that allowed James Joyce's *Ulysses* into the United States, and the 1939 challenge of Jersey City Mayor Frank Hague's right to deny free speech to anyone he considered "radical." The U.S. Supreme Court subsequently ruled that Jersey City's public streets and parks belonged to the people, not Mayor Hague.

In 1942, the ACLU opposed the incarceration of Japanese Americans in concentration camps, calling it "the worst single wholesale violation of civil rights of American citizens in our history." Throughout the 1950s, the ACLU fought a running battle against the government's Cold War loyalty-security program. In 1954, the ACLU joined the legal battle against segregation that resulted in the Supreme Court's *Brown v. Board of Education* ruling. In a variety of ways and places around the country, the ACLU supported the sit-ins and peaceful demonstrations of the civil rights movement.

In 1973, the ACLU was the first national organization to call for the impeachment of President Richard Nixon. In 1981, fifty-six years after the Scopes trial, it successfully challenged an Arkansas statute that required the teaching of biblical creation as a "scientific alternative" to evolution. In 1982, the ACLU successfully lobbied for renewal of the Voting Rights Act of 1965, and in 1987, it changed its policy of neutrality on Supreme Court nominees by opposing the nomination of Judge Robert Bork, saying that he posed an extraordinary threat to constitutional liberties.

Despite, or perhaps because of, public attacks on the ACLU from President George Bush in 1989, the organization added many new members during the Bush administration. ACLU membership was about 150,000 at the end of the 1970s, 200,000 after Reagan's election, and jumped to 300,000 by 1991.

In 1991, after fifteen-year president Norman Dorsen announced that he would not seek another term, Nadine Strossen won the election to become the first female president of the ACLU. She sought to broaden the ACLU's emphasis beyond litigation to lobbying and public education and led the way in opposing campus speech codes, antipornography legislation, school-prayer statutes, and voter initiatives that threatened gay rights.

The most recent and prominent ACLU action was *ACLU v. Reno* (1996), a challenge to the Communications Decency Act, which criminalizes "indecent" communications on the Internet. Ira Glasser, executive director of the ACLU, said, "This is a critical case; nothing less than the future of free expression in the United States is at stake" (*ACLU Spotlight*, Spring 1996, p. 2). The ACLU's national office is located at 132 W. 43rd Street, New York, New York 10036.

REFERENCES: William A. Donohue, *The Politics of the American Civil Liberties Union*, New Brunswick, Transaction Books, 1985; Joel M. Gora, David Goldberger, Gary M. Stern, Morton H. Halperin, *The Right to Protest: The Basic ACLU Guide to Free Expression*, Carbondale, Southern Illinois University Press, 1991.

AMERICAN FAMILY ASSOCIATION   The American Family Association (AFA), formerly the National Federation of Decency, was founded in 1977 to foster a biblical sense of decency in American society by influencing the content of television and radio programs. The AFA consists of over 560 grass-roots organizations throughout the United States. Directed by Reverend Donald E. Wildmon and a staff of twenty-five, the AFA conducts activities such as local letter-writing campaigns to radio and TV networks, broadcasters, and sponsors, protesting sex, violence and profanity in broadcast programming.

The AFA publishes the *AFA Journal*, a monthly report that describes the organization's efforts to improve family programming and examines issues and concerns about the content of television broadcasting. The AFA is located at P.O. Drawer 2440, Tupelo, MS 38803.

REFERENCE: John B. Harer, *Intellectual Freedom: A Reference Handbook*, Santa Barbara, ABC-CLIO, 1992.

ARMSTRONG, SCOTT, 1945–   Scott Armstrong is an investigative journalist and scholar whose career has been distinguished by an unswerving commitment to open government. From 1976 to 1985, Armstrong was a staff writer for the *Washington Post*. He and Bob Woodward coauthored *The Brethren*, an account of the inner workings of the Supreme Court from 1969 through 1976. Armstrong also served as a senior investigator for the Senate Watergate Committee, and his interviews revealed the Nixon White House taping system, which eventually led to Nixon's demise.

In 1985, Armstrong founded the National Security Archive, a nonprofit research institute that provides declassified government information to journalists, scholars, congressional staff, public officials, and the general public. He served as the archive's executive director from 1985 to 1989 and oversaw its public opening in January 1987.

Armstrong is the author or editor of six books and countless articles on foreign affairs, defense, intelligence, and national security issues. His 1991 exposé of secret Saudi arms purchases of American military infrastructure was named "story of the year" by the *Investigative Reporters and Editors Journal*. His cover stories in the *Columbia Journalism Review* revealed the government's heavy-handed control of the press during the Gulf War and the Iran/contra affair, and for his TV coverage of the latter he received an Emmy and a DuPont Silver Baton award.

In 1992, he received the James Madison Award for "championing, promoting and protecting the public's right to know through investigative reporting" and for "prolific and productive use of the Freedom of Information Act." In that same year, he received the President's Award for Service from the Washington Independent Writers' Union. Armstrong has filed numerous public service lawsuits, including suits against Presidents Reagan, Bush, and Clinton that combined to enjoin the White House from destroying the electronic records of the National Security Council and the White House. From 1988 through 1992, Armstrong helped to organize four conferences to reconstruct and document the Cuban missile crisis. Participants included Fidel Castro, members of the Kennedy Executive Committee of the National Security Council, and Soviet officials.

Armstrong is a founder of the Historians' Committee for Open Debate, and during 1992, he became the first executive director of Taxpayers against Fraud, a nonprofit whistleblower organization that used the False Claims Act to recover over $100 million of fraudulent payments to government contractors. From 1990 to 1992, he was the Visiting Scholar of International Journalism at the American University in Washington, D.C., where he organized an international conference on free expression and the global media. The conference gathered several hundred of the world's leading journalists and writers, including Salman Rushdie, to discuss the barriers to free expression in publishing and broadcasting. During this period, Armstrong testified before congressional committees on access to and use of government information.

Since 1993, Armstrong has been the executive director of the Information Trust, a Washington, D.C.–based, nonprofit organization devoted to freedom of expression in the United States and abroad, improving the quality of journalism, increasing accountability of government through open access to information, and reforming abuses of government secrecy. In 1993, the Information Trust facilitated Salman Rushdie's meeting with President Clinton. In 1994, Armstrong's Information Trust convened a two-day symposium at the National Press Club titled "Openness and Secrecy: Estab-

lishing Accountability in the Nuclear Age," which examined declassification efforts by the Department of Energy, whistleblower protections, and strategies for popular participation in government decision making.
REFERENCE: Bob Woodward, Scott Armstrong, *The Brethren: Inside the Supreme Court*, New York, Simon and Schuster, 1979.

ART   Though the modern crisis in art censorship coincided with the government's manipulation of federal funding, censorship of visual artists and their work was rampant in the nineteenth century as well. In post–Civil War New York, a dry-goods clerk named Anthony Comstock led a broad censorship movement that resulted in the antiobscenity law of 1873. After Comstock was appointed as a special postal inspector, he instigated the arrest of prominent art dealer Herman Knoedler, raided the Art Students League for its use of nude models, and warned that indecent photographs and paintings were mistakenly called "art." Such censorship became so common that it came to be known as "Comstockery," a term that endured well into the twentieth century.

By the 1930s, America's Great Depression had changed the focus of censorship from sex to politics. To the consternation of the political and financial establishment, socialism was increasingly seen as a legitimate alternative to capitalism. Many artists had unionized, and class divisions within the broader society were reflected in American art. In 1933, Diego Rivera's gigantic frescoed mural, *Portrait of America*, commissioned for New York's Rockefeller Center, was physically destroyed because it contained a portrait of Lenin. The following year, four artists employed by the New Deal's Public Works of Art Project (PWAP) were accused of Communist tendencies because of left-wing images in their murals.

Of course, the demand for decency in art remained. In 1934, Paul Cadmus's painting *The Fleet's In*, which depicted sailors flirting with prostitutes, was removed from the Corcoran Gallery at the government's request. But political art continued to arouse the greatest controversy within the U.S. government. The Relief Bill of 1940 required a loyalty oath for Federal Arts Project (FAP) artists, and when August Henkel refused to sign it, his murals at the Brooklyn Airport were destroyed. In 1943, Arshile Gorky's Newark Airport murals simply disappeared.

By the end of World War II, the Cold War mentality had defined all leftist artworks as "communistic," a term that came to be applied to most "modernist" or "abstract" art. In 1947, Representative Fred Busbey (R-Ill.) denounced a State Department–funded exhibition of twenty contemporary and abstract artists as "infiltrated by Communists," resulting in the withdrawal of funding. Also during that year, the Photo League was placed on the Solicitor General's list of subversive organizations, denying members virtually any chance of employment.

In 1953, Representative George Dondero (R-Mich.) attacked Anton Refregier's Works Progress Administration (WPA) mural in San Francisco for its allegedly Marxist imagery, and it took the action of arts organizations to save the mural. During the same year, artists Alexander Calder, Georgia O'Keeffe, and Ben Shahn were placed under surveillance by the FBI. In 1957, legislation to create an Arts Advisory Council, as requested earlier by President Eisenhower, was rejected after testimony that the council might be taken over by Communists or "modernists."

By the end of the 1970s, decency had reemerged as the focus of art censorship, accomplished primarily through the manipulation of government funding. Politicians proclaimed that any form of expression supported by taxpayer money could be legislatively silenced, but there was limited legal authority for such a view. In *Perry v. Sindermann* (1972), Justice Potter Stewart had stated:

For at least a quarter-century, this Court has made clear that even though a person has no "right" to a valuable governmental benefit and even though the government may deny him the benefit for any number of reasons, there are some reasons upon which the government may not rely. It may not deny a benefit to a person on a basis that infringes his constitutionally protected interests—especially, his interest in freedom of speech. For if the government could deny a benefit to a person because of his constitutionally protected speech or associations, his exercise of those freedoms would in effect be penalized and inhibited.

Substantial federal funding for the arts did not begin in earnest until 1965, when the National Endowment for the Arts (NEA) was created. The NEA was aware of the need to reflect artistic neutrality in its grants, and toward this purpose it maintained a system of Peer Advisory Panels made up of experts in the fields in which the endowment made grants. The panels sought to ensure that a diversity of artistic styles and philosophies was reflected in the grants, and the endowment usually approved the recommendations of the advisory panels. As a result, the NEA acquired a strong record of support for mainstream excellence in art, and contrary to the claims of conservative politicians, there have been only a handful of controversial grants out of the almost 100,000 given.

From the beginning, there were powerful political forces influencing the endowment's judgments, even in the area of art criticism. In 1981, the NEA reviewed its funding for individual art critics on the basis of charges that the critics had leftist tendencies, and conservatives on the NEA's National Council on the Arts succeeded in completely eliminating the funding after the Reagan administration proposed a 50 percent cut. In 1987, the Center for Arts Criticism in Minneapolis was defunded by the NEA, ending virtually all direct support for art criticism. Nonetheless, by 1992, over two hundred endowment programs provided funding or activities for the arts and humanities. Though federal funding for such programs was dwarfed by private giving, a handful of controversies in 1989 and 1990 led Congress to place substantive limits on the professional discretion of the endowment, something it had not done during the first twenty-five years of its existence.

In 1989, the photographic exhibition "Robert Mapplethorpe: The Perfect Moment" aroused a storm of protest over some of its homoerotic images. The exhibit, which had received a $30,000 grant from the NEA, ran successfully in Philadelphia and Chicago but was cancelled at the Corcoran Gallery in Washington, D.C., due to political pressure and the threat of lost federal funding for the Corcoran's other activities. The exhibit was then transferred to the Washington Project for the Arts, where it included a warning that some of the material might be unsuitable for children. In 1990, the exhibit traveled to Cincinnati's Contemporary Arts Center, where Dennis Barrie, the museum's curator, was taken to trial on obscenity charges. Barrie and the museum were completely exonerated in court (*see also* BARRIE, DENNIS).

Shortly thereafter, another controversial work, Andres Serrano's *Piss Christ*, appeared in an exhibit by the Southeastern Center for Contemporary Arts, which had previously used endowment funds to support the New York photographer. Serrano's inclusion of a photograph of a crucifix in a bottle of urine again brought the endowment under political attack, despite its indirect connection with Serrano. Similar controversy surrounded a subsequent exhibit of paintings and photographs by David Wojnarowicz. That exhibit, produced by Illinois State University with the support of a $15,000 grant from the endowment, was criticized for its inclusion of some sexually explicit scenes.

In the wake of these controversies, Pat Robertson's Christian Coalition initiated a $200,000 advertising campaign designed to end congressional funding for the NEA. Senator Jesse Helms (R-N.C.) then introduced legislation that would bar NEA funding for any obscene or indecent works, or for "material which denigrates the objects or beliefs of the adherents of a particular religion or non-religion" or "denigrates, debases, or reviles a person, group, or class of citizens on the basis of race, creed, sex, handicap, age, or national origin." The Helms legislation also required NEA grant recipients to sign an antiobscenity oath. Since "obscene" expression is not constitutionally protected, the government has clear authority to forbid it, directly or indirectly. The problem with the legislative attempt to ban NEA funding for "obscene" art was that its language adhered closely to the Supreme Court's standard in *Miller v. California* (1973), which said that expression was not obscene if it had "serious literary, artistic, political, or scientific value." But since the endowment was created to award grants to projects that it believed had serious artistic value, none of its projects could, by definition, be obscene (Rodney A. Smolla, *Free Speech in an Open Society*, New York, Knopf, 1992, p. 178).

Many artists and art organizations refused to sign the antiobscenity oath, rejecting $750,000 in grants, and in 1990, the NEA's National Council on the Arts recommended that NEA Chair John Frohnmayer rescind the oath. Frohnmayer refused, but the oath was subsequently ruled unconstitutional in a suit brought by dancer/choreographer Bella Lewitsky and argued by First Amendment lawyer Floyd Abrams. Still, the NEA continued to function under heavy political pressure. When Congress next considered appropriating funds for the NEA, it removed the obscenity stipulation from the earlier Helms provision, but replaced it with a requirement to consider "decency" in approving grants. At this point, Frohnmayer, who had done his best to follow all the political cues from Capitol Hill, said that he would regard the congressional stipulation as merely "advisory," since decency was already a part of the determination of artistic merit. At the same time, Frohnmayer went against long-standing tradition by rejecting four projects that had been approved by advisory panels and the Arts Council. These projects dealt with controversial themes like homosexuality, AIDS, feminism, and religion.

In vetoing grants to artists Karen Finley, Tim Miller, Holly Hughes, and John Fleck, Frohnmayer admitted that "political realities" must be considered in evaluating art. The four artists brought suit against the NEA, claiming that their grants had been denied for political, rather than artistic, reasons. The suit, *Finley v. National Endowment for the Arts* (1992) also included a challenge to the constitutionality of the "general standards of decency" language in the endowment's 1990 reauthorizing legislation. When settled, the suit provided $8,000 to Karen Finley and Holly Hughes, with $5,000 awarded to Tim Miller and John Fleck. Each of the four artists received another $6,000 in damages, while $202,000 was scheduled to go to civil liberties organizations to cover legal fees. The court also ruled that the Helms decency provision was excessively vague. The Bush administration's Justice Department appealed that ruling, and, to the dismay of the arts community, the Clinton adminstration indicated its intention to pursue the appeal.

In his 1993 book *Leaving Town Alive*, John Frohnmayer described the intense political pressure under which he functioned while chairing the NEA. In correspondence dating from 1990, Frohnmayer and President George Bush discussed ways to avoid controversial grants. On June 5, 1990, Frohnmayer wrote to Bush, "There are at least 5 troublesome grants I was/am prepared to deny. The National Council postponed consideration of them until August but I will overrule the Council if they recommend them." On June 19, President Bush responded that he too was troubled by all of the furor. He said that he did not want to see censorship, yet he did not believe that a dime of taxpayers' money should go into art that was "clearly and visibly filth." Frohnmayer's subsequent veto of these "troublesome" grants precipitated the suit previously described, which cost the NEA $252,000 (John Frohnmayer, *Leaving Town Alive*, Boston, Houghton Mifflin, 1993, pp. 160–61).

In July 1993, Martin Mawyer, president of the conservative Christian Action Network, sent letters to all first-term members of Congress urging them to abolish the NEA. The letters attacked a show at New York's Whitney Museum that included works by Robert Mapplethorpe and Andres Serrano as a prime example of the kind of "objectionable art" supported by the NEA. Congress responded immediately by cutting almost $9 million from the endowment's funding, and Mawyer said that the action was a warning against NEA support for "repulsive" art like the Whitney Museum show.

In October 1993, actress Jane Alexander was named as the new chair of the NEA in an attempt to strengthen the endowment's popular and political support. Her first national address, "The Arts Endowment's Agenda," was part of a national teleconference on the partnership between federal and local governments and the arts community, but congressional hostility was unassuaged. In June 1994, Senator Jesse Helms (R-N.C.) wrote to Alexander complaining of awards for prurient, offensive, and/or absurd art. Much of the criticism centered around a Minneapolis show by Ron Athey, an artist who carved a ritual drawing into the back of another man. Athey had simply appeared at a festival that had received some NEA money for operating costs.

In the face of congressional threats, the NEA tiptoed around controversial grants, rejecting a fellowship application from photographer Andres Serrano. "Here we go again," said David Mendoza, executive director of the National Campaign for Freedom of Expression. "We are back to overturning a grant for political reasons despite . . . the opinion of a federal judge that prohibits the NEA from determining grants based on decency" ("NEA Balks at Funding Serrano," *Washington Post*, August 6, 1994, p. C1).

When Congress subsequently imposed a 2 percent cut in NEA funding for 1995, some in the arts community felt fortunate, but the cuts were clearly aimed at specific artists, a direct form of censorship. In describing the funding cut, Senator Robert Byrd (D-W.V.) admitted, "[A]ll of it is directed at those grant programs which have been at the center of recent controversies." Toward that end, areas like theater and the visual arts had their funding slashed, and the resultant cuts in NEA programs included termination of programs for "controversial" artists. Photographer Barbara De Genevieve, whose grant application was rejected after being approved by the visual arts peer panel, said that the cuts were "a thinly veiled attempt at eliminating the most potentially political and controversial programs, and the most experimental and challenging work." She warned that the NEA was becoming "a watchdog for the right" ("Alexander Defends NEA Cuts," *Washington Post*, November 5, 1994, p. D7).

De Genevieve joined with Andres Serrano and Merry Halpern, whose grant requests had also been rejected despite approval by peer panels, to challenge the political nature of the NEA action. The ACLU, the National Campaign for Freedom of Expression, and the Center for Constitutional Rights filed a request with the NEA to have the rejections reconsidered and to obtain copies of all documents relating to the decisions. The NEA refused.

In the meantime, the new Republican Congress, in concert with the religious right, pressed the issue of defunding the NEA. During the summer of 1995, a House appropriations committee recommended the largest

NEA cut ever—40 percent—and proposed ending all grants to individual artists. The Senate Appropriations Committee then approved the House proposals, with the political rhetoric again focused on a single artist, this time Tim Miller, one of the performance artists whose grants had been rejected in 1990 only to be reinstated by the courts. The full Senate subsequently scaled back the NEA cuts, but the final amount was still a staggering 39 percent. In addition, Jesse Helms added a provision that would prohibit the NEA from supporting "obscene or indecent materials or performances denigrating a particular religion." That provision, like his 1990 decency clause, is likely to be tested in the courts if there is anything left of the NEA. Despite the dramatic reduction in NEA funding, Patrick Trueman of the conservative American Family Association complained, "We are very disappointed that the Congress did not zero out the NEA this year. . . . The NEA was in the cross hairs this year, and the Republican leadership refused to pull the trigger."

In early 1996, having failed in the attempt to legislate the NEA out of existence, conservative Republicans suggested a new tack. Representative Ralph Regula (R-Ohio), chairman of the House committee that oversees the endowment's funding, warned NEA Chair Alexander that he could eliminate the agency without a vote by simply holding up a reauthorization bill. The NEA has not been formally reauthorized since 1993, but the Democratic-controlled Congress allowed the endowment to spend money through an exception to the rules. Republicans, said Regula, would simply prevent the agency from spending money.

In May 1996, Alexander told a Senate appropriations subcommittee, "New art is often difficult art. You wouldn't want to cut out total controversy in any case because it is an expression of the variety of who we are as a people." When subcommittee chairman Slade Gordon (R-Wash.) pressed her for a stronger stand against controversial art, Alexander said that the NEA has "enough prohibition right now. We do not fund obscenity, as defined by a court of law. I think that is sufficient." Gordon said that her response was "troubling" ("Senate Panel Has Bad Budget News for Arts Agency," *Washington Post*, May 9, 1996, p. D2).

REFERENCES: Richard Burt, ed., *The Administration of Aesthetics: Censorship, Political Criticism, and the Public Sphere*, Minneapolis, University of Minnesota Press, 1994; Steven C. Dubin, *Arresting Images: Impolitic Art and Uncivil Actions*, New York, Routledge, 1992.

ATTORNEY GENERAL'S COMMISSION ON PORNOGRAPHY
The Attorney General's Commission on Pornography was established in 1985 by then U.S. Attorney General William French Smith, but the commission came to be associated with Smith's successor, Attorney General Edwin Meese III. The commission was chaired by Henry E. Hudson, but Meese assumed responsibility for its work in July 1986. It produced a 1,960–page report that contradicted virtually every conclusion of the 1970 President's

Commission on Obscenity and Pornography, whose report it characterized as "starkly obsolete." Whereas the President's Commission had concluded that erotic material was not a significant cause of crime or sexual deviancy, the Meese Commission claimed that there was a causal relationship between pornography and sexual violence. The Meese Commission said that current laws against obscenity were inadequately enforced, and it recommended particularly harsh penalties for those convicted of obscenity two or more times.

The Meese Commission was more tolerant of erotic literature than it was of film or video, saying that books consisting entirely of text seemed to be the least harmful type of pornography. Still, it recommended grass-roots opposition to all pornography, including picketing, store boycotts, and protests to sponsors of radio and television programs. Meese himself supervised the establishment of a special team of prosecutors to handle pornography cases, and he promised to recommend changes in the federal law to restrict sexually explicit material on cable television and "dial-a-porn" phone services.

REFERENCE: Philip Nobile and Eric Nadler, *United States of America vs. Sex: How the Meese Commission Lied about Pornography*, New York, Minotaur Press, 1986.

BALDWIN, ROGER NASH, 1884–1981   Roger Nash Baldwin was the founder and initial executive director of the American Civil Liberties Union (ACLU). During World War I, he served as director of the American Union Against Militarism and spent one year in prison as a conscientious objector. In 1920, he founded the ACLU and served as its executive director until his retirement in 1950. He authored numerous articles, pamphlets, and books on civil liberties, including the monograph *Civil Liberties and Industrial Conflict*. Baldwin continued as a spokesman on civil liberties until his death in 1981.
REFERENCE: Peggy Lamson, *Roger Baldwin, Founder of the American Civil Liberties Union: A Portrait*, Boston, Houghton Mifflin, 1976.

BARRIE, DENNIS, 1947–   From 1983 to 1993, Dennis Barrie was director of the Contemporary Arts Center (CAC) in Cincinnati, Ohio, following more than a decade of service as the Midwest Area director of the Smithsonian's Archives of American Art. In 1990, Barrie's dedication to displaying important new work of high artistic value precipitated a First Amendment crisis of national proportions when he brought an exhibition of Robert Mapplethorpe's photographs to Cincinnati. The exhibition, "Robert Mapplethorpe: The Perfect Moment," met with organized resistance even before the April 7, 1990, opening to the public.

On March 7, 1990, a group calling itself Citizens for Community Values issued a call to its sixteen thousand members to take action to prevent the opening of the Mapplethorpe exhibit. On March 21, Dennis Barrie held a press conference to affirm the CAC's commitment to presenting the exhibition, but heavy pressure was being brought to bear on Barrie and the museum's board of trustees. There had been threats against Barrie's life and the lives of his staff, public attacks on individual trustees, and even bomb threats. On the day following Barrie's press conference, CACs Board Chairman Chad P. Wick resigned, citing pressure on his employer, the Central Trust Company.

On March 23, Cincinnati law enforcement officials announced that they would review the Mapplethorpe exhibition. Hamilton County Sheriff Simon Leis made public his personal opinion that the Mapplethorpe photographs were "criminally obscene." The CAC, along with the Robert Mapplethorpe Estate and Foundation, then filed a lawsuit requesting a declaratory judgment from a jury that the exhibition did not violate Ohio obscenity statutes. On April 5, plaintiffs filed a motion for summary judgment, but on the following day, Municipal Court Judge Edward Donellon dismissed the suit without explanation.

On April 6, the CAC opened the Mapplethorpe exhibition for a special members' preview, attracting a record crowd of more than four thousand members. On April 7, when the exhibition was opened to the public, a grand jury was impaneled and taken to the CAC to view the exhibition. Shortly before noon, the grand jury issued four criminal indictments, two each to Dennis Barrie and the CAC, for pandering obscenity and illegal use of a minor in nudity-oriented materials.

In a press conference held that afternoon, Sheriff Leis said that the CAC board should remove the 7 photographs deemed obscene. At the same time, about thirty uniformed and plain-clothes police entered the CAC, closed the doors, and presented CAC officials with indictments naming 7 photographs out of 175 as obscene. The police pushed patrons out of the gallery in order to videotape the exhibition as evidence. There was a near riot as angry demonstrators gathered outside, demanding entrance to the exhibition. At 4:10 P.M., the police left the CAC, and the public was once more granted access. That night the CAC filed a civil rights action in federal court, and the following morning U.S. District Court Judge Carl Rubin issued a temporary restraining order barring police from taking action against the CAC or seizing works from the exhibit until after the criminal trial.

In the meantime, CAC broke all attendance records when 28,103 visitors attended during the first thirteen days of the exhibition. A special meeting of the Association of Art Museum Directors (AAMD) was held at the CAC, during which the AAMD's Board of Trustees passed a resolution in support of Dennis Barrie and the CAC for upholding the highest standards of museum professionals.

Barrie's trial made national headlines. The judge appeared to be hostile to Barrie's case when he ruled that the CAC was not a museum because it was not a collecting institution. He also declared that the 7 Mapplethorpe photographs in question could be presented at trial out of the context of the exhibition and their portfolios. He even agreed with the prosecution that an exhibition does not have the kind of intellectual content that a book or play has.

No one who had ever been to the CAC was allowed on the jury. The jurors were not museum patrons, had relatively little formal education, and were considered politically conservative. Nonetheless, during jury selection, the vast majority of them said that they believed that adults have the right to decide for themselves what they can read or see or listen to. On October 5, 1990, the jury found Dennis Barrie and the CAC not guilty on obscenity and child pornography charges.

Barrie recalled: "You have to understand that the Mapplethorpe case was *the* case in our city at that time, even though the Reds were on their way to the World Series. They broadcast the decision over the radios at Riverfront Stadium, and people stood up and cheered. Horns honked all over the city. I walked into a newsroom at Channel 9, a CBS affiliate, and all the staff members stood up and cheered and said, 'The city has been redeemed.' That's an image that will stay with me for a long time" (Dennis Barrie, "The Scene of the Crime," *Art Journal*, Fall 1991, p. 31). Shortly after the trial, Barrie received a 1990 Hugh Hefner First Amendment Award for his role in defending the CAC against government censorship.

The CAC's legal costs were close to $350,000, even with substantial pro bono assistance, but Barrie said: "We did the right thing. There was no alternative. We could not have given in. The down side for our institution is that it was a costly battle—costly in terms of dollars and costly in terms of human health and morale. . . . And we've taken a real hit in the corporate giving, somewhere to the tune of about $110,000. We expect it to be long lasting." Barrie explained: "I think our corporations are scared at the moment because, suddenly [Senator Jesse] Helms and others have made the arts controversial. The arts used to be a very good and safe place to put corporate dollars for public relations purposes and for civic purposes. I think, sadly, that Helms and others have made it a political battleground and, lately, we see corporations shying away from anything controversial."

Barrie said that despite the nightmare he and CAC had endured, he would not do anything differently. "The point is that freedom of expression is at stake here. . . . The issue is to defend the freedom." When asked about similarities between his situation and the attacks on the NEA, 2 Live Crew, and films like *The Last Temptation of Christ*, Barrie said: "I think they're manifestations of the same issue. What we see happening is an assault from the far religious right. And it's a very real political-social agenda, which focuses in some areas on censorship because they want control. . . . It's gone into the entertainment world. It's gone into textbooks. This is all [about] social control" (Allan Parachini, "Victory But No Relief," *Los Angeles Times Calendar*, November 4, 1990, p. 4).

Given Barrie's pessimistic view of future corporate support for the CAC and his identification with the plight of musical groups like 2 Live Crew, it was not a complete shock when he left the Contemporary Arts Center in August 1993 to become director of the Rock and Roll Hall of Fame and Museum in Cleveland, Ohio. Barrie noted that rock music had undergone First Amendment struggles similar to his own defense of the Mapplethorpe exhibition. "[T]he rock world's always pushing the envelope, as they say, in terms of what's permissible or acceptable or even legal in our society. . . . They've put rock groups on trial for the content of their music. Rock's always been a little dangerous for each generation, from Elvis on. So I do think we have something in common" (Chris Willman, "Rock Hall's Chief Has Trivia to Learn," *Los Angeles Times*, August 26, 1993, p. F1).

REFERENCE: Dennis Barrie, "Beyond Mapplethorpe," in *The Cultural Battlefield: Art Censorship and Public Funding*, edited by Jennifer A. Peter and Louis M. Crosier, Gilsum, Avocus Press, 1995.

BLACK, HUGO LAFAYETTE, 1886–1971   Supreme Court Justice Hugo Black, an "absolutist" in support of freedom of speech, began his career in an unlikely way. In 1921, while serving as an attorney in Birmingham, Alabama, Black joined the Ku Klux Klan. He resigned from the Klan in 1925 when he successfully ran for the U.S. Senate, and he remained in the Senate until 1937, when President Franklin Roosevelt appointed him to the Supreme Court. He quickly became known as a champion of First Amendment rights.

Black considered the First Amendment to be "the heart of our government," and he regarded the rights of free speech, press, and assembly to be essential to the maintenance of all other liberties. His "absolutist" belief that the First Amendment barred all government interference with thought or expression brought him into frequent conflict with Justice Felix Frankfurter, who embodied the theory of judicial restraint.

During the 1950s, Black often found himself in the minority on the many loyalty-security cases that came before the Court. For example, Black regularly voted against the majority to overturn restrictions and punishment imposed on Communists because he considered this to be an infringement on freedom of expression. He dissented in May 1950 when the Court upheld the non-Communist oath provision in the Taft-Hartley Act. He dissented the following month when the Court sustained the conviction of eleven Communists under the Smith Act. Black regarded the act's prohibition of teaching or advocacy of communism to be unconstitutional, and in 1957, he wrote a separate opinion maintaining that the entire Smith Act violated the First Amendment.

Black opposed congressional investigations into "anti-American" or subversive beliefs and repeatedly voted to overturn contempt convictions of witnesses who refused to answer investigating-committee questions about their ideas or associations. He joined the majority in two 1957 decisions that set limits on congressional and state investigative powers, but dissented in 1959 when the Court retreated from this position. Black contended that when the House Un-American Activities Committee (HUAC) punished witnesses who were suspected Communists and subjected them to humiliation and public scorn, the committee violated individual rights of free expression and illegally exercised a judicial function.

During the 1960s, many of Black's earlier dissenting views on the First Amendment were accepted by an increasingly liberal Court. He was still in dissent in 1961 when the majority sustained federal laws that required the Communist Party to register with the government and made it illegal to be a member of any party advocating the overthrow of the government. By 1962, however, the Court reversed the contempt-of-Congress convictions of witnesses who refused to answer HUAC questions, and Black concurred in that decision. He also voted with the majority in 1964 to nullify federal laws denying passports to members of the Communist Party and making it a crime for Party members to serve as labor-union officials. In 1965, he joined the majority in voiding a set of New York State teacher loyalty laws.

Black believed that even libelous or obscene expression was protected by the First Amendment. He opposed all government censorship of allegedly obscene materials and asked the Court to protect even malicious criticism of public figures. Though the Warren Court never adopted these views, it narrowed the definition of obscenity and added procedural safeguards against censorship.

Later in his career, Black seemed to take a somewhat conservative position on matters relating to privacy, saying that he could find no right of privacy in the Constitution. He also dissented in 1964 when the Court overturned trespass convictions of civil rights protesters, though he had voted in 1961 and 1963 to void similar convictions. He spoke for the majority in 1966 to sustain the trespass convictions of demonstrators outside a Florida jail, stating that the First Amendment did not give people a right to go wherever they want, whenever they please, without regard to property rights or state law. Black expressed a conservative dissenting view in the landmark case *Tinker v. Des Moines Independent Community School District* (1969), when the Court affirmed the right of school students to nondisruptive political expression. He also objected to a 1971 ruling in which the majority overturned the conviction of a courthouse demonstrator. Still, he denied that his beliefs had moved in a more conservative direction, maintaining his frequently expressed belief that government could regulate the time and place of speech, but not its content.

In a 1970 majority opinion, Black said that a federal law prohibiting actors from wearing U.S. military uniforms in productions critical of the armed forces was a violation of the First Amendment. In three 1971 cases, he voted to invalidate state loyalty oaths, and on June 30, 1971, he joined the majority in the landmark case *New York Times Co. v. United States* that denied a government injunction against publication of the *Pentagon Papers*. In his separate opinion, Black insisted that no judicial restraint on the press was permissible. This was to be Justice Black's final opinion. Shortly thereafter, he resigned because of ill health, and within a week he died at the age of eighty-five.

REFERENCES: Tony Freyer, *Hugo L. Black and the Dilemma of American Liberalism*, Glenview, Scott, Foresman, 1990; Roger K. Newman, *Hugo Black: A Biography*, New York, Pantheon Books, 1994.

BLACK BUDGET   The U.S. Constitution requires of the government that "a regular Statement and Account of the Receipts and Expenditures of all public Money shall be published from time to time." But the public budget that the Pentagon submits to Congress contains hundreds of programs camouflaged under code names, with costs deleted and goals disguised. This "black budget" is the secret budget that funds the programs that the President, the Secretary of Defense, and the Director of the Central Intelligence Agency want to keep hidden from the public. The documentation of the secret accounts is kept sealed in covert compartments of the Pentagon's ledgers.

The origins of the black budget can be traced to the Roosevelt administration's early decision to begin research on the atomic bomb, and those secret methods and procedures remain the blueprint for today's secret spending. President Reagan dramatically expanded the black budget in order to conceal expensive weapons systems. By the end of the Reagan administration, the black budget had grown to $36 billion, larger than the federal budget for transportation or agriculture, twice the budget for education, and more than the entire military budget of any other nation in the world except the Soviet Union. In the 1991 budget, almost twenty cents of every dollar proposed for Pentagon research was "black."

Only a few senior members of Congress have access to the details of the black budget, and they would be subject to censure or expulsion if they discussed such matters on the floor of Congress. The Reagan administration asked that reporters or public officials who published information about black programs be charged with high treason.

In early 1996, a presidential commission took a small step toward exposing the black budget when it advocated disclosing the total amount of money spent by the U.S. intelligence community. But the commission warned that disclosure of additional detail, for example the budgets of the thirteen individual intelligence organizations, should not be permitted because it might reveal vital secrets. Perhaps through oversight, the commission's report included a chart that compared the scope of work at individual intelligence organizations with the work at agencies that had published budgets. Steven Aftergood of the Federation of American Scientists figured out a way to estimate the budgets of the intelligence organizations by analyzing their positions on the chart. "[A]ll of this information is of legitimate public interest," said Aftergood. "It does not disclose any genuine national security secrets. It's a shame that the public has to resort to a kind of subterfuge to get access to this data. The opponents of disclosure are living in a world that has passed" ("Making Connections with Dots to Decipher U.S. Spy Spending," *Washington Post*, March 12, 1996, p. A11).

On April 23, 1996, President Bill Clinton endorsed the modest reforms in the commission's report, authorizing Congress to make public the bottom-line appropriation for U.S. intelligence in the next fiscal year. But in May 1996, when the House made its appropriations for intelligence, the dollar amounts in the bill remained classified. Representative John Conyers (D-Mich.) offered an amendment to declassify the "bottom line," but it was defeated.

All hopes that the Clinton administration would cut the black budget and bring secret programs into the light faded by the end of President Clinton's first term when the part of the black budget that could be glimpsed reached more than $14 billion, close to its 1980s peak. By 1996, the Pentagon was staffed by a substantial number of civilian and military officials with extensive black budget experience, led by Secretary of Defense William Perry, a former defense entrepreneur who is sometimes called "the godfather of Stealth." Estimates are that in 1997, almost ten cents of every dollar that the U.S. Air Force will spend on equipment will be on secret projects. Despite generally lower budgets, the Navy also spends a steady $1.6 billion a year on secret research projects.

Bill Sweetman, a specialist on aerospace and defense matters, says that between 10 and 15 percent of the cost of a black program is absorbed by security measures. Sweetman says, "[O]ne of the program managers told me that Pentagon undercover agents were assigned to contact the spouses of people on the program attempting to find out if anyone had violated the law by answering the questions, 'How was your day at work, dear?' " He believes the black world prospers and becomes ever more established because a compliant administration overrides the judiciary. "Most citizens accept the need for secrecy in times of crisis," says Sweetman. "But the question is whether a secret military should be such a thriving, unaccountable institution when the security of the nation is less threatened than it has been for decades" (Bill Sweetman, "The Budget You Can't See," *Washington Post*, July 7, 1996, C3).

REFERENCE: Tim Weiner, *Blank Check: The Pentagon's Black Budget*, New York, Warner Books, 1990.

BLACKLISTING   The act of excluding qualified persons from employment or other responsibilities on the basis of their political opinions or associations is commonly referred to as blacklisting. Lists of "undesirable" persons are secretly prepared by pressure groups or politicians, who then intimidate employers into firing or rejecting blacklisted persons. The most egregious examples of blacklisting occurred during the 1950s when Senator

Joseph McCarthy (R-Wis.) and the House Un-American Activities Committee (HUAC) hounded anyone with "leftist" views. Senator McCarthy called prominent motion picture producers, directors, writers, and actors before his hearings, demanding that they identify "leftists" in Hollywood.

Numerous actors and writers were fired and denied further employment because their work was judged to be "Communist influenced." Some conservative actors, like John Wayne and Adolphe Menjou, organized the Motion Picture Alliance for the Preservation of American Ideals (MPAPAI) to support HUAC and the blacklisting. Organizations like the American Legion also worked with HUAC to identify undesirables in Hollywood. The Legion published lists of alleged Communists and picketed theaters showing films by "unfriendly" HUAC witnesses, and the movie studios accommodated the Legion by blacklisting anyone so identified. As specified by the Legion, there were five tests that must be met before a person could be removed from the blacklist: (1) The suspect must renounce all Communist sympathies; (2) he must appear before HUAC and make full public disclosure, including naming other suspects; (3) he must join anti-Communist organizations; (4) he must publicly condemn Soviet imperialism; and (5) he must promise not to do it [engage in leftist activities] again.

Other self-promoting blacklisting organizations soon emerged, including the American Business Consultants, which published the booklet *Red Channels*, and AWARE Inc., which published the newsletter *Counterattack*. These publications made money by publishing larger and larger lists of suspected subversives and intimidating the entertainment industry into following their line on all personnel decisions. Motion-picture studios set up departments to politically screen employees, and blacklisted employees were forced to write abject confessions and apologies to blacklisters in order to be removed from their lists. Often, employees were required to make cash payoffs to the blacklisters for the privilege of absolution.

By the end of the 1950s, the practice of blacklisting had virtually disappeared, but those whose reputations had been tarnished never regained their careers. To this day, motion pictures and television remain tame and intimidated as the result of this shameful period of American history. *See also* FAULK, JOHN HENRY.

REFERENCES: Larry Ceplair and Steven Englund, *The Inquisition in Hollywood: Politics in the Film Community, 1930–1960*, Garden City, Anchor Press/Doubleday, 1980; Bernard F. Dick, *Radical Innocence: A Critical Study of the Hollywood Ten*, Lexington, University Press of Kentucky. 1989.

BLACKMUN, HARRY, 1908–   After leaving Harvard Law School in 1932, Harry Blackmun became law clerk for Judge John B. Sanborn in the U.S. Court of Appeals for the Eighth Circuit. Several years later, when Judge Sanborn decided to take senior status, he strongly recommended Blackmun as his successor. After being appointed to the appeals court by President Eisenhower, Blackmun took his seat as a U.S. Circuit Judge on November

4, 1959. More than a decade later, Blackmun was nominated for the U.S. Supreme Court by President Richard Nixon after Nixon's first two nominees, Judges Clement Haynsworth and G. Harrold Carswell, were rejected by Congress. Blackmun joined the Supreme Court on June 9, 1970.

Nixon's decision to nominate Blackmun for the Court was partly based on assurances from Chief Justice Warren Burger that Blackmun, a boyhood Minnesota friend, would be a loyal soldier in Nixon's campaign to move the Court to the right. Indeed, during his first few years on the Court, Blackmun almost always voted in favor of the government on First Amendment cases. During this period, Blackmun's judgments did not suggest the kind of support for the press that would eventually distinguish him. He dissented in the 1971 *Pentagon Papers* case, in which the majority ruled that the government could not stop the *New York Times* from publishing secret documents about the Vietnam War. In his dissent, Blackmun said that the case was rushed through the court system without time for proper analysis.

Despite these early indications of dutiful conservatism, Blackmun soon showed signs of the remarkable transformation that would eventually make him the senior member of the court's liberal wing. Though Blackmun is best known as the author of the 1973 *Roe v. Wade* decision affirming a woman's right to have an abortion, he is also known for his role in decisions protecting the right to free speech. In fact, even his opinion in *Roe* was based on a patient's right to seek and follow the advice of a physician, in addition to the right to privacy.

In 1975, Blackmun spoke for the majority in holding that Tennessee officials had violated the First Amendment by denying the use of a theater for the controversial musical *Hair*. In 1975 and 1976, Blackmun said that Virginia laws prohibiting advertisements for abortion services violated the First Amendment, and he acted independently to invalidate a lower court's gag order on media coverage of a murder case. In the 1976 case *Virginia State Board of Pharmacy v. Virginia Citizens Consumer Council Inc.*, Blackmun wrote the majority ruling establishing that commercial speech enjoys constitutional protection. His opinion said that a state may not suppress the dissemination of truthful information about lawful activity simply out of concern for the information's effect upon its disseminators and recipients. Blackmun's opinion did conclude, however, that commercial speech was not quite equal to political speech and could be regulated if it were false or misleading.

In cases like *Gannett v. DePasquale* (1979) and *Richmond Newspapers Inc. v. Virginia* (1980), Blackmun revealed himself to be a strong proponent of public access to courtrooms. In *Gannett*, Blackmun partially dissented from the majority that found that the right to a public trial was a right enjoyed by the defendant, not the news media and the public. In *Richmond Newspapers*, he joined the majority in finding that closing a criminal court without an overriding interest was unconstitutional under the First and Fourteenth

Amendments. Many believe that Blackmun's dissent in *Gannett* influenced the outcome of *Richmond Newspapers*.

In one of the most important commercial speech cases of the 1980s, *Central Hudson Gas and Electric Corp. v. Public Service Commission of New York* (1980), Blackmun's concurring opinion agreed that scrutiny of commercial speech is appropriate when it is designed to protect consumers, but not when it is designed to suppress information about a product in order to manipulate a private economic decision.

Blackmun dissented in *Cohen v. Cowles Media Co.* (1991), which held that the First Amendment did not protect the news media from breach-of-contract lawsuits over the revelation of confidential sources. He said that the use of the confidentiality claim to penalize the reporting of truthful information was a violation of the First Amendment.

On February 10, 1994, Blackmun lifted a gag order placed on a CBS-TV news show, allowing it to show video footage from an employee's hidden camera in a meat-packing plant. Blackmun, who oversaw the district in which the incident occurred, reiterated the strict burden of proof that must be shown before prior restraint may be imposed. Blackmun announced his retirement on April 6, 1994, and Stephen Breyer was nominated by President Clinton and confirmed by Congress as his replacement.

REFERENCE: *The Burger Court: Political and Judicial Profiles*, edited by Charles M. Lamb and Stephen C. Harpern, Urbana, University of Illinois Press, 1991.

BLANTON, THOMAS S., 1955–   Thomas S. Blanton is executive director of the National Security Archive, a nonprofit Washington, D.C.–based library and research institute devoted to documenting U.S. foreign policy through declassified government documents. After working as a journalist and congressional aide to Representative Gillis Long (D-La.), Blanton came to the archive in 1986 as the organization's first director of planning and research. He was promoted to deputy director in 1989 and became executive director in 1992.

The National Security Archive is the most successful nonprofit user of the Freedom of Information Act (FOIA) to obtain previously classified U.S. government documents and has brought landmark FOIA lawsuits preventing the destruction of the White House electronic mail tapes, exposing the FBI's controversial Library Awareness Program, and halting the government's practice of charging processing fees for FOIA requests by journalists, authors, and public interest groups. Among his many FOIA requests, Blanton personally filed the request and subsequent lawsuit that forced the U.S. government to release Oliver North's diaries in May 1990, an event that generated nationwide headlines. He coauthored *The Chronology: The Documented Day-by-Day Account of the Secret Military Assistance to Iran and the Contras*, and his 1995 book, *White House E-Mail*, was the result of a six-year lawsuit brought by the archive and allied historians, librarians, and public interest attorneys. Blanton has testified before Congress on matters related to government secrecy and has appeared on numerous national broadcasts on the three major networks, as well as the "MacNeil/Lehrer News Hour," "CNN Crossfire," C-SPAN, and National Public Radio.

Blanton also serves on the steering committee of the Brookings Institution's Project on the Costs of Nuclear Weapons and is a member of the Environment and Security Discussion Group of the Woodrow Wilson International Center for Scholars. He has published on such subjects as the Freedom of Information Act, the Iran/contra affair, the war in El Salvador, Eastern European archives, and the government's secrecy network. He has also coauthored several chapters in the American Civil Liberties Union's authoritative litigation manual for open-government laws. He has won several journalism prizes, including the Project Censored award for 1990. See NATIONAL SECURITY ARCHIVE.

REFERENCE: National Security Archive, *Secret Military Assistance to Iran and the Contras: A Chronology of Events and Individuals*, Washington, The National Security Archive, 1987.

BOWDLERIZE   The process of expurgating and revising literary works in order to remove objectionable language or ideas became associated with an English family, the Bowdlers, during the eighteenth and nineteenth centuries, leading to the common use of the term "bowdlerize." That term is still heard today in the United States in describing the censorship of works through expurgation. Among the prominent works expurgated by Thomas Bowdler were *The Family Shakespeare* and *The Family Gibbon*.

REFERENCE: Noel Perrin, *Dr. Bowdler's Legacy: A History of Expurgated Books in England and America*, New York, Atheneum Press, 1969.

BRENNAN, WILLIAM J., 1906–   After earning his law degree from Harvard in 1931, William Brennan joined a New Jersey law firm where he specialized in labor law. He became a judge on the state superior court in 1949 and was appointed to the New Jersey Supreme Court in 1952. In 1956, President Dwight Eisenhower appointed Brennan to the U.S. Supreme Court to replace retiring Justice Sherman Minton.

From the beginning of his term on the Supreme Court, Brennan showed a strong commitment to the First Amendment. Brennan did not share Justice Black's absolutist position on First Amendment rights, but he insisted that a real and substantial government interest be demonstrated before any curtailment of individual rights could be tolerated. In particular, he usually favored the individual in loyalty-security cases. In 1957, for example, he voted in two important cases to reverse contempt convictions against witnesses who had refused to answer questions from congressional or state committees investigating communism.

Brennan dissented in 1958 when the majority upheld the dismissal of municipal employees who had refused to answer questions from superiors about their political activities. He again dissented the following year in two cases where the majority sustained the contempt convictions of witnesses who refused to provide information to congressional and state investigations into subversion. Those investigations, said Brennan, had no valid legislative purpose and were used only to expose and punish the political views of individuals.

Brennan was the primary spokesman for the Court in the landmark obscenity case *Roth v. United States* (1957). His opinion narrowed the definition of obscenity to expression "utterly without redeeming social importance" and appealing to the "prurient interest," when considered by the "average person" applying contemporary community standards. In a 1961 decision, he judged Missouri's censorship system unconstitutional because it allowed the seizure of nonobscene literature along with the obscene. Similarly, his majority opinion in a 1963 case overturned Rhode Island's book-censorship system because it represented an unconstitutional system of prior restraint.

During the 1960s, when a liberal majority emerged within the Warren Court, Brennan wrote some of his most important First Amendment opinions. In March 1964, he spoke for a unanimous Court in *New York Times Co. v. Sullivan*, holding that a public official could not recover damages for a defamatory falsehood relating to official conduct unless the statement was made with "actual malice." Brennan later extended that ruling to cover criminal as well as civil libel and provided a broad definition to the term "public official." In *Time Inc. v. Hill* (1967), Brennan applied the same principle to invasion-of-privacy suits against the press.

Brennan also continued to write the Court's leading opinions on obscenity. In *Jacobellis v. Ohio* (1964), Brennan reaffirmed the obscenity test he had established in *Roth*, extending the community standards of that test to the nation at large. In three 1966 cases, Brennan narrowed the test for obscenity, establishing three criteria for such a judgment: (1) its dominant theme must appeal to the prurient interest, (2) it must be patently offensive, and (3) it must be utterly without redeeming social value.

In 1964, Brennan's plurality opinion reversed an obscenity judgment in Kansas because the materials in question had been seized in a way that endangered nonobscene publications. In 1965, Brennan overturned Maryland's film-censorship system because it provided inadequate safeguards against suppression of nonobscene films. In this opinion, Brennan enunciated strict procedural guidelines for any film-censorship system. Brennan wrote the majority opinion in *National Association for the Advancement of Colored People v. Button* (1963), which said that a Virginia law barring solicitation of legal business resulted in an unconstitutional restriction of the NAACP's rights of free speech and association.

During the 1970s on the conservative Burger Court, Brennan became a frequent and vocal dissenter. In a 1977 *Harvard Law Review* article, he urged litigants to seek protection for individual rights from the state courts, rather than the conservative U.S. Supreme Court. Still, Brennan played a prominent role in a number of First Amendment cases. In a 1976 plurality opinion, he said that the patronage firing of public employees was a violation of their freedom of belief and association. In 1974 and 1976, Brennan objected when the majority narrowed press protections against libel that he had expanded in 1971. He also dissented from several 1973 decisions in which the Court gave the states greater authority to regulate allegedly obscene material. Indeed, Brennan said that in the absence of a clear definition of obscenity, the Court should overturn all obscenity laws for adult audiences.

In July 1990, William Brennan announced unexpectedly that due to the Court's heavy work load and his own failing health, he was retiring immediately. President Bush promptly nominated David Souter, an obscure federal appeals court judge, to replace Brennan, and Souter was easily confirmed by the Senate.

REFERENCES: Kim Isaac Eisler, *A Justice for All: William J. Brennan, Jr. and the Decisions that Transformed America*, New York, Simon and Schuster, 1993; Roger L. Goldman, *Justice William J. Brennan, Jr.: Freedom First*, New York, Carroll and Graf Publishers, 1994.

BROADCASTING   First Amendment rights in broadcasting have a unique fragility, deriving in part from the power of the state to "license" those who would communicate through the broadcast medium. If the government attempted to license newspapers, book publishers, or motion-picture producers, such action would immediately be regarded as prior restraint, the most presumptively unconstitutional form of information control. How, then, can the government, through the Federal Communications Commission (FCC), limit the underlying right to communicate on the airwaves? This authority has traditionally been based on the concept of "spectrum scarcity," the notion that because there are a limited number of frequencies available in the broadcast spectrum, the state must allocate such broadcast space in the public interest. Some have argued that when Congress passed the legislation creating the FCC, it turned all broadcast frequencies into federal property. As the landlord of the property, the state may condition the use of its space in any way it chooses.

In upholding the constitutionality of federal regulation of broadcasting, the Supreme Court has relied upon the unique technical nature of the airwaves and the unique social characteristics of the medium. In *National Broadcasting Company v. United States* (1943), the Court relied upon spectrum scarcity in concluding: "Freedom of utterance is abridged to many who wish to use the limited facilities of radio. Unlike other modes of expression, radio inherently is not available to all. That is its unique characteristic, and that is why, unlike other modes of expression, it is subject to governmental regulation. Because it cannot be used by all, some who wish to use it must be denied."

Again, in *Red Lion Broadcasting Company v. Federal Communications Commission* (1969), the Court relied upon spectrum scarcity in upholding the fairness doctrine: "Where there are substantially more individuals who want to broadcast than there are frequencies to allocate, it is idle to posit an unabridgeable First Amendment right to broadcast comparable to the right of every individual to speak, write, or publish. . . . A license permits broadcasting, but the licensee has no constitutional right to be the one who holds the license or to monopolize a radio frequency to the exclusion of his fellow citizens."

More recently, the FCC has increasingly used its regulatory power to protect the public from "indecent" programming, citing the unique social characteristics of the medium as justification for restraint on speech. The Radio Act of 1927 had stated: "No person within the jurisdiction of the United States shall utter any obscene, indecent, or profane language by means of radio communication." The Communications Act of 1934 retained the Radio Act's wording in this regard, but in 1948, that provision was moved to Section 1464 of the Federal Criminal Code. Its subsequent enforcement has been inconsistent due, in part, to continuing doubts about its constitutionality.

The FCC first applied the concept of indecency in 1970, when it fined a Philadelphia radio station for broadcasting an interview with Grateful Dead star Jerry Garcia in which he used words denoting excrement and sexual intercourse. Rather than attempting to define indecency, the FCC claimed to be using the Supreme Court's *Roth* test for obscenity. The FCC subsequently fined a Chicago station for a program that discussed female sexual habits.

In 1975, the FCC was explicit in identifying what it considered indecent language in a case precipitated by a single complaint lodged with the FCC against a New York radio station for the broadcast of a twelve–minute monologue, "Filthy Words," from an album by humorist George Carlin. The offended listener demanded that indecent speech, such as Carlin's, be prohibited from the airwaves. The FCC subsequently issued a declaratory order ruling that the program had been "indecent," defining indecency to include "language or material that depicts or describes, in terms patently offensive as measured by contemporary standards for the broadcast medium, sexual or excretory activities or organs" (*Pacifica Foundation* [1975]). The FCC also warned the station that its programming would be scrutinized when its license came up for renewal. The owner of the New York station, Pacifica Foundation, appealed the FCC's ruling, which was then overturned by a U.S. court of appeals.

Judge Edward A. Tamm said that the FCC order in the Pacifica case violated the no-censorship provision of the Communications Act and was "overbroad" in that it "sweepingly forbids any broadcast of the seven words [from the George Carlin monologue] irrespective of context or however innocent or educational they may be." Judge Tamm said that the FCC ruling failed to define the "children" it purported to protect and did not distinguish the media within which indecent speech could or could not be expressed. He also rejected the FCC's view that indecent language, when made available to children, cannot have literary, artistic, political, or scientific value. In his concurring opinion, Chief Judge David Bazelon said that the FCC "incorrectly assumes that material regulatable for children can be banned from broadcast."

The FCC appealed the decision to the Supreme Court, which granted certiorari in January 1978. In *Federal Communications Commission v. Pacifica Foundation* (1978), the Court held that the Carlin broadcast was indecent because of the repetitive and deliberate use of words that refer to excretory or sexual activities during an afternoon broadcast that could be heard by children. Because the Court addressed just seven particular "indecent" words, it provided little guidance on how to recognize other indecencies. The FCC therefore chose to apply its indecency concept narrowly to the repetitive use of Carlin's seven dirty words under similar broadcast circumstances. For example, the FCC determined that a broadcast similar to Carlin's monologue would be permissible after 10 P.M.

However, during the 1980s, the FCC significantly increased the frequency and scope of its regulation of indecent programming. On April 29, 1987, the FCC released its Indecency Policy Reconsideration Order, allowing indecent programs to be aired only between midnight and 6 A.M. In its order, the FCC also reaffirmed its previous decisions against three radio stations, one against a Howard Stern morning talk show, another against a broadcast play about AIDS and homosexuality, and a third against a song broadcast after 10 P.M. The order was appealed by a group of petitioners, including Action for Children's Television, as well as commercial networks, associations of broadcasters and journalists, and public interest groups. The petitioners argued that the FCC's definition of indecency was unconstitutionally vague and overbroad, and that the new hours during which indecent broadcasting was banned would effectively prohibit adult access to material protected by the First Amendment.

In *Action for Children's Television v. Federal Communications Commission* (1988), the U.S. appeals court held that the FCC's definition of indecency was not overbroad, but found that the restriction of such programming to the hours from midnight to 6 A.M. was unreasonable. The court therefore returned the case to the FCC for reconsideration of these hours. Soon after the court's decision, Congress passed the Helms Amendment, which became law on October 1, 1988, requiring the FCC to promulgate regulations to enforce a twenty–hour-a-day ban on indecent broadcasting. Indeed, on December 21, 1988, the FCC adopted such a ban, but the action was again appealed by seventeen media and citizen groups led by Action for Children's Television, which sought an injunction against the twenty–hour ban. The D.C. Circuit Court of Appeals initially granted the stay, but subsequently granted the FCC's request to remand the stay pending the release of a report documenting support for the twenty-four–hour ban.

The FCC's report, released on August 6, 1990, stated that a twenty-four–hour ban on indecency was necessary to protect the nation's "children," which it defined to be minors seventeen and under. The report said that alternative methods for protecting children, such as ratings, warnings, or lockout devices, would not be effective, and "time-channeling" could not totally remove the risk of exposing children to indecency.

On May 17, 1991, the appeals court struck down the twenty-four–hour ban, rejecting many of the arguments in the FCC report and concluding that the ban violated constitutional protections on free speech. At issue here was the constitutionality of both the FCC's 1987 indecency standard and the Helms Amendment, which attempted to apply that standard on a twenty-four–hour basis. The court felt compelled by the Supreme Court's *Pacifica* ruling to uphold the FCC's definition of "indecency," but the controls on indecent programming had to be carefully crafted. The D.C. Appeals Court had already stated that the government's only legitimate interest in regulating indecent speech was to facilitate parents' supervision of their children's viewing and listening habits. Even the FCC had taken that position until the Helms Amendment had effectively threatened the FCC with funding cuts if it did not impose the twenty-four–hour ban.

In affirming the right of adult access to indecent material, the appeals court stated: "Broadcast material that is indecent but not obscene is protected by the First Amendment; the FCC may regulate such material only with due respect for the high value our Constitution places on freedom and choice in what the people say and hear." The court thus concluded that the Helms Amendment was unconstitutional, but that, within reasonable restrictions, the FCC's indecency standard did not violate the First Amendment. The court restated its order that the FCC redetermine the times at which indecent material may be broadcast. The court also vacated the FCC's rulings on the two post–10:00 P.M. broadcasts, stating that "in view of the curtailment of broadcaster freedom and adult listener choice that channeling entails, the Commission failed to consider fairly and fully what time lines should be drawn."

As the result of this decision and a similar Supreme Court ruling on March 2, 1992, the FCC was led to reduce its indecency ban to the hours from 6 A.M. to midnight, but this was once again struck down by the appeals court in Washington, D.C. The FCC then proposed a new ban for the hours 6 A.M. to 10 P.M. that was eventually approved by an appeals court. In early January 1996, the Supreme Court refused to review that ruling, rejecting arguments by the broadcasting industry, the news media, and free-speech advocates. FCC Chairman Reed Hundt said that the decision vindicated the FCC's indecency policy and provided a legal foundation for things like enforced children's programming and the V-chip, a microchip that would allow categories of programming to be screened out by parents.

REFERENCE: James R. Bennett, *Control of the Media in the United States: An Annotated Bibliography*, New York, Garland, 1992.

C

CAMPAIGN FINANCING   Despite a long-standing public consensus that America's system of campaign financing is flawed, each attempt at reform has confronted the reality that, to some degree, restrictions on political spending restrict political expression. Though some of these reforms have actually addressed the content of political discourse, most have attempted either to reduce corruption or diminish the influence of special-interest groups or the wealthy on the American political process.

The most serious attempts at campaign-finance reform came in 1974, in the wake of the Watergate scandal, when Congress passed amendments to the Federal Election Campaign Act. The key features of the amended Campaign Act were examined by the Supreme Court in a 1976 decision, *Buckley v. Valeo*. The Court upheld the law's requirement that the identity of persons or organizations contributing to political campaigns be revealed, though it suggested that disclosure requirements might be unconstitutional if they were applied to unpopular or dissident groups. But the most significant issue addressed by the Court in *Buckley* was the distinction between campaign contributions and campaign spending. *Buckley* upheld limits on the former but struck down limits on the latter, concluding that contributions were potentially more dangerous to the integrity of the political process and that limits on them were less intrusive on political expression than limits on campaign expenditures. Any limit on how much money may be spent on a political campaign was judged to be a direct restraint on political speech and therefore in violation of the First Amendment.

Some regard the *Buckley* decision to be an endorsement of the politically privileged position of the wealthy. Indeed, the Court seemed to equate the "marketplace of ideas" with the economic marketplace, ensuring that the rich would always be able to purchase as much political speech as their checkbook allowed. But the Court did uphold limits on how much a person may contribute to a political campaign, claiming that contributions carry with them the possibility of financial corruption. Very large contributions were considered particularly likely to be given with the expectation of a quid pro quo.

Despite the judgment in *Buckley* that limits on campaign spending are unconstitutional, legislative attempts to level the financial playing field within the political process have continued with some success. In *Federal Election Commission v. Massachusetts Citizens for Life, Inc.* (1986), the Court retreated somewhat from its *Buckley* decision. The *MCFL* case, as it is commonly called, involved an incorporated special-interest group, Massachusetts Citizens for Life, which used its funds to lobby against abortion. The Court had previously established that corporations enjoy First Amendment free-speech rights, but a federal statute nonetheless required corporations to make their political expenditures only through special segregated funds, not through their general treasuries.

The Supreme Court struck down that statute in *MCFL*, saying that Massachusetts Citizens for Life resembled a voluntary political association more than a business firm. This suggestion that a more typical corporation might have less First Amendment protection was reinforced by Justice William Brennan's opinion that "[d]irect corporate spending on political activity raises the prospect that resources amassed in the economic marketplace may be used to provide an unfair advantage in the political marketplace." Brennan justified some restraints on the political expenditures of business corporations, because the resources in the corporate treasury were not necessarily an indication of popular support for the corporation's political ideas.

In 1990, the Court once more addressed the issue of corporate expenditures in *Austin v. Michigan Chamber of Commerce*. The Michigan Campaign Finance Act prohibited corporations from using their treasury funds in support of or opposition to candidates for state office. Corporations could create segregated funds for such political expenditures, but they could solicit contributions to such funds only from a specified list of persons associated with that corporation. This law was challenged in 1985 when the Michigan State Chamber of Commerce, a nonprofit corporation, sought to use its general treasury funds to purchase a newspaper advertisement endorsing a candidate for the state legislature.

The state of Michigan followed Justice Brennan's approach in *MCFL*, claiming that corporations would have an unfair advantage in the political marketplace if they could use their general treasuries. The Michigan Chamber of Commerce responded by insisting that the corporate restrictions affirmed in *MCFL* did not apply to a nonprofit corporation.

The Supreme Court, in a 6–3 decision, rejected the arguments of the Chamber of Commerce and upheld the law prohibiting political expenditures from a corporation's general treasury. Justice Thurgood Marshall's opinion distinguished the Chamber of Commerce from the special-interest group in *MCFL*, saying that the latter was virtually free of business influence, while the Chamber of Commerce was an organization for the advancement of business. Justice Brennan concurred, repeating the claim that corporate campaign expenditures do not necessarily reflect the political interests of the shareholders.

Justice Antonin Scalia was emotional in his dissent, characterizing the Court's opinion as "Orwellian" and "incompatible with the absolutely central truth of the First Amendment: that government cannot be trusted to assure, through censorship, the 'fairness' of political debate." Justice Anthony Kennedy wrote a separate dissent, stating: "With the imprimatur of this Court, it is now a felony in Michigan for the Sierra Club, or the American Civil Liberties Union, or the Michigan Chamber of Commerce, to advise the public how a candidate voted on issues of urgent concern to their members."

One seeming contradiction in the Court's judgment in *Michigan Chamber of Commerce* was its acceptance of a "media exception" in the Michigan law. A media corporation, such as a newspaper, was allowed to run an endorsement of a political candidate, but a nonmedia corporation was prohibited from purchasing a political advertisement in the same newspaper, even if it simply reprinted the newspaper's own endorsement.

The Supreme Court has long held that First Amendment rights may not be tied to the identity of the speaker unless the "strict scrutiny" standard is satisfied, requiring that the law be narrowly tailored to serve a compelling state interest. In *Michigan Chamber of Commerce*, the Court claimed that the media exception in the Michigan law served the compelling interest of freedom of the press, but no argument was made that the law was narrowly tailored to accomplish that interest. In any case, critics of the *Michigan Chamber of Commerce* judgment question its apparent conclusion that newspaper speech is more important to society than other corporate speech.

The evolution of the Court's position from *Buckley* to *MCFL* to *Michigan Chamber of Commerce* seems to leave it with an inclination to reject limits on political spending for "leveling" purposes, but to approve controls that would make corporate political expenditures correspond to the views of those who contribute to the corporate treasury. In other words, the rich may still speak with a more powerful political voice than the poor, but the corporate use of shareholders' wealth in the political arena may be regulated.

The Court's position on campaign spending has not diminished the zeal of Capitol Hill reformers, but it has changed the language of reform. In the

1990s, rather than propose strict limits on spending, which would probably be held unconstitutional, Congress has considered a combination of public financing and rewards for "voluntary" spending limits. In 1993, Congress strengthened the system of public funding for presidential campaigns by increasing the public financing available through a checkoff on income-tax returns. Continuing threats of a Republican filibuster, led by Senator Mitch McConnell (R-Ky.), vice chairman of the Senate Ethics Committee, prevented any action on congressional reform, but by the end of 1994, the overwhelming influence of big money was becoming an embarrassment on Capitol Hill. In the 1994 races, candidates for the House and Senate spent a record $586 million, and the campaign spending in the Senate represented a 37 percent increase over 1992. The candidates in one 1994 California senatorial race alone spent almost $30 million. Oliver North spent almost $20 million in his 1994 Senate campaign. These numbers do not include the many millions of dollars raised by so-called independent political committees, nor do they include expenditures by the parties' national committees. An increasing number of wealthy candidates were personally financing their campaigns, and it was no wonder that twenty-eight of the one hundred senators were millionaires.

Senator McConnell maintained his powerful opposition to any spending reforms, noting that the costs of campaign advertising were paltry compared to those of commercial advertising. He claimed that since the Supreme Court regarded spending as speech, involuntary spending limits were unconstitutional. Under McConnell's leadership, the Senate killed a 1994 bill that would have used "voluntary" spending limits, but in late 1995, a conservative Republican, Senator John McCain (Ariz.), and a liberal Democrat, Senator Russ Feingold (Wis.), introduced a more modest bill that avoided public financing, always a problem for Republicans. The new bill would give thirty minutes of free television time to candidates who agreed to spending limits and offer such candidates reduced rates on purchased television time and postage. It would ban free mass mailings by incumbents and limit "soft money," but it would provide ways for candidates to raise additional money if their opponents exceeded spending limits. The bill would also ban political action committees (PACs), but in anticipation of a court ruling against such a ban, it has a fallback position that would limit PAC contributions to $2,000 per election cycle.

Despite continuing opposition from Senator McConnell, Senator Fred Thompson (R-Tenn.) signed on to the bill, and by early 1996, the McCain-Feingold-Thompson bill (S. 1219) had fifteen cosponsors from both parties. McCain and Feingold wrote: "The Supreme Court has ruled that we cannot stop someone who is willing to spend an unlimited amount of money for a federal office from doing so. That is the law of the land, and our bill conforms to it. But the bill does provide strong incentives for candidates to voluntarily comply with spending limits, regardless of personal wealth. Candidates who choose to spend unlimited amounts of their own money receive none of the bill's benefits. Further, the bill raises the individual contribution limits for candidates who comply with the bill's provisions when they run against someone who either refuses to comply with the spending limits or exceeds the personal contribution limit" ("A Better Way to Fix Campaign Financing," *Washington Post*, February 20, 1996, p. A11). Senator McConnell wrote in rebuttal: "Campaign finance reforms . . . would constrict fundamental democratic freedoms to participate in the political process. The campaign reform debate . . . is advanced on the premise that special interest influence is pervasive, corrosive, and must be abated at all costs. But the cost of the alleged reforms in terms of constitutional freedoms for all Americans is high" ("Just What Is a Special Interest?" *Washington Post*, February 21, 1996, p. A19).

In January 1996, the Supreme Court announced that it would hear a First Amendment Challenge to federal limits on political parties' expenditures in general elections. The case arose during a 1986 U.S. Senate race in Colorado when the Federal Election Commission (FEC) fined the Republican Campaign Committee for exceeding a campaign spending cap. In that campaign, Democratic Congressman Tim Wirth became the target of a $15,000 radio ad campaign paid for, not by his Republican opponent, but by the Colorado Republican Party. The Colorado Democratic Party filed a complaint with the FEC that the Republican ads put them over the FEC's spending limit.

The FEC upheld the complaint, ruling that the radio ads were political speech subject to FEC limits, and attempted to impose a civil penalty. The matter was then taken to the district court, which ruled against the FEC, but the appeals court upheld the FEC's position. The Colorado Republican Party, supported by both the national Republican and Democratic parties, then brought the matter before the Supreme Court as *Colorado Republican Federal Campaign Committee v. Federal Election Commission*, arguing not only to overrule the lower-court decision, but to challenge the existing network of campaign expenditure restrictions. The Republicans asked the Court to hold unconstitutional the provision of the federal campaign laws that limits the amount of money political parties may spend on their candidates.

Groups like Common Cause supported the FEC's position, claiming that the Court had already established the correct balance between free speech and government interest in the landmark 1976 case *Buckley v. Valeo*. Ann McBride of Common Cause said, "Speech can be limited when there is a compelling state interest, and in this case . . . the compelling state interest was corruption or the appearance of corruption." McBride said that the removal of state party spending limits would create a loophole, allowing individual donors to funnel unlimited contributions through the national party to the state party and ultimately to a particular candidate. "A $20,000 contribution run through the political party in Colorado has the same corrupting impact as a direct contribution to that candidate," said McBride. Jan Baran, who represented the Colorado Republican Party before the

Supreme Court, said, "This is the core of the First Amendment, and the government rarely, if ever, is able to dictate how much political speech anyone, including a political party, or perhaps especially a political party, may engage in" ("Newshour with Jim Lehrer," Public Broadcasting System, April 15, 1996).

On June 26, 1996, the Supreme Court ruled that political parties could spend unlimited funds on congressional races so long as they acted "independently" of the candidates. This differed from the approach of the lower courts, where the case turned on the question of whether the party spending was "in connection with" a particular candidate. In its 7–2 decision, the Court said that it was a violation of parties' free-speech rights to restrict "independent expenditures" on behalf of their candidates. The Court defined "independent expenditures" to be those that operated independently of a candidate's campaign organization and did not coordinate with the candidate the message, timing, or placement of advertising. The Court's ruling sidestepped the broader question of whether limitations on party spending that is coordinated with individual candidates violated the Constitution. Four justices indicated that they were prepared to remove restrictions on party spending no matter what the circumstances, while two said that they would not, and three said that it was too early to decide that issue.

Justice Stephen Breyer, joined by Justices Sandra Day O'Connor and David Souter, said that there was no evidence that the Colorado Republican Party spending had been coordinated with the candidate. Breyer concluded, "We do not see how a Constitution that grants to individuals, candidates, and ordinary political committees the right to make unlimited independent expenditures could deny the same right to political parties." Chief Justice William Rehnquist and Justices Anthony Kennedy, Antonin Scalia, and Clarence Thomas wanted to go even further and remove all party spending limits. Justices John Paul Stevens and Ruth Bader Ginsburg dissented, saying that spending limits were necessary to avoid corruption and protect equal access to the political arena.

The decision left open the question of whether the 1976 *Buckley v. Valeo* decision allowing contribution limits but barring spending curbs should be reexamined. Justice Thomas urged reversal of *Buckley*, saying, "I believe that contribution limits infringe as directly and as seriously upon freedom of political expression and association as do expenditure limits." Justices Stevens and Ginsburg also endorsed the reversal of *Buckley*, but for the opposite reason, supporting tighter spending limits. "It is quite wrong to assume that the net effect of limits on contributions and expenditures . . . will be adverse to the interest in informed debate protected by the First Amendment," wrote Stevens.

REFERENCES: Thomas Gais, *Improper Influence: Campaign Finance Law, Political Interest Groups, and the Problem of Equality*, Ann Arbor, University of Michigan Press, 1996; Greg D. Kubiak, *The Gilded Dome: The U.S. Senate and Campaign Finance Reform*, Norman, University of Oklahoma Press, 1994; Frank J. Sorauf, *Inside Campaign Finance: Myths and Realities*, New Haven, Yale University Press, 1992.

CHILD PORNOGRAPHY   In *New York v. Ferber* (1982), the Supreme Court ruled that a state could prohibit the dissemination of material depicting sexual acts among children regardless of whether that material was obscene. In addition to New York, nineteen other states have statutes prohibiting the dissemination of such nonobscene material, while fourteen states prohibit the dissemination of such material only if it is obscene. Two states prohibit dissemination only if the material is obscene as to minors, and twelve states prohibit only the use of minors in the production of such material.

In 1988, Congress passed the Child Protection Act, and in 1990, it passed its amended form, the Child Protection Restoration and Penalty Enforcement Act of 1990, making it a crime to produce or possess child pornography and broadening general obscenity enforcement. Introduced by Senator Strom Thurmond (R-S.C.), the act made it illegal for a parent or guardian to permit a child to be engaged in the production of child pornography, made it mandatory for media producers to maintain records of the ages of their models and actors, and defined the sale or transfer of two or more obscene items as an illegal obscenity business. The legislation also strengthened enforcement provisions by placing burdens of proof on businesses. Various civil liberties groups raised objections to the record-keeping provisions of the bill, delaying its enforcement until regulations could be written by the Justice Department.

The Child Pornography Prevention Act of 1996 caused a furor among civil libertarians when it extended the definition of child pornography to include images that do not involve children at all, including adults portraying minors and even computer-generated images. The Act, which took effect on September 30, 1996, outlaws "any visual depiction, including any photograph, film, video image or picture" that "is, or appears to be, of a minor engaging in sexually explicit conduct." The chief defense against prosecution under previous law—proof that participants are of legal age—does not apply under the new law, which prescribes penalties ranging from five years in prison to thirty years for repeat offenders.

Critics of the Child Pornography Prevention Act said it would allow prosecution of legitimate works. Daniel Katz, legislative counsel for the American Civil Liberties Union, said, "[W]hat they're going to do is sweep up a great deal of constitutionally protected activity." The bill also creates an exception to existing laws restricting newsroom searches. Supporters of the new law contend that any images that might incite pedophiles to act out their fantasies should be banned, whether or not those images involve children. But in *Brandenberg v. Ohio* (1969), the Supreme Court rejected the notion that government could ban works that did not directly incite illegal action. To ban works because of what they might inspire others to do "is to reduce the level of the First Amendment to the level of the most perverted criminal among us," said Eric Freedman, a Hofstra University Law profes-

sor ("New Law Expanding Legal Definition of Child Pornography Draws Fire," *Washington Post*, October 4, 1996, A10).
REFERENCES: Shirley O'Brien, *Child Pornography*, Dubuque, Kendall/Hunt Pub. Co., 1983; U.S. Senate Committee on the Judiciary, *Cyberporn and Children: Hearing before the Committee on the Judiciary*, 104th Cong. 1st sess., July 24, 1995.

CHILDREN'S LEGAL FOUNDATION   The Children's Legal Foundation (CLF) was formed in 1957 by Charles Keating as Citizens for Decent Literature. It changed its name to Citizens for Decency through Law in 1973 and adopted its current organizational title in 1989. It is dedicated to fighting pornography, obscenity, and other communications that are deemed harmful to children. Toward this end, the organization conducts public education campaigns about the harmful effects of pornography in publications, broadcasting, and motion pictures. The organization assists local groups in bringing suit against distributors of alleged pornography and supports legislators and law enforcement agencies in passing and enforcing laws against pornography.

The Children's Legal Foundation publishes *The CLF Reporter*, a quarterly publication of foundation activities and research. The president of CLF is Robert J. Hubbard, Jr. The organization is located at 2845 East Camelback Road, Suite 740, Phoenix, AZ 85016.
REFERENCE: John B. Harer, *Intellectual Freedom: A Reference Handbook*, Santa Barbara, ABC-CLIO, 1992.

CHILDREN'S RIGHTS   The courts have failed to provide a clear legal basis for applying the First Amendment rights of adults to minors, in large part because of the long-standing protectionist attitude that American society has taken toward children. This attitude has assigned a special legal status to children, regarding them as the charges of the family and the state. In colonial America, children were treated as servants, holding positions of complete subservience within the family unit. The common law regarded both the infant and the mature teenager as minors, treating them as the virtual property of their parents. This extremity has been rejected by the Supreme Court in recent years, but without an analysis of the full relationship between the child and the state. Areas in which children's rights have been tested in the courts include the mass media, personal privacy, and the schools.

In *Ginsberg v. New York* (1968), the Court tested the constitutionality of a state law that defined certain material to be obscene only if it was sold to minors under the age of seventeen. The magazines in question were not considered obscene for adults. In determining that the state has the power to apply "variable obscenity" standards, the Court claimed that even where there is an invasion of protected freedoms, "the power of the state to control the conduct of children reaches beyond its authority over adults." In his concurring opinion, Justice Potter Stewart stated: "I think a State may permissibly determine that, at least in some precisely delineated areas, a child . . . is not possessed of that full capacity for individual choice which is the presupposition of First Amendment guarantees."

This expansive view of the state's power over children rested upon two assumptions: first, the recognition that parents' authority over the children within their household is basic to our society; second, the belief that when parental control cannot be exercised, society's transcendent interest in protecting the welfare of children justifies "reasonable" regulation of the sale of material to them. Finally, the Court declared that pornography in the hands of children was obscene, and since obscenity was not protected speech, the New York statute did not violate constitutional rights. However, the Court made clear that such restraint on speech was narrowly defined. The *Harvard Law Review* warned that *Ginsberg* should not be interpreted as supporting broad state restrictions on the access of minors to nonobscene material such as violent films, even if the state judged them to be injurious to minors.

The electronic media were soon seen as a greater threat to children than the print media. In *Federal Communications Commission v. Pacifica Foundation* (1978), the Court once more approved restrictions on nonobscene speech within the public media by judging it in relation to children. The case arose when the Federal Communications Commission issued a declaratory ruling concerning the broadcast of a recording by humorist George Carlin, played on a noncommercial radio station, WBAI-FM, in New York City. A parent who heard the recording on his car radio while driving with his fifteen-year-old son complained to the FCC.

The FCC ruling did not impose any fines or forfeiture upon WBAI-FM, but declared a general ban on "indecent" programming during daytime hours. The FCC conceded that the Pacifica broadcast was not obscene, but claimed authority to regulate indecent speech during those broadcast hours when children might be in the audience. The Court ruled that indecent speech may be prohibited from daytime radio during hours when children are presumed to be in the audience, but it went to great lengths to distinguish "obscene" from "indecent," suggesting that indecent speech is constitutionally protected speech that nonetheless may be restricted in order to protect children.

Pacifica thus interpreted the First Amendment to allow controls on adult speech in the general marketplace so long as children might be exposed to that speech, justifying such government control on the basis of the pervasive influence of broadcasting and its easy accessibility to children. This potentially broad sweep was subsequently narrowed in *Sable Communications of California, Inc. v. Federal Communications Commission*, which examined legislation prohibiting "dial-a-porn" telephone messages. *Sable* rejected a congressional ban, pointing out that *Pacifica* did not approve a total ban on indecent material, requiring only that the material be broadcast during times when children would be unlikely to hear it.

In the area of personal privacy, the Supreme Court has ruled that the state may not constitutionally impose a blanket parental-consent requirement as a condition for an unmarried minor's abortion. In *Planned Parenthood of Central Missouri. v. Danforth* (1976), the Court rejected a portion of a Missouri statute requiring parental consent, noting that "constitutional rights do not mature and come into being magically only when one attains the state-defined age of majority. Minors, as well as adults, are protected by the Constitution and possess constitutional rights."

In *Bellotti v. Baird* (1979), the Court addressed the constitutionality of a Massachusetts statute that required unmarried minor girls to gain the approval of both parents before having an abortion. The 8–1 opinion, written by Justice Lewis Powell, began: "A child, merely on account of his minority, is not beyond the protection of the Constitution. . . . Whatever may be their precise impact, neither the Fourteenth Amendment nor the Bill of Rights is for adults alone." Though the Court in *Bellotti* concluded that the Massachusetts law was unconstitutional because it offered minors no alternative to parental authorization, it nonetheless outlined three justifications for limiting the rights of children. First, "The State is entitled to adjust its legal system to account for children's vulnerability and their needs." Second, children are unable "to make critical decisions in an informed, mature manner." Third, the system of parental authority accepted by the American legal system "is not inconsistent with our tradition of individual liberty."

Perhaps the most complex context in which to define children's First Amendment rights is within the school environment. In *Pierce v. Society of Sisters* (1925), the Court struck down mandatory public school attendance, stating: "The fundamental theory of liberty upon which all governments in this Union repose excludes any general power of the state to standardize its children by forcing them to accept instruction from public teachers only. The child is not the mere creature of the state."

Not until 1940, in the flag-salute case *Minersville School District v. Gobitis*, did the Supreme Court go beyond *Pierce* in clarifying the limits of state authority over schoolchildren. In *Gobitis*, the children of a Jehovah's Witnesses family had refused to join the flag-salute ceremonies at their school, claiming that they were following the biblical prohibition against bowing down to graven images. After the Gobitis children were expelled from school, their parents brought the suit decided by the Supreme Court in 1940. The Court ruled that the school authorities did have the right to require participation in the flag salute, and that the religious beliefs of the Jehovah's Witnesses did not represent a First Amendment exemption. Justice Harlan F. Stone, dissenting in *Gobitis*, declared, "[T]here are other ways to teach loyalty and patriotism . . . than by compelling the pupil to affirm what he does not believe."

In *West Virginia State Board of Education v. Barnette* (1943), the Court overruled *Gobitis* and established a legal restraint on the power of school officials to impose their "socialization" process on students. Justice Robert Jackson's repudiation of Felix Frankfurter's *Gobitis* opinion suggested clear limits upon the authority of school officials. "That they are educating the young for citizenship is reason for scrupulous protection of constitutional freedoms of the individual, if we are not to strangle the free mind at its source and teach youth to discount important principles of our government as mere platitudes."

In *Tinker v. Des Moines Independent Community School District* (1969), the Court addressed the authority of school officials to prohibit students from wearing black armbands to silently express their opposition to the Vietnam War. The principals of the Des Moines schools announced that any student wearing such an armband would be asked to remove it, and if the student refused he or she would be suspended from school. One group of students, including John and Mary Beth Tinker, wore the armbands to school, where they were told to remove them in accordance with the principals' edict. They refused, and were ordered to leave school. The students subsequently returned to school without their armbands, but only after filing suit in federal court.

The Tinkers lost their case at both the district-court level and in the U.S. court of appeals, but the U.S. Supreme Court reversed these decisions. In the Supreme Court's clearest affirmation of First Amendment rights for schoolchildren, the majority opinion held that school officials may not place arbitrary restraints on student speech in public schools. Justice Abe Fortas wrote: "First Amendment rights, applied in light of the special character of the school environment, are available to teachers and students. It can hardly be argued that either students or teachers shed their constitutional rights to freedom of speech or expression at the schoolhouse gate."

The Court did not renounce its traditional deference to school authority on matters of student conduct, but it noted that the action of the students in *Tinker* did not intrude upon the work of the school or the rights of other students. The Court concluded: "Students in school as well as out of school are 'persons' under our Constitution. They are possessed of fundamental rights which the State must respect, just as they themselves must respect their obligations to the State. In our system, students may not be regarded as closed-circuit recipients of only that which the State chooses to communicate. . . . In the absence of a specific showing of constitutionally valid reasons to regulate their speech, students are entitled to free expression of their views."

In *Tinker* the Court made no attempt to distinguish between the First Amendment rights of adults and minors, as Justice Stewart did in *Ginsberg*. This may have been because the two cases considered different forms of expression, one involving obscenity and the other involving political expression. Even so, one member of the *Tinker* Court did express some confusion, stating, "I cannot share the Court's uncritical assumption that . . . the First Amendment rights of children are coextensive with those of adults. Indeed, I had thought the Court decided otherwise just last term in *Ginsberg*."

Indeed, just three years later, the Court seemed to move back toward the broad paternalism in *Ginsberg*. In *Wisconsin v. Yoder* (1972), Chief Justice Burger wrote for an almost unanimous Court in affirming the right of Amish parents to withhold their children from compulsory schooling beyond the age of fourteen, regardless of the children's desire. In dissenting in *Yoder*, Justice William O. Douglas warned: "It is the student's judgment, not his parents,' that is essential if we are to give full meaning to what we have said about the Bill of Rights and of the right of students to be masters of their own destiny." Douglas expressed concern that the child's choices and judgments be respected before allowing the imposition of Amish attitudes: "Where a child is mature enough to express potentially conflicting desires, it would be an invasion of the child's rights to permit such an imposition without canvassing his view."

The federal courts have also tested children's rights in the area of book and curricular censorship. In *Zykan v. Warsaw Community School Corporation* (1980), a student brought suit to reverse school officials' decision to prohibit the use of certain textbooks, to remove a book from the school library, and to delete certain courses from the curriculum. The suit was dismissed by the district court, and the Court of Appeals for the Seventh Circuit upheld the school board's right to establish a curriculum on the basis of its own discretion so long as it did not impose a "pall of orthodoxy" on the classroom. Here the court held that "two factors tend to limit the relevance of 'academic freedom' at the secondary school level. First, the student's right to and need for such freedom is bounded by the level of his or her intellectual development. . . . Second, the importance of secondary schools in the development of intellectual faculties is only one part of a broad formative role encompassing the encouragement and nurturing of those fundamental social, political, and moral values that will permit a student to take his place in the community." Following this argument, the court concluded that "complaints filed by secondary school students to contest the educational decisions of local authorities are sometimes cognizable but generally must cross a relatively high threshold before entering upon the field of a constitutional claim suitable for federal court litigation."

Two years later, a similar case went to the Supreme Court, producing a judgment more sympathetic to the rights of students than did *Zykan*. In *Board of Education, Island Trees Union Free School District No. 26 v. Pico* (1982), five students from the local junior high school and high school brought suit to challenge the school board's action in removing nine books from the school library. The district court initially granted summary judgment in favor of the Board of Education, but in October 1980, the U.S. Court of Appeals for the Second Circuit reversed the decision and remanded the case back to the district court for trial. The school board responded in 1981 by requesting that the Supreme Court review the *Pico* case, and certiorari was granted. By a 5–4 vote, the Supreme Court affirmed the appeals court ruling that the board's removal of books from the libraries denied the students their First Amendment rights. Justice William Brennan wrote the plurality opinion, with Thurgood Marshall and John Paul Stevens joining, Byron White concurring, and Harry Blackmun concurring in part. Brennan acknowledged that all First Amendment rights accorded to students must be construed in light of the "special characteristics of the school environment," but he said that school boards had no authority "to extend their claim of absolute discretion beyond the compulsory environment of the classroom, into the school library and the regime of voluntary inquiry that there holds sway."

In his *Pico* dissent, Justice William Rehnquist was joined by Warren Burger in rejecting such rights within the special circumstances of the school: "When it acts as an educator, at least at the elementary and secondary school level, the government is engaged in inculcating social values and knowledge in relatively impressionable young people. . . . In short, actions by the government as educator do not raise the same First Amendment concerns as actions by the government as sovereign." Rehnquist distinguished between the First Amendment rights of high-school students as opposed to college students, drawing upon the conclusion in *Zykan* that high-school students lack the intellectual skills necessary to take full advantage of the marketplace of ideas. Their need for academic freedom is therefore bounded by their level of intellectual development.

Rather than go back to trial, as the *Pico* plurality ordered, the School Board voted to return all of the banned books to the library shelves, effectively ending the dispute. The opinions in *Pico* documented a fundamental philosophical dispute between two entrenched factions within the Court. The faction led by Justice Brennan regarded education as having an analytic objective that should not be subordinated to indoctrination. Such education would require that teachers and students work together in a joint search for truth. On the other hand, the faction led by Chief Justice Burger regarded elementary and secondary education to be indoctrinative or prescriptive in purpose, within which the teacher and the curriculum serve to convey prescribed truths. Burger's characterization of schools as vehicles for inculcating the fundamental values of the American political system caused Brennan to fear that students would become nothing more than "closed-circuit recipients of only that which the State chooses to communicate."

Perhaps because of the fractured plurality in *Pico*, it did not establish a clear precedent in support of students' First Amendment rights. The power of school officials to control student expression was reasserted just four years after *Pico* in *Bethel School District No. 403 v. Fraser* (1986). Here the Court rejected a student's claim that his First Amendment rights had been violated when he was disciplined for an alleged sexual innuendo in his speech nominating another student for school office. In supporting the school board, Burger advised: "The undoubted freedom to advocate unpopular and controversial views in schools and classrooms must be balanced against the society's countervailing interest in teaching students the boundaries of socially appropriate behavior. . . . It does not follow . . . that simply because the use of an offensive form of expression may not be prohibited to adults making what the speaker considers a political point, that the same latitude must be permitted to children in a public school." Writing for the majority, Burger concluded: "Surely it is a highly appropriate function of public school education to prohibit the use of vulgar and offensive terms in public discourse. . . . The determination of what manner of speech in the classroom or in school assembly is inappropriate properly rests with the school board."

The most severe legal restraint on student expression came in the 1988 *Hazelwood School District v. Kuhlmeier* decision. Here the Court saw no constitutional restraint on a Missouri school principal who removed portions of a student newspaper produced as part of a high-school journalism class. When the principal removed pages containing articles on pregnancy and divorce from the high-school newspaper, the student staff filed suit, claiming violation of their First Amendment rights. The school principal claimed that he was properly protecting the privacy of pregnant students described, but not named, in the articles, and also that he was protecting younger students from inappropriate references to sexual activity and birth control. The principal also claimed that since a school-sponsored newspaper could be perceived as an expression of official school opinion, censorship was justified to protect the school from possible libel action. The Supreme Court held that the principal acted reasonably and did not violate the students' First Amendment rights. The Court declared that a school need not tolerate student speech "that is inconsistent with its 'basic educational mission,' even though the government could not censor similar speech outside the school."

Because the newspaper was part of the journalism curriculum, it was held to be subject to control by a faculty member. The newspaper was thus regarded not as a forum for the free expression of ideas but "as supervised learning experience for journalism students." The Court ruled that "educators do not offend the First Amendment by exercising editorial control over the style and content of student speech in school-sponsored expressive activities so long as their actions are reasonably related to legitimate pedagogical concerns." The Court did caution, however, that this authority does not justify school action "to silence a student's personal expression that happens to occur on the school premises. . . . It is only when the decision to censor a school-sponsored publication, theatrical production, or other vehicle of student expression has no valid educational purpose that the First Amendment is so 'directly and sharply implicate[d]' as to require judicial intervention to protect students' constitutional rights." *Hazelwood* therefore established that teachers, principals, and school boards may take action within the school's educational mission that might otherwise be unconstitutional.

Within a year of *Hazelwood*, the fears that it would lead the courts to place school censorship outside of First Amendment protections seemed realized. In *Virgil v. School Board of Columbia County* (1989), the Eleventh Circuit applied the Supreme Court's approach in *Hazelwood*, upholding a school board's removal of a previously approved textbook because of alleged vulgarity and sexual explicitness in two textbook selections, *The Miller's Tale* by Chaucer and *Lysistrata* by Aristophanes. Some parents in the community objected to the court's apparent willingness to allow the complaints of a few people to determine what could be read by all of the students in the school. On November 24, 1986, the ACLU brought suit against the board on behalf of a parent named Moyna Virgil. The case, *Virgil v. School Board of Columbia County*, argued that the removal of the textbook suppressed free speech and free thought while advancing religion through the public schools.

The defense relied on *Hazelwood*, while the ACLU counted on *Pico*. U.S. District Judge Susan Black ruled that *Hazelwood* was the relevant Supreme Court precedent, concluding that its interpretation of the limited scope of students' First Amendment rights compelled her to decide in favor of the school board. The ACLU appealed, arguing that *Hazelwood* applied to student writing, not literary classics, but the U.S. Court of Appeals for the Eleventh Circuit upheld Black's decision, stating, "Of course, we do not endorse the Board's decision. Like the district court, we seriously question how young persons just below the age of majority can be harmed by these masterpieces of Western literature. However, having concluded that there is no constitutional violation, our role is not to second guess the wisdom of the Board's action."

Today, *Hazelwood* remains the controlling precedent on student expression, though there have been some contrary opinions. In *McCarthy v. Fletcher* (1989), a teacher, a student, a parent, and a general taxpayer brought suit against the administrators and trustees of the Waco Union High School District after school officials banned two novels from use in a twelfth-grade English class. The trial court granted summary judgment in favor of the school officials, but the California Court of Appeal reversed the lower court's judgment, saying that the possible violation of the First Amendment rights of teachers and students needed to be examined in a full trial, rather than the summary judgment rendered. In remanding the case for trial, the court said that even under the *Hazelwood* standard, school officials may not act to "prescribe what shall be orthodox in politics, nationalism, religion, or other matters of opinion. . . . [T]he educational unsuitability of the books . . . must be the true reason for the books' exclusion and not just a pretextual expression for exclusion because the board disagrees with the religious or philosophical ideas expressed in the books." The court concluded that such

dissembling would enable school officials to "camouflage religious 'viewpoint discrimination' . . . which we do not believe *Hazelwood* intended."
REFERENCE: Herbert N. Foerstel, *Banned in the U.S.A: A Reference Guide to Book Censorship in Schools and Public Libraries*, Westport, Greenwood Press, 1994.

COMSTOCK, ANTHONY, 1844–1915 Anthony Comstock was a religious fundamentalist who left his career as a New England dry-goods clerk to begin a crusade to root out vice and pornography. In 1873, Comstock created what came to be called "vice squads" when he originated the New York Society for the Suppression of Vice. That organization subsequently inspired the creation of the Boston-based New England Watch and Ward Society. Comstock was also the moving force behind the passage of the federal obscenity statute, also known as the Comstock Act, which barred from the mails any obscene, lewd, or indecent material. Appointed as a special agent of the Post Office, he was authorized to carry a gun and attack pornographers nationwide.

Comstock estimated that he arrested more than 3,500 people under the act, though few were found guilty. His aggressive and self-righteous public behavior, mimicked and ridiculed, came to be known as "Comstockery," a term coined by George Bernard Shaw to describe "a self-appointed protector of other people's morals."
REFERENCES: Heywood Broun and Margaret Leech, *Anthony Comstock, Roundsman of the Lord*, 1927; Robert W. Haney, *Comstockery in America: Patterns of Censorship and Control*, New York, Da Capo Press, 1974 [c.1960].

CONCERNED WOMEN FOR AMERICA Concerned Women for America (CWA) is an educational and legal foundation founded in 1979 to promote traditional American family values. The organization was created by wives of evangelical Christian ministers, but its membership now numbers about 600,000 women of various faiths. CWA organizes political action through what it calls "kitchen table lobbyists," which are local groups using letter-writing campaigns to attack feminism, including the Equal Rights Amendment (ERA), and liberal policies in public education, such as restraints on prayer in school and the inclusion of indecent or un-Christian curricular and library materials. In 1991, CWA formed a network of legal offices, called the American Justice League, to counteract the activities of the American Civil Liberties Union.

Concerned Women for America publishes a monthly newsletter for its membership. The organization is located at 370 L'Enfant Promenade, SW, Suite 800, Washington, DC 20024.
REFERENCE: *Encyclopedia of Associations*, Detroit, Gale Research Co., 31st ed., 1996.

CONTEMPT OF CONGRESS Whereas contempt of court restricts speech or conduct that would interfere with the administration of justice, contempt of Congress occurs when a witness summoned before Congress fails to appear or refuses to answer any question pertinent to the matter under inquiry. Title 2, Section 192 of the *U.S. Code* reads: "Every person summoned as a witness by the authority of either House of Congress to give testimony or to produce papers upon any matter under inquiry before either House, or any joint committee established by a joint or concurring resolution of the two Houses of Congress, or any committee of either House of Congress, who wilfully makes default, or who, having appeared, refuses to answer any question pertinent to the question under inquiry, shall be deemed guilty of a misdemeanor, punishable by fine of not more than $1,000 nor less than $100 and imprisonment in a common jail for not less than one month nor more than twelve months."

This congressional power to force the appearance and testimony of citizens was upheld by the Supreme Court in *Barenblatt v. United States* (1959), in which a contempt conviction arising from a refusal to answer questions from the House Committee on Un-American Activities was upheld. However, in *Watkins v. United States* (1957), the Supreme Court said that Watkins, who had appeared before the same Un-American Activities Committee, could not be convicted of contempt of Congress if he refused to answer questions about other people's alleged associations with Communist organizations.

REFERENCE: Carl Beck, *Contempt of Congress: A Study of the Prosecutions Initiated by the Committee on Un-American Activities, 1945–1957*, New Orleans, Hauser Press, 1959.

CONTEMPT OF COURT   Contempt of court is a restriction on free speech imposed within a courtroom to avoid words or actions that would interfere with the administration of justice. For example, criticism of the judge or other court officers expressed within the courtroom could be punishable as contempt. The same criticism, expressed outside the courtroom, might be protected speech.

If, in the view of the court, an individual's expression unreasonably interferes in an immediate sense with the administration of justice, such expression is outside of First Amendment protections. Inside the courtroom, judges have the power to punish such speech directed at the judge or other officers of the court. Even outside the court, there are some restraints, though such speech may only be restricted as contempt if it constitutes a clear and present danger to the administration of justice.

REFERENCE: Christopher J. Miller, *Contempt of Court*, 2d ed., New York, Oxford University Press, 1989.

CRIMINAL SYNDICALISM   Several states have criminal syndicalism laws that prohibit and punish anarchism, the violent overthrow of the government, and other forms of rebellion or revolution. In *Gitlow v. New York* (1925), the Supreme Court upheld such a statute in New York, stating,

"That utterances inciting to the overthrow of organized government by unlawful means, present a sufficient danger of substantive evil to bring their punishment within the range of legislative discretion, is clear. . . . It cannot be said that the State is acting arbitrarily or unreasonably when in the exercise of its judgment as to the measures necessary to protect the public peace and safety, it seeks to extinguish the spark without waiting until it has enkindled the flame or blazed into the conflagration."

Despite its willingness to suppress political speech, *Gitlow* did establish that freedom of speech and press were among the rights protected by the due process clause of the Fourteenth Amendment. In dissent, Justices Oliver Wendell Holmes and Louis Brandeis voiced the "clear and present danger" test. *Brandenburg v. Ohio* (1969) subsequently refined the Court's view by holding that a state criminal syndicalism statute violated the First Amendment by punishing advocacy without a showing of imminent danger: "The constitutional guarantees of free speech and free press do not permit a state to forbid or proscribe advocacy of the use of force or of law violation except where such advocacy is directed to inciting or producing imminent lawless action, and is likely to incite or produce such action."
REFERENCE: Eldridge F. Dowell, *A History of Criminal Syndicalism Legislation in the United States*, New York, Da Capo Press, 1969 [c.1939].

CRYPTOGRAPHY Cryptography has been defined as the science of protecting the privacy and authenticity of information in a hostile environment. Historically, cryptography was the exclusive domain of an elite cadre of secret government scientists who sought to protect their nation's official communications while breaking the codes of other nations. Today, the field has burgeoned, with unlimited applications to private life and business. Everything from ATMs to interactive TV to the secured communications of corporate executives uses encrypted data.

Cryptography has emerged as the most severely restricted form of scientific communication, and the implications for personal privacy are ominous. As the federal government increases its reliance on the technology of surveillance, its insistence that effective cryptography, the public's only defense against surveillance, be denied to the private sector strongly suggests that the state intends to manipulate science against the privacy interests of American citizens.

Even the scholars producing this research have been forced to struggle with the government for the right to communicate freely with their peers. The early battles against government-imposed secrecy in cryptography came from the cryptographers themselves, who sought to publish accounts of their spectacular accomplishments. The first American superstar in cryptography was Herbert Osborne Yardley. In 1917, Yardley assumed command of Section Eight of Military Intelligence (MI-8), which had responsibility for all code and cipher work during World War I. After the war, the supersecret bureau he created became known as the Black Chamber.

Yardley quickly gained the complicity of companies like Western Union in monitoring America's domestic communications, but in 1929, President Herbert Hoover's Secretary of State, Henry L. Stimson, discovered the details of the Black Chamber's machinations and closed down the operation, declaring, "Gentlemen do not read each other's mail." Now out of a job, Yardley began work on a book describing his exploits. The War Department warned Yardley not to proceed, but Bobbs-Merrill agreed to publish the book, and the *Saturday Evening Post* serialized it during April and May of 1931.

Yardley immediately began a second book, *Japanese Diplomatic Secrets, 1921–22*. The State Department now approached the publisher to prevent the appearance of the book, and Bobbs-Merrill agreed to withdraw it. An officer from the War Department then called on Yardley at his home and demanded that he surrender his new manuscript and all source documents. Yardley refused and instead offered his manuscript to another publisher, Macmillan. At this point, a young assistant in the U.S. Attorney's Office, Thomas E. Dewey, interceded to suppress the book. Dewey, who would later come within a hair of being elected President, seized Yardley's manuscript from Macmillan, an unprecedented action by the American government. Yardley was then summoned to Dewey's office, where he was told that if he continued to pursue publication of his book, he would face prosecution under the Espionage Act. A dejected Yardley complied with Dewey's demands, and his manuscript remained impounded for almost fifty years.

To avoid similar incidents in the future, the State Department pressed for legislation to criminalize the publication of any information on government codes. In 1933, H.R. 4220 was quietly passed and signed by President Roosevelt. When the press learned of the bill, there were charges that it violated the First Amendment, but it remains on the books today.

After the closing of the Black Chamber, its functions were simply shifted from Military Intelligence to a variety of new, ultrasecret agencies. By the end of World War II, all private cable companies were secretly sharing the public's communications with these agencies. In 1952, President Truman created the National Security Agency (NSA), and, like the Black Chamber, the NSA indulged in prior restraint of cryptographic literature. When amateur cryptologist David Kahn signed a contract with Macmillan to write a book titled *The Codebreakers*, the NSA devised a set of options to stop publication, including (1) hiring Kahn, thus making him subject to prepublication review and criminal statutes; (2) purchasing the copyright to Kahn's book; or (3) stealing Kahn's manuscript through a black-bag job on his home. Under pressure from the entire American intelligence community, Macmillan agreed to turn Kahn's manuscript over to the Pentagon, just as it had done with Yardley's manuscript almost forty years earlier. The Pentagon and the NSA then forced Kahn to agree to a series of deletions before approving publication.

The censorship of communications on cryptography has been reinforced through draconian export controls that restrict the exchange of information as well as products. For export purposes, cryptographic information is conveniently defined as "munitions." The Munitions Control Act, the Arms Export Control Act, and the International Traffic in Arms Regulations (ITAR) have all been invoked to prevent scholarly publications, meetings, symposia, or even private conversations on cryptography. In 1977, the NSA used the ITAR as a rationalization for imposing a censorship system over private cryptographic research, despite the Justice Department's admission that the existing provisions of ITAR were unconstitutional insofar as they established a prior restraint on disclosure of cryptographic ideas and information developed by scientists and mathematicians in the private sector.

The NSA has persistently attempted to control academic research in cryptography. In 1978, the NSA forged an unfortunate gentleman's agreement with the National Science Foundation (NSF) under which the NSF transferred responsibility for funding unclassified cryptographic research to the NSA. In 1980, the NSA pressured the American Council of Education to form the Public Cryptography Study Group (PCSG) to consider prepublication review of all papers in cryptography. The NSA wanted a statute permitting it to censor a "central core" of nongovernmental cryptographic research, but the PCSG's final report recommended a system under which authors would "voluntarily" refrain from publishing such papers. If the author refused, a five-member advisory committee appointed by the Director of the NSA and the President's science adviser would make the final decision.

In 1980, cryptography expert David Kahn told Congress that public research in cryptography improves America's overall cryptographic skills, produces spin-off advances in mathematics and computer science, and provides database security for America. "For all of these reasons, then," he concluded, "I feel that no limitation should be placed on the study of cryptology. Besides all of these reasons, it seems to me that something more fundamental will in the end prevent any restrictions anyway. It is called the First Amendment" (*The Government's Classification of Private Ideas: Hearings before a Subcommittee of the Committee on Government Operations, House of Representatives*, 96th Cong., 2nd Session, 28 February, 20 March, 21 August 1980, Washington, D.C., U.S. GPO, 1981, 410).

After the collapse of the Soviet Union in 1990, the United States relaxed some of its export controls. The exporters of mass-market software, the kinds of products that can be bought at any local computer store, were generally granted export licenses with few restrictions unless that software used any form of encryption. Cryptographic software, even that on the mass market, is treated like weapons, appearing on the U.S. Munitions List. A manufacturer of software containing an encryption algorithm must therefore go through an elaborate review process for an export license.

Among the agencies that must approve such a license is the NSA, which insists that the encryption be easily broken before it may be exported. The actual NSA review process is classified.

A violation of the export restrictions on encryption software can result in a maximum criminal penalty of $1 million and ten years in prison or a maximum civil penalty of $500,000 and a three-year export ban. Unlike the United States, most countries do not regulate encryption software. The new post-Communist Constitution in Russia actually felt it necessary in this new world order to explicitly forbid governmental restriction on the use of cryptography.

The Clinton administration embraced two policy positions on cryptography: (1) the continuation of long-standing restrictions on the export of encryption software that the NSA cannot crack, and (2) support for the NSA-developed Clipper Chip as the encryption standard for government and private industry. The disturbing privacy implications of these policies were underscored by the administration's simultaneous endorsement of an FBI proposal to require telecommunications firms to build wiretapping capabilities into their new technologies.

The controversial Clipper Chip plan is an attempt to replace the Data Encryption Standard (DES) that since the 1970s has been the mandatory cipher for all federal agencies requiring cryptographic protection. On April 16, 1993, the White House issued a press release announcing that a state-of-the-art microcircuit called the Clipper Chip had been developed by government engineers. The government claimed that the new chip could be used in relatively inexpensive encryption devices attached to an ordinary telephone. The new wrinkle in the Clipper Chip was a "key-escrow" system that would provide two unique keys to allow authorized government agencies to decode messages encoded by any private encryption device.

The White House press release said that in order to allow law-enforcement and other government agencies to collect and decrypt electronically transmitted information, the President was directing the Attorney General to request manufacturers of communications hardware that incorporates encryption to install the U.S. government-developed key-escrow microcircuits in their products. The White House statement claimed that commercial encryption would not be prohibited outright, but it ridiculed the idea that "every American, as a matter of right, is entitled to an unbreakable commercial encryption product."

The Clipper Chip contains a sixty-four-bit block encryption algorithm called Skipjack, designed by NSA and classified secret. The algorithm uses eighty-bit keys and has thirty-two rounds of scrambling, giving it sixteen million more keys and twice as much scrambling as DES. The power of the Clipper Chip is not in dispute, but there are widespread doubts about the constitutionality of imposing a trap door, whether in escrow or not, on America's encrypted communications. The trustworthiness of the government as guarantor of American privacy is also a matter of concern, given the long history of systematic and secret violations of the public trust in this regard.

Many have questioned the "voluntary" nature of the Clipper Chip proposal, noting the government's intention to use its overwhelming market power and export controls to drive out any alternatives. Private industry would be allowed to export only Clipper Chip or weak technology. The American Civil Liberties Union (ACLU) believes that any prohibition on encrypted communications raises substantial First Amendment problems, and it questions the constitutionality of the government's export controls on cryptography. "This technology is speech protected by the First Amendment and the government must meet strict First Amendment standards before imposing such a licensing scheme, which is essentially a prior restraint that operates as censorship," said the ACLU (American Civil Liberties Union, Statements before the Computer System Security and Privacy Advisory Board, National Institute of Standards and Technology, May 28, 1993, p. 4).

The First Amendment arguments against restraints on cryptographic expression are convincing, but it is the American business community that is generating the major opposition to Clipper. Shortly after the White House announced its initiative, the Computer and Business Equipment Manufacturers Association (CBEMA) questioned whether the American people would accept an arrangement under which every telephone call, electronic mailing, or fax transmission was open to interception by the government. CBEMA also claimed that the government's cryptographic policies have effectively created an international embargo against U.S. encryption products and fostered foreign encryption production.

On July 20, 1994, Vice President Gore wrote a conciliatory letter to a congressional opponent of Clipper, saying that the administration was willing to explore alternatives to Clipper. In his letter, Gore said that the administration would initiate a pair of presidential studies to reassess existing export controls and would work with private industry to develop an alternative key-escrow system. Indeed, in August and September 1995, the government met with computer-industry executives to try to devise a compromise alternative to Clipper, but they found little common ground. Clinton administration officials said that they were willing to let companies export more sophisticated encryption if a private organization would hold a spare key to be made available to the government after a court order. But company officials, like Bill Gates of Microsoft Corporation, said that overseas customers would not accept keys to their information held by organizations authorized by the U.S. government. In any case, said the critics, the controls were impractical, since the software could be purchased in a U.S. shopping mall and carried abroad in floppy disks or sent in a few seconds on the Internet.

In the meantime, American companies are faced with two alternatives: either manufacture two different encryption products, a strong one for domestic consumption and a weak one for export; or choose the lowest common denominator, a single product that can be marketed at home and overseas. In practice, cost considerations have forced virtually all companies to choose the single-product approach, avoiding additional manufacturing costs by dumbing down their product to meet export restrictions.

Senator Patrick Leahy (D-Vt.) has proposed a bill that would do away with export licenses for any encryption technology that is generally available or in the public domain. He said that encryption policy should not be controlled by executive decree but by legislation. Law enforcement, said Leahy, must simply keep ahead in the technology, not try to hold back private industry. American companies were losing billions of dollars in revenues and thousands of jobs because they were handicapped in the global market. Leahy's bill and others like it received a boost on May 30, 1996, when the National Research Council issued its long-awaited report on encryption. Commissioned by Congress, the report that said the government should encourage, not hamper, the general use of encryption technology. The study concluded that current controls harm national security by making it difficult for U.S. businesses and citizens to protect their data and communications against criminals and industrial spies. It therefore recommended that companies be allowed to manufacture and sell encryption technology with fifty-six-bit keys, such as the Data Encryption Standard, rather than the forty-bit technology to which they are currently limited. Computer experts say that American intelligence agencies can break a forty-bit key in 0.0002 seconds and a fifty-six-bit key in 12 seconds.

In June 1996, the Electronic Systems Data Corporation (EDS), which specializes in encryption, began running an advertisement in major newspaper under the headline, "When governments hamper encryption, they hamper commerce." The ad charged: "Archaic, Cold War U.S. regulations limit export and global use of effective encryption. These regulations were once considered a vital tool to protect information from enemies and enhance our military security. However, these regulations hurt businesses and consumers by limiting their ability to protect themselves in international commerce. In doing so, they actually help criminals and undermine the nation's *economic* security."

The ad warns that foreign cryptographic technology may become the global standard unless American companies are unleashed. It concludes, "To enhance America's military and economic security, we should encourage the spread of stronger encryption, not discourage it" ("When Governments Hamper Encryption, They Hamper Commerce," *Washington Post*, June 20, 1996, A25).

The following month, the Clinton administration responded with proposals that continued to rely on some form of key escrow. Vice President Gore said the administration would consider allowing companies to export more sophisticated encryption, provided it involved a spare key. Companies would be allowed to hold their own spare key. Gore also suggested that "trustworthy" firms in select industries might be allowed to export encryption without spare keys, providing they made "real, measurable commitments" to building key systems. Meanwhile, said Gore, the government would develop its own key program ("Administration Says It May Shift Stance on Encryption," *Washington Post*, July 13, 1996, F2).

Netscape Communications Corporation quickly announced plans to begin sales over the Internet of software containing advanced encryption, but requests from abroad to download the software would be rejected. Netscape executives said the State Department had approved their plan, which requires customers to affirm that they are U.S. citizens or green-card holders. The Clinton administration said its approval of the plan was not a change of government policy, but was a way of showing flexibility while still preventing unauthorized exports.

REFERENCE: Herbert N. Foerstel, *Secret Science: Federal Control of American Science and Technology*, Westport, Praeger, 1993.

D

DECLASSIFICATION   Declassification is the process of removing the access restrictions on national security information previously imposed through the classification process. The unmanageable mountain of classified information that has accumulated since World War II can be attributed in part to excessive classification, but the major problem has always been the absence of an effective declassification process. Despite the fact that the sensitivity of information tends to diminish over time, few American presidents have provided for adequate declassification in their executive orders on classification, and those orders that specified declassification schedules have tended to be honored in the breach.

Traditionally, classification rules have specified that when a document is classified, the length of time it is to remain classified should be pegged, if possible, to a particular date or event, such as a military invasion date or the first public use of a new military weapon. If such a date or event could not be determined, then the newly classified document would be marked for declassification upon review at some time in the future. Steven Garfinkel, Director of the Information Security Oversight Office (ISOO), has said that this approach has been disastrous, primarily because classifiers find it much easier to classify documents for indefinite periods than to think about a determining date or event. (Note: All references to statements by Steven Garfinkel in this entry are derived from his lecture, "National Security Information," April 24, 1995, Univeristy of Maryland, College Park. Tapes of the lecture are maintained by the University's College of

Library and Information Science.) As a result, almost all classified documents are marked for review by placing the designation "OADR" (originating agency determination required) at the bottom of the document.

Under President Nixon's executive order, any documents classified as confidential were to be declassified in six years; material that was classified as secret was to be downgraded to confidential in two years and declassified in a total of eight years; top secret material was to be declassified in ten years. President Nixon was faced with a tremendous accumulation of World War II–era classified documents, but most of this was information on military operations, making its sensitivity very short-lived. Nixon's declassification plans would therefore have been much more easily implemented than the proposals of later Presidents, who faced massive amounts of material generated by a worldwide intelligence apparatus and strategic alliances like NATO. Nonetheless, Steven Garfinkel, Director of ISOO, has said that the Nixon declassification schedules were ignored by classifiers.

President Nixon's executive order was the first to include the concept of what was called "systematic review." Under the Nixon order, documents classified before the issuance of that order had to undergo review after thirty years. The only information that was to be automatically declassified after thirty years was information classified during the reign of the Nixon order, beginning in 1972. Thus the huge universe of classified material that had accumulated under prior administrations was not subject to automatic declassification. Since the Nixon order was superseded long before its thirty-year declassification schedule was implemented, few of its declassification provisions had any effect. In any case, because the federal bureaucracy never had the will or the resources to conduct the reviews called for, classifiers have usually chosen, by default, to leave things classified.

President Carter's executive order, issued in 1978, appeared to effectively address the need for a dramatic reduction in the growth of classified materials. The Carter order said that all documents should be declassified within six years or less of the date of classification. An infrequent exception was provided in the event that a person authorized to classify at the top secret level believed that a document was so sensitive that it should be marked for review in twenty years. Unfortunately, the liberal Carter declassification policy was ignored by the people making the classification decisions. They arbitrarily changed the category "declassify in six years" to "review in six years." Steven Garfinkel said that these classifiers arbitrarily invented a term that had no foundation in law. If, after six years, such documents had been taken before a judge, the judge would have said that the document was declassified because there is no authority for a six-year "review" in the executive order. Garfinkel said that about 35 percent of all the information classified during the Carter years was marked "review in six years." About 60 percent was being marked for twenty-year review, the supposedly "special" case. Thus, only 5 percent of the classified documents followed the general rule for declassification. Garfinkel concluded that as a result, there really was no rule.

We have seen that despite occasional attempts by Presidents to codify requirements for declassification, the bureaucratic secrecy system ignored them, and the mountain of classified documents grew out of control. The problem is that historically, in order to declassify information, agency heads had to commit resources, people, and money from their budgets. It was always easier and cheaper to let information remain classified. President Clinton's 1995 executive order may have changed all of that. As of October 1995, any permanently valuable classified material that is twenty-five years old or older will be permanently declassified without the need for review or public request. The only way an agency will be able to keep such information classified is to commit resources, people, and money to justify why a particular document should remain classified after twenty-five years. Otherwise, that document will, by law, become automatically declassified. Any exception to the twenty-five-year rule will be carefully scrutinized. The agency head who is authorized to make an exception must have that exception reviewed by someone outside of that agency.

The Clinton order says that all newly classified material must be marked for declassification at ten years or less, but there are exceptions to that rule. The exceptions are relatively narrow, compared to what previous executive orders allowed, but it would be naive to assume that classifiers will not find ways to exploit them. Steven Garfinkel hopes that the Clinton ten-year rule will be honored at least half of the time.

Garfinkel said that excessive photocopying and computer duplication have severely complicated the process of declassification, producing a mountain of classified information all over the world. FBI agents take the view that if only 300 copies of a classified document are distributed, that material is considered very well controlled. But if the original document is declassified at its original site, the other 299 copies remain classified. Eventually these copies will be reviewed, probably by someone other than the person who classified the original document. Garfinkel advocates a requirement that the original classifier be notified or consulted before a classified document could be copied. What is really needed is a database of all declassified documents, something that the National Archives has been considering for years.

REFERENCE: Steven Cohen, *Secrecy and Democracy*, Cambridge, Educators for Social Responsibility, 1990.

DEFAMATION   Defamation is a form of unprotected speech that occurs when written or spoken words injure a person's reputation, character, integrity, or morality, causing public hostility, ridicule, or financial loss. The truth of such injurious words is not of itself a sufficient defense against a charge of defamation, so long as the words were intended to injure someone and can be shown to have caused pain and suffering to a person. A private person may bring suit against defamation and earn a financial judgment, while public figures must prove "actual malice" before an award for defamation may be given. *See also* LIBEL.

REFERENCE: Sheldon Halpern, *The Law of Defamation, Privacy, Publicity, and Moral Right*, 2d ed. [s.l.], S. W. Halpern, 1993.

DERIVATIVE CLASSIFICATION   The practice of restricting access to unclassified information that is derived from currently classified information or is, in substance, similar to information currently classified is called derivative classification. President Clinton's 1995 executive order on classification defines derivative classification as "the incorporating, paraphrasing, restating or generating in new form information that is already classified and marking the newly developed material consistent with the classification markings that apply to the source information. The duplication or reproduction of existing classified information is not derivative classification." Typically, derivative classification occurs when a person creates a new document using information taken from a classified document. That person is usually bound by the decision of the original classifier, even if he or she believes that the new document does not warrant classification. Ninety-five percent of all classification occurs derivatively, with only five percent coming from original classification. *See also* NATIONAL SECURITY INFORMATION.

REFERENCE: John D. Baxter, *State Security, Privacy, and Information*, New York, St. Martin's Press, 1990.

DERSHOWITZ, ALAN, 1938–   Alan Dershowitz has been one of America's most prominent First Amendment attorneys since the 1960s, when he began arguing controversial free-speech cases for the American Civil Liberties Union. He has represented clients from across the political spectrum, from antiwar activist Dr. Benjamin Spock to the racist genetic theorist William Shockley. Dershowitz has been the defense counsel in two famous pornographic-film cases. He successfully argued against the ban of the Swedish film *I Am Curious (Yellow)* and defended actor Harry Reems against charges of conspiracy to promote and distribute obscenity.

Dershowitz is a graduate of Yale Law School, where he was editor of the *Yale Law Review*. He subsequently clerked for a number of federal judges, including Supreme Court Justice Arthur Goldberg. He joined the faculty of Harvard Law School in 1964, where he became the youngest law professor to earn tenure in the school's history.

One of his most important First Amendment cases involved Frank Snepp, a former CIA agent and author of *Decent Interval*. In *Snepp v. United States* (1980), Dershowitz defended Snepp's right to publish a book critical of the CIA without being sued by the government. The CIA did not challenge Snepp's claim that his book contained no classified information, but it sued him for violating a secrecy agreement imposed on agency employees. An injunction prohibiting him from speaking or writing about the CIA for the rest of his life was overturned by an appeals court, but reinstated by the Supreme Court.

REFERENCES: Alan M. Dershowitz, *The Best Defense*, New York, Random House, 1982; Alan M. Dershowitz, *Contrary to Popular Opinion*, New York, Pharos Books, 1992.

DEWITT, HUGH, 1930–   Hugh DeWitt is a nuclear physicist who worked at the prestigious Lawrence Livermore National Laboratory for forty years, during which his First Amendment struggles at the laboratory became legendary. The American Federation of Science has honored him as "the conscience of the Livermore laboratory."

DeWitt's most famous battle occurred in 1978 when he opposed the government's prior restraint of an article about the hydrogen bomb in the magazine *The Progressive*. The Justice Department's attempt at official censorship went to the courts as a legal test of the "born classified" concept embodied in the Atomic Energy Act, and DeWitt played two significant roles in defense of publication. First, he and several other Livermore scientists submitted an affidavit challenging the government's claim that a layman's article on the H-bomb, based on unclassified sources such as the *Encyclopedia Americana*, would jeopardize national security. Second, when *The Progressive*'s managing editor, Sam Day, went to California to obtain the supporting affidavit, the Department of Engery (DOE) claimed that it could only be carried by someone with a security clearance, and DeWitt was the only such person willing and available. He volunteered to carry a suitcase containing the "classified" material to the U.S. Attorney, even though he considered the government's secrecy rigamarole to be preposterous.

Years later, DeWitt recalled the highly publicized court case. "It soon became clear," he wrote, "that the real issue was the censorship power of the U.S. Government. The court actions preventing publication of the H-bomb article appeared to be a major threat to the publication rights of the American press and . . . to the First Amendment." The government eventually withdrew its injunction, allowing the article to be published. Despite the government's claims of disastrous consequences, the article did nothing more than bring the light of day to the atomic weapons industry bureaucracy. DeWitt concluded, "The mystique of secrecy surrounding nuclear weapons work was largely broken" (Erwin Knoll, "The Good It Did," *The Progressive*, February 1991, p. 4).

DeWitt's bold defense of free expression made him the target of government administrators at the Livermore Laboratory, but he continued to act on principle. He knew that his years of major public activity had made his situation precarious, but he vowed to keep at it. In 1987, despite his long and distinguished service, DeWitt received an unsatisfactory personnel rating at Livermore. In 1988, the laboratory again told DeWitt that his work was "unsatisfactory" and that if it did not improve that year, he would have to leave. Again, the laboratory's threats failed to silence DeWitt. Finally, in March 1994, DeWitt was summoned to the laboratory's security office and stripped of the badge that gave him access to classified areas, including his own office. He was charged with publishing an article containing classified information, even though that information came from public sources, including congressional releases. DeWitt wrote to Secretary of Energy Hazel O'Leary, complaining that he was being harassed. O'Leary agreed and ordered a review that resulted in the restoration of his clearance just two months later.

In 1995, DeWitt was invited to talk to the Energy Department's Fundamental Classification Policy Review panel, where he described his long history of disputes over inappropriate classification of DOE material. He cited examples of nontechnical nuclear weapons information available in the public domain but still considered classified by DOE. DeWitt suggested that matters openly debated before Congress should not be regarded years later as classified. On February 27, 1996, the Livermore Laboratory's Safeguards and Security Department cited him for a "Category A" security infraction, the highest-level violation, because of his remarks to the panel. On March 20, he received a letter of warning, a formal disciplinary action. Once again, Energy Secretary O'Leary, the champion of openness in the DOE, had to calm the waters. A department spokesperson said that "there is a difficult balance to be struck between openness and nonproliferation [of nuclear materials], but [O'Leary] was outraged about how the scientists were treated before, and if the facts are similar this time, she will have the same reaction" (Al Kamen, "In the Loop," *Washington Post*, April 19, 1996, p. A23).

REFERENCE: Hugh DeWitt, "A View of Nuclear Policy from Inside a Weapons Laboratory," in *Science, Technology, and the Arms Race*, audiocassette, Washington, American Association for the Advanceemnt of Science, 1984.

DIAL-A-PORN   The 1980s saw a massive growth of 900–number phone services, an industry that provides phone messages covering everything from financial advice to the Psychic Network. Only when sexual messages were offered on 900 numbers did controversy arise. These "dial-a-porn" numbers provided erotic messages, usually read by women for men, lasting up to two minutes. New York City alone has registered as many as seven million dial-a-porn calls per month. In 1983, claiming the need to keep minors away from indecent phone messages, Congress passed an amendment instructing the FCC to create regulations to control access to such messages. In response, the FCC issued a *Report and Order* in June 1984, requiring dial-a-porn to be restricted to the hours of 9 P.M. to 8 A.M. and requiring advance payment by credit card.

One affected company, Carlin Communications, Inc., filed suit in the Second Circuit, challenging the FCC's order and claiming that it violated the First Amendment by proscribing "any obscene or indecent communication." The court distinguished telephone messages from broadcasting, the regulation of which had been found constitutional in *Federal Communications Commission v. Pacifica Foundation* (1978). Telephone messages, said the court in *Carlin Communications, Inc. v. Federal Communications Commission* (2d Cir. 1986), were not "uniquely pervasive," and the controls on expression approved in *Pacifica* were not applicable outside the broadcast context. Noting that the FCC had barred the phone messages during daytime hours when children were likely to be in school, the court concluded that the FCC had failed to demonstrate that its regulatory scheme was "tailored to its ends or that those ends could not be met by less drastic means."

A few years later in *Sable Communications of California, Inc. v. Federal Communications Commission* (1989), the Supreme Court dealt with a congressional attempt to eliminate dial-a-porn. The Court in *Sable* noted that unlike broadcasting, which "can intrude on the privacy of the home without prior warning as to program content, and is 'uniquely accessible to children, even those too young to read,'" the dial-a-porn medium "requires the listener to take affirmative steps to receive the communication." The Court stated that in the absence of a captive audience, "Placing a telephone call is not the same as turning on a radio and being taken by surprise by an indecent message. Unlike an unexpected outburst on a radio broadcast, the message received by one who places a call to a dial-a-porn service is not so invasive or surprising that it prevents an unwilling listener from avoiding exposure to it" (*Sable Communications of California, Inc. v. Federal Communications Commission,* 109 S. Ct. 2829, 2837 [1989]).

A similar judgment was rendered the following year in *American Information Enterprises Inc. v. Thornburgh* when a district court granted a preliminary injunction against the enforcement of legislation (the Helms Amendment) that would have outlawed indecent telephone services unless provisions were imposed to limit access. In *Thornburgh,* the court once more found that the state had failed to employ the "least restrictive" means to protect children from indecent speech.

REFERENCE: Cindy Peterson, "The Congressional Response to the Supreme Court's Treatment of Dial-a-Porn," *Georgetown Law Journal,* August 1990, pp. 2025–55.

DOBSON, DR. JAMES C., 1936–   Dr. James Dobson was a member of the notorious Attorney General's Commission on Pornography, often called the Meese Commission, which published a *Final Report* in 1986 recommending action against a broad range of "pornographic" books, magazines, television shows, and other forms of communication. Dobson later formed the conservative organization Focus on the Family, which advocates a return to "family values," including tight control of information and literature available in public school curricula, libraries, and the general publishing industry. Dobson's Focus on the Family is twice the size of the Christian Coalition, and his radio show is the second most widely syndicated program in America. He has his own publishing house, a monthly church bulletin, a magazine for teachers, a magazine for physicians, and a mass-market monthly for single parents. He has written a number of books on the dangers of a permissive society, including *Fighting for the Minds of Our Children: America's Second Civil War*.

REFERENCE: Michael Cromartie, ed., *No Longer Exiles: The Religious New Right in American Politics*, Washington, Ethics and Public Policy Center, 1993.

DORSEN, NORMAN, 1930–   Norman Dorsen is among this nation's most principled, and at times controversial, advocates of civil liberties. His vision in this regard was evident when he served as a law clerk to Supreme Court Justice John Marshall Harlan, and it matured in his subsequent career in academia and during his years of leadership in the American Civil Liberties Union (ACLU). Dorsen served on the ACLU Board of Directors from 1965 until his retirement in 1991, and he became the organization's guiding force as its general counsel (1969–76) and president (1976–91).

It was Dorsen who presided over the most difficult and divisive stand ever taken by the ACLU, the decision to support the right of the American Nazi Party to march through the town of Skokie, Illinois. Dorsen argued that the ACLU had a principled obligation to protect unpopular expression, but ACLU membership declined immediately after the Skokie incident.

Dorsen's teaching at New York University and his numerous books, essays, law-review articles, briefs, and arguments to the Supreme Court and other courts made him a respected constitutional scholar. Among the U.S. Supreme Court cases that he argued was *In re Gault* (1967), which raised the question of whether the constitutional protections afforded to criminal defendants applied to juvenile court proceedings.

REFERENCES: Norman Dorsen, *Frontiers of Civil Liberties*, New York, Pantheon Books, 1968; Norman Dorsen, ed., *The Evolving Constitution: Essays on the Bill of Rights and the U.S. Supreme Court*, Middletown, Wesleyan University Press, 1987.

DOUGLAS, WILLIAM ORVILLE, 1998–1980   William O. Douglas worked his way through Columbia Law School, spent a brief period in private practice, and taught at Columbia and Yale law schools before serving as chairman of the Securities and Exchange Commission from 1937 to 1939. In March 1939, Douglas became President Franklin Roosevelt's fourth Supreme Court appointee, filling the vacancy left by the retirement of Louis Brandeis.

Douglas and Hugo Black are considered to be the strongest champions of the Bill of Rights in the history of the Supreme Court. Douglas's long service on the Court influenced the legal philosophy of Chief Justice Earl Warren, contributing significantly to the liberal decisions of the Warren Court. Despite his background in business law, Douglas soon became one of the foremost civil libertarians on the Court. He believed that First

Amendment rights were the cornerstone of a free society, and he rarely found government interference with these rights to be justified.

In 1948, Douglas spoke for the majority to overturn a local ordinance banning the use of sound trucks as an unconstitutional restraint on free speech. The following year, Douglas again wrote for the majority in overturning the disorderly-conduct conviction of a speaker whose statements almost caused a riot. In that controversial opinion, Douglas said that free speech must be guaranteed even to a speaker who "stirs the public to anger, invites dispute, brings about . . . unrest or creates a disturbance" (*Terminiello v. Chicago* [1949]).

Douglas also tended to oppose most loyalty-security measures. In 1951, he dissented when the Court upheld the conviction of Communist Party leaders for violation of the Smith Act. He argued that the defendants were charged only with conspiring to teach and advocate overthrow of the government, which represented no "clear and present danger" to the government that would justify denial of free speech. Douglas also opposed the deportation of aliens solely because they had once been Communist Party members. In a 1952 dissent, he said that a New York law that prohibited members of subversive organizations from teaching in public schools was a threat to free thought and expression.

During the 1950s, Douglas went beyond the "clear and present danger" rule in free-speech cases, espousing the absolutist view that the First Amendment barred all government restraint on expression unless it was tied to illegal action. He spoke increasingly as the protector of the individual against big government, and he maintained his strong opposition to all loyalty-security programs. In 1958, he wrote the majority opinion to overturn the State Department's policy of denying passports to members of the Communist Party. Douglas dissented in two 1961 cases where the majority upheld contempt-of-Congress convictions for witnesses who refused to answer questions before the House Un-American Activities Committee.

In a series of important obscenity cases in 1964 and 1966, Douglas teamed with Justice Black to reaffirm their earlier position that the First Amendment prohibited all government regulation of allegedly obscene materials. Douglas also joined concurring opinions in two 1964 cases that protected even malicious criticism of public officials. In 1966, when the Court upheld the trespass convictions of demonstrators protesting outside a Florida jail, Douglas wrote the dissenting opinion, stating that a jail could be an appropriate place for a protest.

Of all the justices on the Court, Douglas was the most aggressive in claiming the existence of a constitutional right to privacy. In his controversial opinion for the Court in *Griswold v. Connecticut* (1965), he overturned an anticontraceptive law because it violated the right to marital privacy.

Throughout his long service on the Court, Douglas maintained his absolutist position on the First Amendment, opposing all loyalty and obscenity laws and favoring wide protection for symbolic expression, including flag desecration. He believed that freedom of the press was unassailable and voted with the Court to reject the government's request for an injunction against the publication of the *Pentagon Papers*.

Douglas retired from the Court in 1975 after suffering a stroke during the previous year. He had served for thirty-six years on the bench, longer than any other justice in the Court's history.

REFERENCE: William O. Douglas, *The Court Years, 1939–1975: The Autobiography of William O. Douglas*, New York, Random House, 1980.

DRAFT CARD BURNING In 1948, Congress passed a law prohibiting anyone from forging, altering, or changing a Selective Service certificate. The law was amended in 1965 to add the words "knowingly destroys" or "knowingly mutilates."

On March 31, 1966, David Paul O'Brien and three friends burned their draft cards in front of the South Boston Courthouse. An FBI agent who observed the act arrested O'Brien and charged him with violating federal law. O'Brien appealed his conviction to the Supreme Court, claiming that he had burned his draft card as political protest and that the law was censoring his freedom of speech. The Court upheld O'Brien's conviction, claiming that whenever speech and nonspeech elements were combined, as in draft-card burning, the government was permitted to regulate that action under the following conditions: (1) the regulation must be within the constitutional power of government and must further an important or substantial government interest; (2) the government interest must be unrelated to the suppression of free expression, and any incidental restriction on First Amendment freedoms must be no greater than is essential to the furtherance of that interest.

The Court concluded that the orderly administration of the draft was a constitutional power of the government and that preventing the destruction of draft cards was a reasonable act in support of government interests. Critics of the *O'Brien* decision have noted that the rigorous "strict scrutiny" or "clear and present danger" tests usually applied to free-speech cases were not used here. In *United States v. O'Brien*, the government was required to show only an "important" or "substantial" interest, not the usual "compelling" interest. On its surface, even the requirement that the government's interest be "unrelated to the suppression of free expression" affords little First Amendment protection, since virtually all laws restricting expression claim to be motivated by unrelated matters, such as national security, violence, privacy, or morality. A more appropriate interpretation of the Court's words may concern the distinction between the speech and nonspeech aspects of O'Brien's action.

If the government's regulation of draft-card burning is grounded solely in the noncommunicative aspects of that action, then its interests are unrelated to free expression. In *O'Brien*, the Court provided four nonspeech interests served by laws against draft card burning. First, draft-cards are a necessary proof of draft registration. Second, the card bears the registrant's indentification number and the address of his draft board, facilitating communication between the two. Third, the card serves as a reminder to the registrant that he must notify his draft board of any change of address or status. Finally, the laws against destroying or mutilating draft cards serve a government interest in forgery detection, since it is more difficult to trace forgeries or alterations of a card if it has been destroyed or mutilated.

The problem with the Court's attempt to explain the nonspeech basis for the laws against draft-card burning was that it was in direct conflict with Congress's admitted purpose in passing the laws, namely, to discourage dissenters from persuading others to resist the draft. Few outside the Court pretended that the laws had any original purpose other than to control political expression, and even the Court conceded as much by stating that "this Court will not strike down an otherwise constitutional statute on the basis of an alleged illicit legislative motive." In an expression of contempt for Congress, the Court said that it would serve no purpose to declare void a law that Congress could simply reenact "if the same or other legislator made a 'wiser' speech about it." In other words, the Court believed that Congress would simply reenact the statute, this time disguising its true intent to suppress speech.

REFERENCE: Michael Useem, *Conscription, Protest, and Social Conflict: The Life and Death of a Draft Resistance Movement,* New York, Wiley, 1973.

DWORKIN, ANDREA, 1946–   Andrea Dworkin is a feminist author and antipornography crusader who helped to draft antipornography statutes in several cities, including Indianapolis and Minneapolis. Working with her attorney, Catharine MacKinnon, Dworkin crafted unique statutes that purported to criminalize the exploitative process of creating pornography, rather than the expression itself. Unfortunately, where these statutes have been applied, they have punished pornographic expression in the same way that the traditional antipornography statutes have always done.

Both Dworkin and MacKinnon lecture nationally against pornography and offer assistance to any government authorities who wish to write antipornography legislation. In addition, Dworkin is a prolific writer, best known for her 1986 novel *Ice and Fire* and feminist treatises such as *Woman Hating* and *Pornography: Men Possessing Women.* She was also a contributor to the prominent feminist text *Take Back the Night.*

REFERENCE: Patricia Smith, ed., *Feminist Jurisprudence,* New York, Oxford University Press, 1993.

EAGLE FORUM   The Eagle Forum, founded in 1975 by Phyllis Schlafly, is a conservative organization that is frequently involved in censorship disputes as part of its national effort to remove immoral content from textbooks. Schlafly had been an early opponent of the Equal Rights Amendment, saying that it was antifamily and antiwoman. The Eagle Forum claims to stand for God, Country, and Family, and it opposes groups that it considers antifamily, antireligion, antimorality, antichildren, antilife, and antidefense.
REFERENCE: Phyllis Schlafly, *Eagle Forum*, videocassette [s.l.], Eagle Forum, 1984.

EDUCATIONAL RESEARCH ANALYSTS   Educational Research Analysts is a conservative textbook research and review organization founded in 1961 under the direction of Mel and Norma Gabler. The Gablers operate out of Longview, Texas, where they check and certify textbooks for school boards in Texas and around the country, exposing those that conflict with "traditional values," including the Judeo-Christian ethic. The Gablers oppose any mention of the changing sex roles, including the representation of women in "men's jobs," and they remove all mention of negative aspects in American history, such as slavery, the depression, and discrimination.

The organization is not open to formal membership, but it has a staff of eight that examines school textbooks under consideration by the Texas Educational Agency. The very severe religious and cultural restrictions that the Gablers impose on curricular materials in Texas are exported to other states through a consulting network that has involved itself in numerous challenges to existing and proposed textbooks around the country.

Many conservative school officials and private citizens have come to use *Mel Gabler's Newsletter* as their primary source of textbook reviews. The newsletter, published twice a year, lists objectionable portions of textbooks by page. The Gablers have also published the books *Textbooks on Trial, What Are They Teaching Our Children?* and *Are Textbooks Harming Our Children?* Educational Research Analysts is located at P.O. Box 7518, Longview, TX 75607–7518.

REFERENCE: Educational Research Analysts, *Recommended Reading/Literature*, Longview, Educational Research Analysts, 1988.

EDWARDS, DON (W. DONLON EDWARDS), 1915–   No member of Congress in this century has been more closely associated with the struggle for constitutional liberties than Representative Don Edwards (D-Calif.). He began his thirty-two–year congressional career in 1962 when he was elected to the U.S. House of Representatives. His background did little to suggest that he would be a crusader for First Amendment rights. Edwards was a businessman who had never before held elective office. He had served two years as an FBI agent and four years during World War II as a Navy officer. Though he ran for Congress as a Democrat, he had earlier been the president of the California Young Republicans during Richard Nixon's 1950 Senate race.

Almost immediately after joining the House, he became one of only twenty members who voted to kill the House Un-American Activities Committee. Many thought that this principled but unpopular vote would end his career, but he went on to win fifteen more elections. Edwards voted for the landmark Civil Rights Act of 1964 and sponsored the Voting Rights Act of 1965. In 1967, he was one of only sixteen legislators to vote against a bill making it a federal crime to desecrate the American flag. He was subsequently vindicated when the Supreme Court ruled the bill to be a violation of the First Amendment to the Constitution. When President Bush advocated a constitutional amendment to prohibit flag burning, Edwards successfully led the fight against the amendment.

More recently, Edwards opposed campus speech codes that sought to restrict speech expressing bias toward women, blacks, and other minorities. He said that such codes had "civil liberties problems" and recommended counseling and communication as better remedies for offensive speech.

Until the Republican takeover of Congress in 1995, Edwards had served as chairman of the House Judiciary Subcommittee on Civil and Constitutional Rights for more than two decades, during which period he turned down numerous opportunities to lead other committees. He preferred to remain in the position that would allow him to monitor violations of civil rights by federal agencies like the FBI. Edwards also turned down a seat on the Select Committee on Intelligence, explaining that it required secrecy oaths that would interfere with his free speech.

Civil liberties columnist Nat Hentoff said of Edwards, "I consider him the congressman from the Constitution. Don is very low-key, but he's about the most passionate person I've ever known in politics about the Bill of Rights." When Edwards retired in January 1995, he looked back with pride: "When I came here the 11 states of the Old South practiced apartheid. There was a House UnAmerican Activities Committee. And the FBI was out of control threatening individual liberties. This is a much better country today" (Albert R. Hunt, "The Congressman from the Constitution," *Wall Street Journal*, September 29, 1994, p. A13).
REFERENCES: Don Edwards, "Why Has the Constitution Endured So Long?", in *The Constitution: Perspectives on Contemporary American Democracy*, Arlington, Close Up, 1986; Robert Pear, "A Champion of Civil Liberties Lays Down His Lance," *New York Times*, April 3, 1994, Section 4, p. 7.

EROTICA   Erotica is distinguished from other categories of sexual expression, like indecency, pornography, or obscenity, on the basis of its relative respectability. The *Random House Dictionary* characterizes erotica as "literature or art dealing with sexual love." The *American Heritage Dictionary* defines erotica as "literature or art concerning or intending to arouse sexual desire."

Some examples of "classic" erotica are Henry Miller's *Tropic of Cancer* and *Tropic of Capricorn*; D. H. Lawrence's *Lady Chatterley's Lover*; John Cleland's *Fanny Hill, or, Memoirs of a Woman of Pleasure*; and James Joyce's *Ulysses*. All of these books were subjects of court cases stemming from their banning. More recent examples of quality erotica include Marco Vassi's *The Erotic Comedies* (1981); David Steinberg's *Beneath This Calm Exterior* (1982); and Lili Bita's *Fleshfire: Love Poems* (1984). Contrary to the popular impression, there is a good deal of contemporary erotica written by and for women. Some recent anthologies are *Ladies's Own Erotica* (1984), *Herotica: A Collection of Women's Erotic Fiction* (1988), and *Deep Down: The New Sensual Writing by Women* (1988).

There are a number of prominent American research collections of erotica, including Indiana University's Kinsey Institute for Sex, Gender, and Reproduction. As of 1991, this collection included a library of over 70,000 print volumes, of which about 25,000 were considered to be "erotic." In addition, there were about 30,000 pieces of erotic art, 100,000 photographs, 6,500 films, and 600 videocassettes. Another major research collection of erotica is at the Institute for Advanced Study of Human Sexuality, located in San Francisco. This collection includes 160,000 books, 110,000 periodicals, and 90,000 audiovisual materials.

The New York Public Library's General Research Division has a collection of erotic magazines, pulp novels, pamphlets, and comics on microfilm. These items are initially purchased from bookstores in the New York area that specialize in pornography. The Library of Congress maintained a separate erotica collection called the Delta Collection until 1964, when it was dismantled and integrated into the Rare Books and Special Collections Division. Most of these materials now fall under the subject classification for family, marriage, and women, but the division also houses hundreds of erotic paperback books and photography books that were once part of the Delta Collection.

The University of North Carolina in Charlotte has a collection of 100 cataloged erotic works, including classics by writers such as D. H. Lawrence, Frank Harris, and Norman Douglas. Cornell University houses a collection of homosexual erotica assembled by the Mariposa Education and Research Foundation. The materials, which include books, journals, films, and artifacts, were donated to Cornell University to support the multidisciplinary Center for the Study of Human Sexuality.

Clearly, erotica has a legitimate place in scholarly repositories, but aside from the emphasis on literature and art, what makes erotica good, or at least socially acceptable, and pornography bad? Many writers have concluded that it comes down to this: "What turns me on is erotic; what turns you on is pornographic."

REFERENCES: Martha Cornog, ed., *Libraries, Erotica, Pornography*, Phoenix, Oryx Press, 1991; *Erotica: An Illustrated Anthology of Sexual Art and Literature*, edited by Charlotte Hill and William Wallace, New York, Carroll and Graf, 1992.

EXECUTIVE PRIVILEGE   The President of the United States has historically claimed an executive privilege to maintain the confidentiality of certain communications with his staff. Though that right was mentioned neither in the Constitution nor in the constitutional debates, it was claimed by America's first president, George Washington, when he attempted to withhold from Congress certain documents about a military expedition. The dispute was resolved without legal recourse when Washington chose to share the information with Congress.

The eventual legal basis for executive privilege was laid in the landmark case *Marbury v. Madison* (1803), which established the doctrine of judicial review. In that case, Chief Justice John Marshall stated that it "is emphatically the province and duty of the judicial department to say what the law is." The judiciary first addressed the specific issue of executive privilege in 1808 in the case of *United States v. Burr*, when the Court held that incumbent President Thomas Jefferson was subject to a subpoena seeking certain presidential documents in connection with Aaron Burr's treason trial. When Jefferson initially objected to the release, the court stated that it was the judiciary's duty to determine the validity of the executive privilege claim. In reality, the legal issue was never definitively resolved because Jefferson provided the documents "voluntarily," rather than under compulsion by the judiciary.

Indeed, it took almost 170 years before President Richard Nixon's use of executive privilege during his ill-fated second term brought the issue to a resolution in the Supreme Court. Nixon refused to release taped conversations concerning the Watergate burglary of Democratic National Headquarters to a special prosecutor or to the House committee considering his impeachment. Nixon claimed an absolute privilege to maintain the confidentiality of communications between a President and his aides, but in *United States v. Nixon* (1974), a unanimous Supreme Court ordered him to surrender the tapes.

In *Nixon*, the Court for the first time attempted to define when a President can be compelled to release confidential information. That case originated in *United States v. Mitchell*, in which the Watergate special prosecutor served a subpoena *duces tecum* upon Nixon requesting the release of White House tapes. In response to the subpoena, the U.S. Attorney General, on behalf of the President, filed a motion to quash on the grounds that the President could not be compelled to surrender the tapes. After the motion to quash was denied by the district court, Nixon appealed, and the Supreme Court granted certiorari.

The Court recognized that executive privilege was constitutionally based, but nonetheless rejected Nixon's claim on the basis that neither the separation of powers doctrine nor the need for confidentiality was sufficient to justify an absolute privilege. The Court concluded that because the Nixon tapes contained no diplomatic, military, or sensitive foreign policy information, their necessity to the criminal prosecutions at hand outweighed the President's executive privilege.

Twenty-five years later, another controversial case involving executive privilege occurred during what has been called the Irangate scandal. Once again, a President was being compelled to reveal information relevant to a criminal trial. This time, the criminal defendants included former National Security Adviser John Poindexter and White House aide Oliver North, who were charged with a series of crimes stemming from involvement in the Iranian arms-for-hostages deal and secret aid to the contra rebels in Nicaragua. Poindexter claimed that President Reagan's personal diaries were necessary to his defense, and North served subpoenas on President Ronald Reagan and President-elect George Bush, compelling both to testify in the case. In addition, a subpoena *duces tecum* was served upon President Reagan to compel production of his diaries.

At a preliminary hearing in January 1989, Reagan was ordered to hand over the diaries, but when Reagan claimed executive privilege, the U.S. Attorney General moved to quash all of the subpoenas. U.S. District Judge Gerhard Gesell quashed the subpoenas for Reagan's diary and Bush's testimony, but held in abeyance the subpoena to compel Reagan's testimony. In *United States v. North* (D.D.C. Jan. 27, 1989), Gesell relied upon the *Nixon* case in stating, "As for the power of the Court to require the testimony of former President Reagan or President Bush for that matter I

didn't think there was any legal question. I thought the Court's power in that regard was clear, indisputable."

Nonetheless, while reaffirming the authority of the judicial branch to force presidential compliance with a subpoena, Judge Gesell chose not to exercise that power. Gesell noted that President Reagan had cooperated with the independent counsel and North's defense, and he concluded that North's need for the President's testimony did not overcome the right of executive privilege. Though Gesell's decision in *North* reiterated the judgment in *Nixon* that executive privilege is not absolute, the court in fact deferred completely to that privilege, leading many to conclude that the *North* decision set the President above the law. By basing its decision on documents screened by the executive branch, the court in *North* may not have protected the judiciary's role as guardian of legitimacy and authorization.

In January 1989, at the conclusion of his second term, President Reagan administered a parting blow to the public's right to know when he issued Executive Order 12667, dramatically extending his right of executive privilege over his presidential papers and allowing his successors to have the same privilege. Executive Order 12667 essentially skirted a 1978 law that had made Reagan's papers and those of his successors public property. Now, presidents would be allowed to shield their papers from disclosure unless otherwise instructed by court order.

The most recent claim of executive privilege occurred in May 1996 when President Bill Clinton withheld subpoenaed documents from a House committee investigating White House travel office firings. After the committee voted to cite a White House lawyer for contempt of Congress for refusing to deliver the documents, the White House Counsel complained to committee chairman William Clinger, Jr. (R-Pa.), "You have unilaterally determined that this president is not entitled to any confidential legal communications." Clinger responded, "If this claim of a blanket privilege over an unidentified group of documents . . . is allowed to stand, how is this congressional committee to have oversight of the alleged misdeeds of this White House?" Clinger concluded, "The culture of secrecy must end" ("House Panel Votes for Contempt Citation," *Washington Post*, May 10, 1996, p. A4).

REFERENCE: Mark J. Rozell, *Executive Privilege: The Dilemma of Secrecy and Democratic Accountability*, Baltimore, Johns Hopkins University Press, 1994.

EXPORT CONTROLS   Throughout the Cold War, the Departments of Defense and Commerce frequently complained of "technology transfer," the flow of unclassified technical information to U.S. adversaries. Almost any high-technology information was considered to be defense related, and the CIA said that it made no difference whether technical data were copied from open journals in a public library or stolen by agents of a foreign power.

The government's export-control laws were seen as the best way to stem the flow of unclassified technical information to foreign powers. Contrary to popular perception, export controls restrict the flow of information even more frequently than they control products. The Arms Export Control Act (1976) and the Export Administration Act (1979) provide the authority to prevent foreign dissemination of scientific and technical data, as defined in the Export Administration Regulations (EAR), the Military Critical Technologies List (MCTL), and the International Traffic in Arms Regulations (ITAR). Through the years, the web of export controls grew to the point where the National Academy of Sciences warned: "Such restrictions have the effect of creating de facto a new category of unclassified but restricted information. These new, more comprehensive technical data restrictions have had a chilling effect on some professional scientific and engineering societies" (Herbert N. Foerstel, *Secret Science*, Westport, Praeger, 1993, p. 156).

For example, the ITAR restricts the dissemination of broadly defined unclassified "technical data," which the Department of Defense admitted "would cover virtually everything done in the United States." The term "export" is defined to have occurred whenever technical data are mailed, shipped, or carried by hand outside the United States or are disclosed through visits abroad by American citizens involved in briefings, symposia, or plant visits.

The First Amendment implications of the ITAR have not been fully clarified in the courts. In *United States v. Donas-Botto* (1973), the defendants were charged under the ITAR with conspiracy to export technical data without an export license. The defendants claimed that the ITAR restrictions on technical knowledge violated the First Amendment, but the court concluded, "[W]hen matters of foreign policy are involved the government has the constitutional authority to prohibit individuals from divulging 'technical data' relating to implements of war to foreign governments."

In *United States v. Edler Industries, Inc.* (9th Cir., July 31, 1978), the defendant, Edler Industries, Inc., was charged with unlicensed export of technical data to a French aerospace firm. Edler Industries contended that the Munitions Control Act and the ITAR were overly broad and imposed an unconstitutional prior restraint, but the court held both to be constitutional so long as they prohibit only the export of data significantly and directly related to items on the Munitions List.

In 1981, then Assistant Attorney General John Harmon revisited the *Edler* decision and expressed concern that there was no mechanism to provide prompt judicial review of federal restraints on communication. Harmon concluded, "The general principle we derive . . . is that a prior restraint on disclosure of information generated by or obtained from the government is justifiable under the First Amendment only to the extent that the information is properly classified or classifiable. . . . [T]he existing ITAR provisions we think fall short of satisfying the strictures necessary to survive close scrutiny under the First Amendment" (*The Government's Classification of Private Ideas*, Hearings before a Subcommittee of the Committee on Government Operations, House of Representatives, 96th Congress, 2nd session, 28 February, 20 March, 21 August 1980, Washington, D.C.: U.S. GPO, 1981, p.273–74).

Export controls are deliberately written broadly to ensure that anything of importance can be controlled. As a result, they inevitably reach much information that is at best remotely or indirectly related to national security concerns. The effect has been to suppress speech well beyond the scope of the export controls. Though it has not yet been definitively tested in the courts, the prior restraint imposed by export controls is likely to be even less acceptable to the courts than prior restraint by judicial injunction because both the EAR and ITAR place the power of restraints in the hands of executive-branch civil servants with little judicial oversight. The licensing decision is, in fact, made by an employee whose job it is to suppress information and who will be held accountable for any harmful consequences of approved communication.

The most effective pressure for change in the oppressive structure of American export controls has come not from traditional free-speech advocates, but from the American business community. American companies believe that the export controls imposed on them are based not on national security grounds but on questionable or outdated foreign policy objectives. The result of such controls has been a steady erosion of American competitiveness internationally that has turned the businessman into a First Amendment activist.

REFERENCES: Kent A. Jones, *Export Restraint and the New Protectionism: The Political Economy of Discriminatory Trade Restrictions*, Ann Arbor, University of Michigan Press, 1994; *Breaking Down the Barricades: Reforming Export Controls to Increase U.S. Competitiveness: Final Report of the Project on Export Controls in a Changing World*, Project Chairman, Boyd J. McKelvain, Washington, D.C., Center for Strategic and International Studies, 1994.

F

FAIRNESS DOCTRINE   In 1949, the Federal Communications Commission introduced regulations requiring radio and television broadcasters to provide coverage of issues of public importance and to present contrasting views. This "fairness doctrine," as it was commonly called, required reasonable balance in a station's overall programming, measured over weeks or months, when there had been significant discussion of a controversial issue of public importance. Though failure to comply could risk possible loss of a broadcaster's license, the doctrine was largely self-enforcing, leaning on citizen-broadcaster conciliation as a prerequisite to FCC involvement. In those cases where the FCC did become involved, the remedy was usually more speech, rather than fines or license revocations. For this reason, the Supreme Court ruled in *Red Lion Broadcasting Company v. Federal Communication Commission* (1969) that the fairness doctrine did not violate the First Amendment, though the Court noted that its ruling was subject to reconsideration if there was evidence that it was causing a reduction in the volume and quality of coverage.

The FCC abandoned the fairness doctrine in 1987, claiming that it disserved both the public's right to diverse sources of information and the broadcaster's interest in free speech. There were several congressional attempts to revive the doctrine, and one such bill was passed in 1988, but it was subsequently vetoed by President Ronald Reagan. Another attempt to revive the fairness doctrine came through a legal appeal by the Syracuse Peace Council, a group that had a programming dispute with a television station in Syracuse, New York. In 1989, the U.S. Circuit Court of Appeals for the District of Columbia rejected the appeal, stating that the fairness doctrine was no longer needed to assure expression of a variety of viewpoints and that it discouraged broadcasters from airing controversial topics. An FCC statement called the court's decision "a victory for the free speech rights of all Americans," vindicating "the public's right to receive press coverage free from government influence" ("Repeal of Fairness Doctrine by F.C.C. Upheld in Court," *New York Times*, February 11, 1989, p. A30).

That decision was appealed to the Supreme Court, which was asked to decide whether the fairness doctrine was mandated by the 1934 Communications Act, and, if so, whether it was constitutional. The FCC and broadcasters urged the Court to deny the appeal, arguing that broadcast licensees were still required to provide "issue responsive" programming for their communities. On January 8, 1990, the Court unanimously denied the appeal, effectively ending the fairness doctrine.

REFERENCES: Thomas G. Krattenmaker and Lucas A. Powe, Jr., *Regulating Broadcast Programming*, Cambridge, MIT Press, 1994; Ford Rowan, *Broadcast Fairness: Doctrine, Practice, Prospects*, New York, Longman, 1984.

FAULK, JOHN HENRY, 1913–1990   John Henry Faulk was born on August 21, 1913, in Austin, Texas. His father, Henry, a prominent attorney known for his liberal politics and support for civil rights, received national publicity for his role in the 1911 Supreme Court case that broke Standard Oil's monopoly. Like his father, young John Henry took a passionate interest in equal rights for all.

During World War II, John Henry Faulk served initially in the Merchant Marine and the Red Cross and later in the Army as a medic. While on furlough from the Army during Christmas of 1945, he was introduced by his friend Alan Lomax to a number of New York radio executives who were fascinated by his salty humor and storytelling skills. In April 1946, Faulk began a weekly radio series on CBS called "Johnny's Front Porch."

In the early 1950s, Faulk began appearing on TV shows in addition to his radio show, which climbed near the top of the Nielsen ratings. But the politics of paranoia soon came to threaten his success. The practice of blacklisting radio, TV, and movie performers became widespread, and Faulk's network (CBS) and union (the American Federation of Radio Artists [AFRA]) began to investigate the "loyalty" of their employees and members. In 1951, AFRA merged with the television actors' union to form the American Federation of Television and Radio Artists (AFTRA) and passed a resolution to expel any members who refused to answer questions from a congressional investigating committee. As the practice of blacklisting became a part of the broader witch-hunt conducted by Senator Joseph P. McCarthy (R-Wis.) and his House Un-American Activities Committee (HUAC), concerned members of AFTRA realized that they needed to choose their leadership from among people who had served their country during the war, had not been involved in union politics, and were "squeaky clean." John Henry Faulk fit the bill perfectly.

In the summer of 1955, Faulk's "Middle-of-the-Road" slate of AFTRA officers was announced: Newsman Charles Collingwood would run for president; Comedian Orson Bean, first vice president; and John Henry Faulk, second vice president. During the campaign for the union elections, Faulk said that the primary interest of a union should be the employment and security of its members, not blacklisting them. In December 1955, a record number of AFTRA voters gave the "Middlers," as they were called, twenty-seven of the thirty-five seats on the board.

Shortly after the election victory, Faulk was accused of Communist activities by a right-wing organization called AWARE. AWARE had already used innuendo and guilt by association to destroy the careers of entertainers it regarded as soft on communism, and it claimed that Faulk's opposition to blacklisting was really opposition to the exposure of communism. When a major sponsor pulled its advertising from Faulk's radio show, Faulk chose to hire Louis Nizer's law firm to challenge the lies that AWARE was circulating about him. The case was filed in the New York Supreme Court on June 26, 1956, with a plea for $500,000 in compensatory damages, later increased to $1 million. The legal complaint charged that AWARE had conspired with the advertising agencies and the networks to defame Faulk's reputation, destroy his livelihood, and remove him from AFTRA.

Faulk received wide public support for his suit, and when his ratings went up, many thought that he had beaten AWARE. However, the lawsuit had made him more controversial than ever. Soon, even some of the members of Faulk's Middle-of-the-Road AFTRA group began to lose their nerve. When influential columnist and TV host Ed Sullivan removed Orson Bean from a scheduled appearance on his show and CBS cancelled his pilot series, Bean called Faulk and said that in order to save his career, he would have to resign from the AFTRA slate. Bean soon reappeared on Ed Sullivan's TV show.

AWARE made it clear to Faulk that if he would name union members that he suspected of having Communist ties, things might go better for him. Faulk refused, saying that AWARE was a bunch of blackmailers who preyed on entertainers, using patriotism as a smokescreen. CBS was putting pressure on Faulk to drop his suit against AWARE, but Edward R. Murrow encouraged him and helped pay the legal fees. Murrow told him, "Let's get this straight, Johnny. I am not making a personal loan to you of this money. I am investing this money in America."

In 1958, despite generally good ratings for his radio show, Faulk was summarily fired by CBS. He was suddenly unemployable. Meanwhile, he proceeded with his lawsuit against AWARE, which used its close relationship with HUAC to have him subpoenaed. The subpoena was eventually cancelled, but its issuance alone was publicized in such a way as to further close all avenues of employment for Faulk. His income for 1958 declined to $2,061, and his savings were soon exhausted. Even his wife's long-time employment with an advertising firm was threatened by AWARE, and she eventually had to take a job as a waitress.

At the end of 1959, heavily in debt and facing an eviction notice from his landlord, Faulk returned to his hometown of Austin, Texas, where he worked at odd jobs to eke out a living. Finally, in April 1962, his suit against AWARE was brought to trial in the New York Supreme Court. Prominent performers like Gary Moore testified to Faulk's "rare form of talent," saying that he might have earned anywhere between $200,000 and $1 million a year had he not been blacklisted.

When the members of the jury returned from their deliberations, they surprised the courtroom by asking the judge if it was permissible to award more money in damages than the plaintiffs had requested. On June 27, 1962, the jury awarded $3.5 million, the largest libel judgment in history as of that time. *Look* magazine editorialized: "The guilt for John Henry Faulk's ordeal is shared by all—magazines, newspapers, radio and television, advertising agencies and just plain citizens. He who made no protest at the time has no license for smugness now. Let us hope that we have learned our lesson well" (Joseph P. Blank, "The Ordeal of John Henry Faulk," *Look*, May 7, 1963, p. 96, concluding editorial).

As it turned out, Faulk saw very little of the record-breaking settlement because AWARE had insufficient money to pay more than a fraction of the judgment. Most of what Faulk received was used to cover legal fees and pay off the debts he had incurred in six years of unemployment. Even after his court victory, job offers were not forthcoming because the networks now regarded him as an embarrassing reminder of their shameful collaboration.

In 1963, Faulk wrote *Fear on Trial*, a book about his ordeal and that of the many others blacklisted for their lack of political orthodoxy. After a painful divorce, he remarried in 1965 and returned to Austin, Texas, to start a new life. Twelve years later, his book was made into a TV docudrama shown on CBS. The movie led to renewed interest in Faulk as a performer, including regular appearances on the TV show *Hee Haw* (1975–80) and on National Public Radio.

Faulk also toured the country as a lecturer on First Amendment rights, often showing the parallel between blacklisting performers and censoring books or artwork. "My blacklisting wasn't about whether I was a subversive or wasn't a subversive," Faulk said. "It was about repression of our basic freedoms . . . a way of shutting off the dialogue in this country and destroying dissent" (Michael C. Burton, *John Henry Faulk: The Making of a Liberated Mind*, Austin, Eakin Press, 1993, p. 168).

In January 1980, Faulk and his friends Eric Sevareid and Walter Cronkite formed the First Amendment Congress, a national forum organized to protect free expression and the separation of church and state. Among the awards Faulk received were the National Press Club Certificate of Appreciation (1955), the Eleanor Roosevelt Freedom of Speech Award (1976), the

James Madison First Amendment Award (1980), a Freedoms Foundation at Valley Forge Award (1985), and a Hugh M. Hefner First Amendment Award for Individual Conscience (1989).

John Henry Faulk died on April 9, 1990, and the University of Texas at Austin subsequently established a fund in his name to support programs on the Bill of Rights. That university also sponsors "The John Henry Faulk Conference on the First Amendment," held every two years.

REFERENCES: Michael C. Burton, *John Henry Faulk: The Making of a Liberated Mind: A Biography*, Austin, Eakin Press, 1993; John Henry Faulk, *The Uncensored John Henry Faulk*, Austin, Texas Monthly Press, 1985.

FEMINISM AND PORNOGRAPHY   There is no single feminist position on pornography, but during the 1980s, the debate on this issue became polarized in ways that are likely to persist. On one side are the anticensorship feminists, whose support for intellectual freedom has historical roots in the liberal politics of the women's suffrage movement. On the other side are the feminists whose attempts to prohibit pornography have their origins in Victorian concepts of decency, family values, and the protection of women, attitudes that, until recently, were most common among conservative, fundamentalist, and antifeminist women. But in the 1980s, some feminists introduced a new political paradigm that appeared to place less emphasis on the indecency of pornography and more emphasis on the political and social consequences of the pornographic process and product. Through a complex, legalistic argument, this new approach attempts to avoid the stigma of censorship by characterizing the fight against pornography as a civil rights struggle.

The influential writings of the antipornography feminists have been further elevated by dramatic legislative initiatives. The feminist ordinances redefined pornography in various ways, always placing it outside the protection of the First Amendment. The notorious Minneapolis pornography ordinance, drafted by feminist author Andrea Dworkin and law professor Catharine MacKinnon, was passed by a 7–6 vote of the Minneapolis City Council on December 30, 1983. It amended the city's civil rights ordinance to include pornography as a violation of women's civil rights, claiming that pornography promotes civil inequality between the sexes, systematic exploitation and subordination based on sex, and acts of aggression, bigotry, and contempt.

Under the Minneapolis ordinance, individuals could file complaints with the Civil Rights Commission seeking damages or an injunction to prevent the production, sale, distribution, or showing of pornography. Individuals could also file complaints if they were physically hurt as a direct result of pornography or had pornography forced upon them in public places or at home. Women could sue the producers of pornography or husbands who forced pornography on them. Even librarians appeared to be subject to penalties if they distributed materials falling within the ordinance's definition of pornography. The Minneapolis ordinance defined pornography as

the sexually explicit subordination of women, graphically depicted, whether in pictures or in words that also includes one or more of the following:

(A) women are presented dehumanized as sexual objects, things, or commodities; or

(B) women are presented as sexual objects who experience sexual pleasure in being raped;

(C) women are presented as sexual objects who enjoy pain or humiliation;

(D) women are presented as sexual objects tied up or cut up or mutilated or bruised or physically hurt;

(E) women are presented in postures of sexual submission or sexual servility, including inviting penetration;

(F) women's body parts—including but not limited to vaginas, breasts, and buttocks—are exhibited, such that women are reduced to those parts;

(G) women are presented as whores by nature;

(H) women are presented being penetrated by objects or animals;

(I) women are presented in scenarios of degradation, injury, torture, shown as filthy or inferior, bleeding, bruised, or bruised [sic], or hurt in a context that makes the condition sexual.

The use of men, children, or transsexuals in the place of women is pornography for the purposes of this statute.

The Minneapolis ordinance was vetoed by the mayor, who feared that it would be struck down as unconstitutional. The ordinance never became law, but this new legislative attack on pornography was given prominent coverage in the media. In April 1984, the Indianapolis City-County Council passed a similar ordinance, drafted again by Catharine MacKinnon, treating pornography complaints as sexual discrimination complaints and referring them to the city's Equal Opportunities Board, which would have the authority to seek a court injunction against distribution of the material. If the court order was ignored, the distributor would be subject to penalties, including civil damages for anyone harmed by a pornography user. The ordinance prohibited the production, sale, exhibition, or distribution of pornography or the coercion of persons into the performance of pornographic acts. Exhibitions in public or educational libraries were for the most part excluded from the provisions of the ordinance, but "special displays" in a library could be regarded as an act of sexual discrimination.

The Indianapolis mayor signed the ordinance into law on May 1, 1984, but an immediate lawsuit caused a federal district judge to enjoin the city from enforcing the ordinance. On November 19, the federal district court ruled that "pornography," as defined in the Indianapolis ordinance, was protected speech, not conduct, as the feminists argued. In declaring the ordinance unconstitutional, the court stated that the state's interest in prohibiting sexual discrimination did not outweigh an individual's interest in free speech. The judgment was immediately appealed, but the district court's ruling was affirmed on August 27, 1985. The appeals court specifically held that the feminists' new definition of pornography outside of the "obscenity standard" was unconstitutional, and it declared, "Any other answer leaves the government in control of all of the institutions of culture, the great censor and director of which thoughts are good for us."

The appeals court concluded that the ordinance discriminated in a vague and arbitrary way on the basis of the content of speech: "Speech treating women in the approved way—in sexual encounters 'premised on equality'—is lawful no matter how sexually explicit. Speech treating women in the disapproved way—as submissive in matters sexual or as enjoying humiliation—is unlawful no matter how significant the literary, artistic, or political qualities of the work taken as a whole. The state may not ordain preferred viewpoints in this way. The Constitution forbids the state to declare one perspective right and silence opponents" (*American Booksellers Association v. Hudnut* [1985]). On February 24, 1986, the Supreme Court summarily affirmed the judgment of the appeals court.

REFERENCE: *Dirty Looks: Women, Pornography, Power*, edited by Pamela Church Gibson and Roma Gibson, London, BFI Pub., 1993.

FIRST AMENDMENT   After the drafting of the American Constitution at the federal convention in 1787, a series of contentious state ratifying conventions attempted to resolve the remaining conflicts. The omission of a declaration of rights was a particular source of controversy that threatened ratification. During the Massachusetts convention, the presiding officer, John Hancock, avoided defeat of the draft constitution by suggesting that a resolution accompany ratification recommending to Congress the adoption of certain amendments to the Constitution. Hancock's proposal suceeded and became a model for other state constitutions.

During the Virginia convention, governor Patrick Henry argued: "If we must adopt a constitution ceding away such vast powers, express and implied, and so frought with danger to the liberties of the people, it ought at least to be guarded by a bill of rights; . . . Congress might think it necessary, in order to carry into effect the given powers, to silence the clamors and censures of the people; . . . what then would become of the liberty of speech and of the press?" (William Wirt, *Sketches of the Life and Character of Patrick Henry*, 2d ed., Philadelphia, William Brown, 1818, p. 204.)

Following Henry's arguments, a resolution was introduced drafting amendments and a Declaration of Rights including: "That the people have a right to freedom of speech, and of writing and publishing their sentiments; that freedom of the press is one of the greatest bulwarks of liberty, and ought not to be violated" (Jonathan Elliot, *The Debates in the Several State*

Conventions on the Adoption of the Federal Constitution, New York, Burt Franklin Reprints, 1974, vol. 3, p. 659).

Agreement on the final wording of the First Amendment required compromise between the libertarian views represented by spokesmen like James Madison and the more conservative forces represented by Alexander Hamilton. Hamilton and others believed that English common law, despite its narrow focus on prohibiting prior restraint, provided adequate protection for free speech. James Madison argued that "freedom of the press and rights of conscience, those choicest privileges of the people, are unguarded in the British constitution." Madison proposed a constitutional amendment stipulating: "No State shall violate the equal rights of conscience or the freedom of the press." When his concept of "rights of conscience" was rejected, Madison proposed the following wording: "The people shall not be deprived or abridged of their right to speak, to write, or to publish their sentiments; and the freedom of the press, as one of the great bulwarks of liberty, shall be inviolable" (*Annals of Congress, 1789–1791*, Washington, D.C., Gates and Seaton, editors and compilers, 1834, vol. 1, p. 453).

As finally ratified on December 15, 1791, the First Amendment states: "Congress shall make no law respecting an establishment of religion, or prohibiting the exercise thereof; or abridging the freedom of speech, or of the press; or the right of the people peaceably to assemble." The wording embodied the common law view that freedom of speech was protected against prior restraint by the national government, but it gave no explicit protection from punishment for what one might speak in print. For example, libelous or defamatory speech or publications were not constitutionally protected speech. Even libelous statements against the government, called "seditious libel," were left open to punishment.

Within a decade after ratification of the First Amendment, the issue of protected speech was tested when Congress passed the Alien and Sedition Acts of 1798, making it a punishable crime to make "any false, scandalous writing against the government of the United States." Though Thomas Jefferson argued that the Sedition Act was unconstitutional, the Supreme Court upheld its constitutionality, along with the common law concept of "seditious libel." Not until the 1930s did the Supreme Court begin to question the use of common law principles in construing the First Amendment.

In many ways, the interpretation of the First Amendment remains a work in progress. By the end of World War II, a minority of the Supreme Court was arguing for a citizen's First Amendment "right to know," under which not only free expression was guaranteed, but an affirmative right of access to government information and facilities was assumed. Though the "right to know" has not yet been affirmed by a majority of the Court, the growing apparatus of state secrecy has made it a continuing focus of debate among First Amendment scholars, the press, and the general public.

REFERENCE: *The First Amendment: A Reader*, edited by John H. Garvey and Frederick Schauer, St. Paul, West Pub. Co., 1996.

FLAG DESECRATION   Laws attempting to ban flag desecration have been persistently tested during this century, with the debate inevitably turning on the question of whether flag burning or other desecration was political expression. Under the administration of President George Bush (1988–92), the United States saw the most serious federal attempts to ban and criminalize flag burning through statutes and Constitutional amendments. Until that time, the Supreme Court had never clearly defined the extent to which desecration of the flag could be penalized by the government. In 1907, in *Halter v. Nebraska*, the Supreme Court had upheld a Nebraska law forbidding the representation of the American flag in advertising or upon commercial products. In a comment that seemed to condone vigilante violence against flag desecrators, the Court noted that "insults to a flag have been the cause of war, and indignities put upon it in the presence of those who revere it, have often been resented and sometimes punished on the spot." On the other hand, in *Stromberg v. California* (1931), the Court struck down a state statute that barred displaying a red flag as a symbol of opposition to government, saying that the statute threatened "the opportunity for free political discussion."

In *Minersville School District v. Gobitis* (1940), Justice Felix Frankfurter wrote the opinion upholding the expulsion from school of two children who refused to salute the flag or recite the Pledge of Allegiance on the grounds that it violated their religious rights as Jehovah's Witnesses. "The flag is the symbol of our national unity," said Frankfurter, "transcending all internal differences, however large, within the framework of the Constitution." Frankfurter concluded that the Constitution could not deny government the power to promote that "unifying sentiment without which there can ultimately be no liberties, civil or religious."

Just three years later, the Court retreated from that position in *Taylor v. Mississippi* (1943). In the middle of World War II, when one would have expected little tolerance for antipatriotic expression, two cases, decided on the same day, affirmed the right to political dissent. In *Taylor v. Mississippi* (1943), a group of men who had distributed leaflets opposing the flag salute were convicted of violating a Mississippi law prohibiting communications that "create an attitude of stubborn refusal to salute, honor or respect the flag or government of the United States or of the State of Mississippi." One of the defendants, R. E. Taylor, particularly aroused the ire of the local community when he told two mothers who had lost sons in the war that their sons had died in vain and that Americans should stop worshipping the flag and the government.

The second case decided on that day, June 14, 1943, was *West Virginia State Board of Education v. Barnette*, in which a group of Jehovah's Witnesses challenged a West Virginia law that required children to salute the flag each morning at school. In both *Taylor* and *Barnette*, the Court struck down state laws imposing patriotic restraints on expression. In his opinion for the Court in *Barnette*, Justice Robert Jackson declared: "If there is any fixed star in our constitutional constellation, it is that no official, high or petty, can prescribe what shall be orthodox in politics, nationalism, or other matters of opinion or force citizens to confess by word or act their faith therein." The Court in *Barnette* stated that the flag salute was "a form of utterance" and thus established that the symbolic gesture of saluting fell within the constitutional definition of "speech."

The *Taylor* decision, concerning a criminal conviction for unpatriotic speech, was unanimous, while *Barnette*, which dealt with forced patriotic ritual, was decided 6–3. Neither dealt with the physical desecration of national symbols. Such a case arose on June 6, 1966, when Sidney Street publicly burned an American flag in protest after learning of the shooting of civil rights leader James Meredith. Street was arrested and convicted on the charge that "he did wilfully and unlawfully cast contempt upon, and burn an American flag . . . and shouted, 'If they did that to Meredith, we don't need an American flag.' "

Street was convicted of "malicious mischief," but in *Street v. New York* (1969), the Supreme Court reversed the conviction, emphasizing that the indictment concerned Street's words as well as his action in burning the flag. Indeed, the Court did not establish whether a conviction based on flag burning alone would have been sustained.

In 1974, the Supreme Court addressed two flag-desecration cases, *Smith v. Goguen* and *Spence v. Washington*. In the former, Valarie Goguen was arrested in the state of Massachusetts for wearing a four-by-six-inch patch representing the American flag on his trousers. He was charged under a Massachusetts law that imposed a $100 fine and up to a year's imprisonment against anyone who "publicly mutilates, tramples upon, defaces or treats contemptuously the flag of the United States . . . , whether such flag is public or private property." Goguen was convicted and sentenced to six months in prison, but the Supreme Court overturned the conviction.

Justice Lewis Powell, who wrote the opinion in *Goguen*, did not regard Goguen's action as political expression, but said that the statute under which he had been convicted was too broad in its reference to "contemptuous" conduct. The Court thus once more failed to address the question of whether a more narrowly drawn statute against flag desecration would be constitutional.

Spence v. Washington dealt with the action of a college student, Harold Spence, who hung a United States flag upside down from the window of his apartment, attaching to it a peace symbol made from black tape. Spence had attached the peace symbol to protest American policy in Southeast Asia. Though the state of Washington had a flag-desecration statute, Spence was charged instead under a statute controlling the appropriate display of the flag. That statute prohibited the placing of "any word, figure, mark, picture, design, drawing, or advertisement of any nature upon any United States flag" or "exposing to public view any such decorated flag."

Spence was convicted, but the Supreme Court held that the conviction violated the First Amendment because the display was on Spence's property and involved no risk of breach of peace. The state of Washington conceded that the display was an action of expression, a concession the Court said was "inevitable." The Court emphasized that Spence's action was an expression of anguish about the government's domestic and foreign affairs, not "an act of mindless nihilism." There was no evidence, said the Court, that anyone had been upset or offended by the flag display, and anyone so inclined could simply have looked elsewhere. The Court concluded that "the public expression of ideas may not be prohibited merely because the ideas are themselves offensive to some of their hearers."

Still, the Court suggested circumstances under which the state might pursue its interest in protecting a national emblem, such as the prevention of the use of the flag to imply governmental endorsement for a particular product or viewpoint. Or the state might have an interest in protecting the universal symbolism of the national flag from physical destruction or disfigurement. Clearly, the endorsement issue was not involved in this case, and since Spence had not been charged under the Washington desecration statute, that issue was also not implicated. Thus the Supreme Court once more avoided a direct consideration of the constitutionality of flag-desecration laws. It was not until 1989 that the Supreme Court squarely addressed the issue.

In *Texas v. Johnson* (1989), the Supreme Court reviewed the conviction of Gregory Lee Johnson, who had burned a flag in protest during the 1984 Republican National Convention in Dallas. The convention was about to renominate President Ronald Reagan, and Johnson was part of a group demonstrating against the policies of the Reagan administration. The protesters marched to the Dallas City Hall, where Johnson set fire to a kerosene-soaked American flag. Johnson was arrested and charged with violation of a Texas statute titled "Desecration of a Venerated Object" that made it a criminal offense to intentionally desecrate a public monument, a place of worship or burial, or a state or national flag. The statute defined "desecration" to mean defacing, damaging, or physically mistreating an object in a way that would seriously offend one or more persons who might observe or discover the act. Johnson was convicted and sentenced to one year in prison and a fine of $2,000.

In *Johnson*, the Court established that laws banning the desecration of flags control the content of expression and must therefore be subject to the exacting scrutiny of the "clear and present danger" tests. Further, *Johnson* established that the government's desire to promote "political cohesiveness" and "national unity" did not, of itself, justify curtailing speech. The attorney for the state of Texas argued that its antidesecration law protected the integrity of a symbol of national unity while also preventing a breach of the peace. But Justice Antonin Scalia responded that Johnson's action did not destroy the symbolic character of the flag. It simply showed disrespect for it. "You want not just a symbol, you want a venerated symbol," Scalia told the Texas attorney.

Texas continued to claim that the statute was designed to protect the "physical integrity" of the flag, despite the fact that Johnson was charged with desecrating the flag as a symbol. Justice Anthony Kennedy attacked the state's argument that privately owned flags are somehow public property, and Scalia agreed, stating, "I never thought that the flag I own is your flag."

In a 5–4 decision, *Texas v. Johnson* held that Johnson's conviction was inconsistent with the First Amendment. Justice William Brennan wrote the opinion for the majority, stating that when flag burning is overt political expression, its restriction will be subject to "the most exacting scrutiny." Brennan found that Johnson's conviction was not content neutral because it was directly related to the message conveyed. The conviction was thus inconsistent with "a bedrock principle underlying the First Amendment . . . that the Government may not prohibit the expression of an idea simply because society finds the idea itself offensive or disagreeable."

Brennan asserted that nothing in the Court's precedents "suggests that a State may foster its own view of the flag by prohibiting expressive conduct relating to it." The government may foster unity through persuasion, but not through criminal law. "It is the Nation's resilience, not its rigidity, that Texas sees reflected in the flag—and it is that resilience that we reassert today," wrote Brennan. America, he admonished, does "not consecrate the flag by punishing its desecration, for in doing so we dilute the freedom that this cherished emblem represents." Liberal Justices Brennan, Harry Blackmun, and Thurgood Marshall were joined by conservatives Scalia and Kennedy, the latter writing an eloquent concurring opinion that stated, "It is poignant but fundamental that the flag protects those who hold it in contempt."

Chief Justice William Rehnquist's dissent, joined by Justices Byron White and Sandra Day O'Connor, characterized the Texas statute as an unintrusive government regulation that forced no one to be patriotic, only to avoid antipatriotic acts against the nation's flag. Rehnquist claimed that Johnson's act was "no essential part of any exposition of ideas, and at the same time it had a tendency to incite a breach of the peace." He conceded that Johnson's act did communicate a criticism of his government, but noted that it was not necessary to burn a flag in order to express that dissent. Rehnquist compared burning the flag to "an inarticulate grunt or roar" that was unlikely to express any particular idea. He concluded, "Uncritical extension of constitutional protection to the burning of the flag risks the frustration of the very purpose for which organized governments are instituted."

Justice John Paul Stevens filed a separate dissent in *Johnson* in which he insisted that Johnson had not been prosecuted for his expression, but for the method he chose to express himself. Stevens revisited the idea of the flag as public property, comparing flag burning to spray-painting the Lincoln Memorial. In either case, said Stevens, the government had a legitimate interest in preserving the quality of an important national asset. Stevens admitted that in this case the national asset, a privately owned flag, was "intangible," but said that its protection served the same interest.

The Court's judgment on flag desecration had finally been rendered, but in a divided opinion that left an opening for political opportunists in Congress. Some called for a constitutional amendment to protect the flag. Others suggested a federal statute that would presumably patch up the constitutional flaws in the Texas law. In 1989, flag waving was good politics, and even those members of Congress who supported the *Johnson* decision knew better than to defend it publicly.

Congress produced a federal law, the Flag Protection Act of 1989, that specified, "Whoever knowingly mutilates, defaces, physically defiles, burns, maintains on the floor or ground, or tramples upon any flag of the United States shall be fined under this title or imprisoned for not more than one year, or both." President George Bush, who capitalized on his opposition to the *Johnson* decision, nonetheless opposed the Flag Protection Act because he was certain that it would not pass constitutional scrutiny. Bush was contemptuous of the congressional pretense that the act did not curtail expression, and he felt that only a constitutional amendment could do the job.

On October 28, 1989, the moment the Flag Protection Act became law, a group of demonstrators in Seattle burned an American flag in front of a post office. The demonstration was publicized by leaflets describing the law as an attack on political protest and dissent. Because the flag was owned by the post office, the protesters were charged with destruction of federal property and violation of the Flag Protection Act of 1989.

Just two days later, another group of protesters desecrated flags on the steps of the U.S. Capitol. Among those protesters was Gregory Lee Johnson, fresh from his Supreme Court victory. This time, however, Johnson was unable to get his flag to burn and was charged with no crime. The other protesters, like those in Seattle, distributed leaflets explaining their opposition to compulsory patriotism and enforced reverence for the flag. One of the protesters, David Gerald Blalock, a Vietnam veteran, said that he burned his flag to protest American policy in Indochina.

In both the Seattle and Washington, D.C., cases, the local courts struck down the convictions, holding that the Flag Protection Act of 1989 differed little from the Texas law that had been found unconstitutional in the *Johnson* case. Nonetheless, in 1990, the Supreme Court agreed to review the two consolidated cases, *United States v.Eichman* and *United States v. Haggerty*, on a special schedule outside the normal Court calendar. On June 11, 1990, the

Court struck down the Flag Protection Act in a 5–4 decision that retained the same alignment as in the *Johnson* decision. Justice Brennan once more wrote the majority opinion, with Justice Stevens this time writing the dissenting opinion. Brennan wrote, "Although Congress cast the Flag Protection Act in somewhat broader terms than the Texas statute at issue in *Johnson*, the Act still suffers from the same fundamental flaw: it suppresses expression out of a concern for its likely communicative impact."

The government in *Eichman* and *Haggerty* seemed to acknowledge its inability to distinguish the Flag Protection Act from the Texas statute. It asked the Court to reconsider its opinion in *Johnson* because of the negative public reaction to that decision. In response to the government's claim that a "national consensus" existed to prohibit flag burning, Brennan wrote, "Even assuming such a consensus exists, any suggestion that the Government's interest in suppressing speech becomes more weighty as popular opposition to that speech grows is foreign to the First Amendment."

Justice Stevens's dissent was restrained and respectful, stating that the case was a question of judgment on which reasonable judges may differ. The Court's deliberations showed little of the emotion and bitterness that appeared in *Johnson*, and even the dissenting justices seemed resentful of the opportunistic congressional tactics that had produced the Flag Protection Act. Indeed, Stevens went so far as to chastise those politicians "who seem to advocate compulsory worship of the flag even by individuals whom it offends, or who seem to manipulate the symbol of national purpose into a pretext for partisan disputes about meaner ends."

No sooner was the Flag Protection Act buried than the idea of a constitutional amendment was resurrected by Congress. After much posturing by members of both political parties, the measure came to a vote in the House on June 21, 1990, just ten days after the Supreme Court had disposed of the Flag Protection Act. When the House defeated the proposed amendment by a vote of 254–177, Republicans announced that they would take the issue directly to the public. Despite the fact that the amendment was dead, the Senate proceeded with a symbolic vote, and once more the measure was defeated.

True to their promise, Republicans took the flag-burning issue to the public in 1992, with predictable popular support. Over the next few years, many state legislatures passed resolutions urging Congress to reintroduce a constitutional amendment against flag burning. Vermont bucked the national trend in 1995 by defeating such a resolution and replacing it with an affirmation of First Amendment freedoms.

In June 1995, Senators Orrin Hatch (R-Utah) and Howell Heflin (D-Ala.) announced that they would lead the effort to reintroduce a constitutional amendment against flag burning. The House Judiciary Committee quickly endorsed a constitutional amendment that read, "The Congress and the states shall have the power to prohibit the physical desecration of the flag of the United States." The committee vote was 18–12, split along party lines, to send the vote to the House floor.

For the first time in two hundred years, Congress was attempting to amend the First Amendment to the Constitution, with little motivation other than personal pique and political opportunism. There was no threat to the nation. After all, there had been only a handful of flag-burning incidents since an amendment had first been proposed. In testimony before a Senate subcommittee, Assistant Attorney General Walter Dellinger presented the Clinton administration's objections to the amendment, warning that there would be litigation challenging its scope, the definition of some of the words used, and its relationship to the First Amendment. Even if those problems could be corrected, said Dellinger, the amendment was ill advised.

On June 28, 1995, the House easily passed the flag-burning amendment, 312 to 120, surpassing by 24 votes the two-thirds majority needed to approve a constitutional amendment. Critics were concerned about the vagueness of terms like "flag" and "desecration," especially since each state would be free to define the terms as it wished. Was a flag napkin a flag, and would you desecrate it when you blew your nose? What about a cake made in the image of the flag? Would you desecrate it by eating it? House Judiciary Chairman Henry Hyde (R-Ill.) brushed aside such concerns, comparing a ban on flag burning with existing restraints on obscenity, libel, and perjury.

On July 20, 1995, the Senate Judiciary Committee approved the flag-burning amendment by a 12–6 vote, sending it to the full Senate for a vote. On December 12, the Senate voted 63 to 36 in favor of the amendment, but it was 3 votes short of the two-thirds needed to propose an amendment for ratification by the states. Just before voting on the amendment, the Senate made a final attempt to ban flag desecration through legislation, but the bill was rejected 71 to 28, in large part because it was widely assumed to be unconstitutional. President Clinton had opposed the flag amendment, though aides said that he would be open to further attempts to craft legislation against flag desecration. Senator Hatch, floor manager for the amendment, blamed Clinton for the amendment's defeat and vowed to reintroduce it.

REFERENCE: Robert J. Goldstein, *Saving "Old Glory": The History of the American Flag Desecration Controversy*, Boulder, Westview Press, 1995.

FREEDOM OF INFORMATION ACT   The Freedom of Information Act (FOIA) was signed into law by President Lyndon Johnson on July 4, 1966, and went into effect on July 4, 1967. Johnson said, "This legislation springs from one of our most essential principles: a democracy works best when the people have all the information that the security of the Nation permits. No one should be able to pull the curtains of secrecy around decisions which can be revealed without injury to the public interest."

Attorney General Ramsey Clark added, "If government is to be truly of, by, and for the people, the people must know in detail the activities of government. Nothing so diminishes democracy as secrecy" (L. G. Sherick, *How to Use the Freedom of Information Act (FOIA)*, New York, Arco, 1978, p. 7).

The FOIA was intended to make information from most federal agencies (Congress and the judiciary were exempted from FOIA) available to the public, providing such information upon request, unless it fell within the following statutory exemptions:

1. Matters that are specifically authorized by executive order to be kept secret in the interest of national defense or foreign policy and are properly classified pursuant to such an order
2. Matters that are related solely to the internal personnel rules and practices of an agency
3. Matters that are specifically exempted from disclosure by statute
4. Matters that are trade secrets and commercial or financial information obtained from a person and privileged or confidential
5. Matters that are interagency or intraagency memorandums or letters that would not be available by law to a party other than an agency in litigation with the agency
6. Matters that deal with personnel and medical files and similar files the disclosure of which would constitute a clearly unwarranted invasion of personal privacy
7. Matters that are investigatory records compiled for law-enforcement purposes, when the revelation of such records would (*a*) interfere with enforcement proceedings, (*b*) *deprive a person of a right to fair trial or impartial adjudication,* (*c*) constitute an unwarranted invasion of personal privacy, (*d*) disclose the identity of a confidential source or confidential information furnished only by the confidential source in the course of a criminal or national security intelligence investigation, (*e*) disclose investigatory techniques or procedures, or (*f*) endanger the life or physical safety of law-enforcement personnel
8. Matters related to reports prepared by, on behalf of, or for the use of an agency responsible for the regulation or supervision of financial institutions
9. Matters involving geological and geophysical information and data, including maps, concerning wells

Because the FOIA was immediately unpopular with the federal bureaucracy, and Presidents Nixon, Ford, and Reagan gave little support to it, the law did not really work. It contained no deadlines for compliance and no penalties for violation. Many federal agencies instituted crippling delays in compliance with requests, and others imposed high fees as a means of discouraging requestors. In 1974, Congress attempted to fix some of the obvious loopholes through a series of amendments that covered the areas of index publication, record identification, search and copying fees, attorney fees, court review, response to complaints, expedited appeals, sanction, administrative deadlines, national defense and foreign policy exemptions, annual reports by agencies, segregable portions of records, and expansion of agency definition. President Ford vetoed the bill to strengthen FOIA, claiming that it was unconstitutional and unworkable, but it was passed over his veto.

The FBI has often expressed its discomfort with the FOIA, and in 1984 the bureau was the prominent voice in hearings on a proposed amendment to significantly weaken the FOIA. After two years of congressional haggling, three amendments were enacted in 1986. One of the amendments substituted the general term "records or information" for "investigative records," a change intended to ensure that law-enforcement procedures could be kept from the public. A subsection was added allowing a law-enforcement agency to withhold records concerning any ongoing and undisclosed criminal investigation and records maintained under an informant's name. A new provision was added concerning the FBI's foreign intelligence, counterintelligence, or international terrorism investigations, stating that the agency would have no obligation to acknowledge the existence of such records in response to a request.

Despite the 1986 weakening amendments and continuing problems with agency compliance, the FOIA remains the people's most effective challenge to government secrecy. In January 1989, Representative Don Edwards, chairman of the House Subcommittee on Civil and Constitutional Rights, used the *Congressional Record* to rebut a court decision to deny a reporter's FOIA request on the grounds that oversight committees like his own could adequately serve the public's interest. "The subcommittee has never sought to substitute itself for an informed public or an alert press," said Edwards. "Nor does the subcommittee see its access to executive branch information as a substitute for the rights of access established by the Freedom of Information Act. . . . In conclusion, Mr. Speaker, the FOIA and the congressional oversight are sometimes complementary, but the principle of public accountability does not depend solely on the Congress. The public is entitled to direct access to information about its Government and the actions of the Government's agents" ("The FOIA and Congressional Oversight," *Congressional Record—House*, January 27, 1989, p. H108).

REFERENCE: United States Congress, House, Committee on Government Reform and Oversight, *A Citizen's Guide on Using the Freedom of Information Act and the Privacy Act of 1974 to Request Government Records*, Washington, D.C., U.S. G.P.O., 1995.

FREEDOM TO READ FOUNDATION The Freedom to Read Foundation was created in 1969 as an organization of individuals, associations, and corporations committed to the protection of the freedoms of speech and press, with particular emphasis on the First Amendment rights and obligations of librarians and libraries. The foundation's primary purpose is to promote the role of libraries as repositories of knowledge and their right to make available to the public any legally acquired publications. The foundation provides legal counsel and support to librarians and libraries whose collections are challenged by outside groups or authorities.

The Freedom to Read Foundation publishes *News*, a quarterly newsletter that documents foundation activities, reports on censorship incidents, and analyzes federal and state laws affecting First Amendment rights. The organization's executive director is Judith Krug, and it is located at 50 East Huron Street, Chicago, IL 60611.

REFERENCE: Leon Hurwitz, *Historical Dictionary of Censorship in the United States*, Westport, Greenwood Press, 1985.

G

GARFINKEL, STEVEN, 1945– Steven Garfinkel has served four Presidents as Director of the Information Security Oversight Office (ISOO) since his appointment by President Jimmy Carter in 1978. In his capacity as Director of ISOO, he is responsible to the President for the administration and monitorship of the entire federal system of national security controls on information and personnel, including the governmentwide information-classification system and the National Industrial Security Program.

Steven Garfinkel was born on June 18, 1945, in Washington, D.C. Before heading ISOO, Garfinkel served for almost ten years in the Office of General Counsel of the General Services Administration (GSA), where his positions included Chief Counsel for the National Archives and Records Service, Chief Counsel for Information and Privacy, and Chief Counsel for Civil Rights. He is a member of the District of Columbia bar, and among the awards he has received are sixteen commendations or citations from Presidents Bush, Reagan, Carter, and Ford. These include the Presidential Rank Award to a Meritorious Federal Executive. He has also received commendations from the National Security Council, the Departments of Defense and Justice, the Office of Personnel Management, GSA, and a number of nongovernmental professional and service organizations. In 1989, the American Defense Preparedness Association presented Garfinkel with its first Security Man of the Year Award.

Critics of America's vast federal secrecy system may be inclined to hold Garfinkel accountable for the government's excessive classification of information and its intrusive personnel security program, but the federal guidelines for secrecy come primarily from presidential executive orders, which Garfinkel's office is required to uphold. In fact, in the post–Cold War era, Garfinkel has argued for a relaxation of such procedures, and President Clinton's 1995 Executive Order 12958 represents an important move in that direction. Garfinkel's March 1994 report to the President stated, "The submission of this Report occurs while we are in the final stages of shaping the first post–Cold War security classification system: a system intended to reduce significantly the amount of information that we classify in the first place, and to reduce dramatically through declassification the amount of older classification that has built up over the decades."

REFERENCE: Information Security Oversight Office, *Report to the President*, annual.

GLASSER, IRA, 1938–   Ira Glasser has been the executive director of the American Civil Liberties Union (ACLU) since 1978, when he replaced Aryeh Neier. Glasser's early studies were in mathematics and philosophy, and he served as associate director of *Current*, a liberal public affairs journal. In 1967, he joined the staff of the New York ACLU, becoming its director in 1970 and serving in that capacity until 1978, when he became executive director of the national ACLU.

Throughout his tenure as national executive director, Glasser criticized the policies of the Reagan and Bush administrations and the Burger and Rehnquist Courts as betrayals of Americans' political freedoms and civil liberties. During the Bush administration, he led the charge against a constitutional amendment prohibiting flag desecration. He has characterized a woman's right to choose an abortion as a constitutional right, not a democratically elected freedom, and he has been in the forefront of support for the separation of church and state. In his 1991 book *Visions of Liberty: The Bill of Rights for All Americans* (Boston, Little, Brown and Co., 1991, p. 273), he examined the history and modern application of the Bill of Rights, concluding, "If the Bill of Rights has developed from little more than a parchment barrier in 1791 to an enforceable set of legal restrictions today, it is to those who fought when the fight seemed hopeless that we owe the most gratitude.... Those who do not have liberty often see it more clearly. We could do worse than use them as our guides."

REFERENCE: Ira Glasser, *Visions of Liberty: The Bill of Rights for All Americans*, Boston, Little, Brown and Co., 1991.

GOLDBERG, DANNY, 1950–   Danny Goldberg is a leading First Amendment advocate within the entertainment industry. A New York native, Goldberg enrolled at the University of California at Berkeley in 1967, but dropped out to join the counterculture of Vietnam, Bob Dylan, the Beatles, long hair, psychedelics, and civil rights. For Goldberg, rock-and-roll music was the common thread. He began his career as a music journalist, free-lancing for the *Village Voice* and *Rolling Stone*. He later worked for *Billboard* and *Record World* and then became managing editor for *Circus*.

Goldberg soon became interested in public relations, joining the New York firm of Solters and Roskin, where his main client was the British band Led Zeppelin. He later formed his own company, Danny Goldberg Inc., signing such prestige clients as Bonnie Raitt, Nirvana, and Sonic Youth. In 1979, Goldberg and a partner formed Modern Records, which was distributed by Atlantic Records. Also in 1979, he organized the "No Nukes" concert at Madison Square Garden, featuring stars like Bonnie Raitt, Jackson Browne, Graham Nash, and John Hall. The "No Nukes" concert established Goldberg's reputation as a liberal activist.

In 1985, Goldberg joined forces with the American Civil Liberties Union (ACLU) to form the Musical Majority, a coalition of rock artists and industry figures who opposed attempts to place warning labels on music albums containing sexually explicit lyrics. Within the entertainment industry, the Musical Majority soon became a popular means of organizing on behalf of First Amendment rights generally. Goldberg was also one of four cofounders of Show Coalition, a four-hundred–member Hollywood-based group that creates interaction between elected officials and political policy experts on the one hand and the entertainment and business communities on the other.

In speeches and articles, Goldberg explained that the very occasional appearance of an offensive rock lyric should not characterize the music, nor did such occurrences fall under any conventional definition of pornography. He was particularly concerned when congressional hearings were scheduled in September 1985 to consider proposals for mandatory ratings on musical records and tapes. As Capitol Hill issued vague threats of legislative controls over music, Goldberg warned that erosions of freedom in show business and the media have not usually come through legislation, but from intimidation by extremists, often channeled through congressional hearings. He cited the infamous period of blacklisting in movies and television during the 1950s. At that time, he noted, patriotism was the cloak for censorship. Today, "concern for children" is the excuse given. "In both cases," said Goldberg, "the real reason for antagonism is a conflict between the American tradition of free expression and the quest by a well-organized few to squash that freedom and create cultural orthodoxy" (Danny Goldberg, "Pressure Groups Squeeze Music Biz," *Variety*, October 28, 1986, p. 3).

In 1987, Goldberg became the youngest person ever named chairman of the American Civil Liberties Foundation of Southern California. Goldberg was enthusiastic about his new role. "I frankly jumped at it," he said. "I was overwhelmed by the vision of how [the ACLU] used the court process as a tool of political activism. And, for me personally, it was a great step because it wasn't just rock and roll. . . . This gave me a chance to get involved with a wider range of issues" (Elaine Woo, "The Rock Activist," *Los Angeles Times*, February 10, 1989, pp. V6–V7). In 1990, Goldberg received a Hugh

Hefner First Amendment Award for his work in galvanizing the recording industry and consumers to oppose the muzzling of recording artists and the labelling of records.

In 1992, Goldberg became senior vice president of Atlantic Records, with a contractual agreement allowing him to spend up to 10 percent of his time on management of non-Atlantic artists. As a corporate executive and as an individual, Goldberg attempts to get people to distinguish between what they do not like and what should be denied to others. For example, he did not approve of 2 Live Crew because of their frequent disparagement of women and gays, yet he strongly supported signing 2 Live Crew on the Atlantic label, saying: "It was a statement that pressure groups and Florida sheriffs are not going to decide what's available to the American public. . . . The whole nature of music is diversity, and people have different tastes. . . . I'm not going to be some taste policeman at Atlantic records" (Paul Green, "Danny Goldberg's Hat Trick," *Musician*, August 1992, p. 34).

REFERENCE: John B. Harer, *Intellectual Freedom: A Reference Handbook*, Santa Barbara, ABC-CLIO, 1992.

GRIFFIN, ANTHONY, 1955–   Anthony Griffin is a lawyer and adjunct professor at the University of Houston Law Center who gained national prominence in 1993 when, at great personal risk, he defended the right of the Ku Klux Klan to keep its membership lists private. While serving as a volunteer general counsel for the American Civil Liberties Union, Griffin represented Michael Lowe, the grand dragon of the Waco-based Klan, after Lowe had been ordered to produce the Klan's membership lists and financial records. Griffin's principled defense of the First Amendment rights of the Klan was all the more striking because, as a black attorney and head of the Texas State Conference of the NAACP, his action was regarded by many as a conflict of interest.

Griffin saw no conflict and, indeed, compared the Klan case to two famous cases in 1958 and 1959, when Alabama and Florida attempted to obtain NAACP membership rolls. Nonetheless, Griffin was asked to resign as volunteer general counsel of the NAACP. He refused, saying that though he detested the Klan, his own rights to free speech would be at risk if he did not defend the Klan's rights. "I can't stand them," he said. "I wish they didn't exist. But it's very easy to give the First Amendment to groups we like and make us feel good. It's very difficult to apply those principles to people who anger us. . . . The First Amendment is not to protect me from you, but us from the government" ("Klan Leader and NAACP Counsel Make an Odd Couple of Civil Rights," *Washington Post*, September 9, 1993, p. A3). A Texas district court initially ruled against Griffin and the Klan, but in June 1994, the Texas Supreme Court struck down that ruling, saying that it violated the Klan's rights.

Griffin has received numerous awards, including the first Justice William J. Brennan, Jr., Award; the Galveston Chapter NAACP Peace and Role

Model Award; the Black Heritage Committee's Citizen of the Year Award; and the Hugh M. Hefner First Amendment Award.

REFERENCE: Anthony Griffin, "The First Amendment and the Art of Storytelling," in *Speaking of Race, Speaking of Sex*, New York, New York University Press, 1994.

HATCH ACT   The 1939 Hatch Act stipulated the limits on permissible political activities for federal employees. These statutory limitations on political expression were originally justified as a form of protection for employees against intimidation by supervisors, but many regarded the Hatch Act as a violation of the First Amendment.

Under the Hatch Act, federal employees could not take an active part in partisan political activities, except to vote. They were prohibited from serving as candidates for nomination or election to a national or state office, or even from campaigning for or against a candidate. A federal employee could not serve as an officer of a political party nor as a member of a local committee of a political party or club. He or she could not handle contributions or other political funds nor work at the polls on behalf of a candidate or party. Federal employees were also prohibited from endorsing or opposing candidates through advertisements, broadcasts, or campaign literature, and they could not use a personal automobile to drive voters to the polls on behalf of a candidate or party. Despite the severity of these restraints on otherwise protected expression, the Supreme Court has consistently upheld their constitutionality (e.g., *Oklahoma v. United States Civil Service Commission* [1947] and *United States Civil Service Commission v. National Association of Letter Carriers* [1973]).

In 1993, Congress passed and President Clinton signed the Hatch Act Reform Amendments. Taking effect in 1996, the amended Hatch Act continues the ban on politicking by federal workers on the job, prohibits them from running for partisan office, and bars them from soliciting or accepting political contributions from the public, but among the activities now permitted are:

1. Contributing money to political organizations.
2. Attending political fund-raising functions.
3. Stuffing envelopes with campaign literature that includes an appeal for political contributions.
4. Giving a speech at a fundraiser, so long as the speech does not include an appeal for political contributions.
5. Serving as a treasurer of a campaign or political organization if the duties are limited to preparing financial disclosure forms.
6. Helping to organize a fund-raiser, so long as the employee does not solicit or accept political contributions.
7. Voluntarily contributing to a political action committee through a payroll deduction.
8. Soliciting and receiving political contributions for a candidate in a local nonpartisan election.

Republicans opposed liberalizing the Hatch Act, fearing that it would expand the power of employee unions to help Democrats. As a result, the reform amendments were a compromise that gave federal employees many of the political rights enjoyed by other Americans, while leaving them as second class citizens in the political arena.

REFERENCE: James R. Eccles, *The Hatch Act and the American Bureaucracy*, New York, Vantage Press, 1981.

HATE SPEECH   "Hate speech" is a term used to describe speech that attacks individuals or groups on the basis of their race, ethnicity, religion, or sexual orientation. The courts have made clear that acts of discrimination or hatred may be prevented or punished under the Constitution. For example, discrimination, including racist speech, may be prohibited in the workplace, both public and private, in order to safeguard the economic and social relationship between employees, coworkers, and supervisors. Here the courts claim that they are not regulating the content of speech but protecting the economic rights of employees.

Even in the broader social context, the government may constitutionally restrain itself from racist speech to avoid imposing an onerous stigma on a class of citizens. For example, in rejecting school segregation in the landmark 1954 case *Brown v. Board of Education*, the Court said that segregation on the basis of race caused feelings of inferiority in black children that may never be undone. The argument was made that when black children were denied the right to attend desegregated schools, a "message" was sent that black children were unfit to attend school with white children.

In *Regents of University of California v. Bakke* (1978), Justice William Brennan denied that the university's purposes contravened the cardinal principle that racial classifications that stigmatize—because they are drawn on the presumption that one race is inferior to another or because they put the weight of government behind racial hatred and separatism—are invalid without more." That principle seems to have been embraced by subsequent Courts as well.

But what of private hate speech? Here the Court has been less than clear. In *Chaplinsky v. New Hampshire* (1942), the Court attempted to define limited classes of speech, the prevention and punishment of which are fully constitutional. These included "the lewd and obscene, the profane, the libelous and the insulting or 'fighting' words—those which by their very utterance inflict injury or tend to incite an immediate breach of the peace." Hate speech would certainly seem to fall within the unprotected categories cited in *Chaplinsky*.

In *Beauharnais v. Illinois* (1952), the Court addressed a libel case involving an Illinois statute that criminalized any published portrayal of "depravity, criminality, unchastity, or lack of virtue of a class of citizens, of any race, color, creed or religion" and that subjects them "to contempt, derision, or obloquy or which is productive of breach of the peace or riots." The defendant in *Beauharnais* was the president of a racist organization that had distributed leaflets calling on the mayor of Chicago to halt the further invasion of white people by the "Negro." The leaflets characterized "Negros" as mongrels, rapists, robbers, and drug addicts.

The defense in *Beauharnais* claimed that the "clear and present danger" standard should be applied in this case to judge the threat posed by the leaflets. The Illinois court refused to accept that approach and found Beauharnais guilty. The U.S. Supreme Court affirmed that decision in an opinion by Justice Felix Frankfurter that distinguished between restrictions on political speech and restrictions on speech relating to "race, color, creed or religion." Frankfurter believed that the hate speech under consideration had no "political" component and was therefore unprotected by the First Amendment.

Current law no longer permits the broad prohibitions on hate speech approved in *Beauharnais*. Today's Court would require narrowly drawn restrictions involving either "fighting words," a "clear and present danger" of violence, illegal discriminatory conduct, or private hate speech with no component of general public concern.

In *Brandenburg v. Ohio* (1969), the Court reviewed the prosecution of a Ku Klux Klan leader under an Ohio law that made it illegal to advocate a crime or to gather "with any group or assemblage of persons formed to teach or advocate the doctrines of criminal syndicalism." The Court held the Ohio law to be unconstitutional because the Klan rally represented no direct physical threat to anyone. No one was present at the rally other than the Klan members and a television crew. The Court concluded that the constitutional guarantees of free speech and free press "do not permit a State to forbid or proscribe advocacy of the use of force or of law violation except where such advocacy is likely to incite or produce such action."

In *Cohen v. California* (1971), the Court raised the standard required for the prohibition of "offensive" speech, restating the "fighting words" doctrine of *Chaplinsky* while imposing the rigorous "clear and present danger" test from *Brandenburg*. The Court said that the First Amendment protected the display of the words "Fuck the Draft" on a jacket because those who saw the words would not regard them as a personal insult and there was no danger of reactive violence. The decision in *Cohen* suggested that a verbal attack on an individual that represented incitement to violence could be punished or prevented.

Perhaps the most controversial hate-speech case grew out of the 1977 Nazi march in Skokie, Illinois. Frank Collin, leader of a neo-Nazi organization called the National Socialist Party of America, asked Skokie officials for permission to stage a rally in front of the village hall to protest a local ordinance. The protesters planned to wear Nazi uniforms with swastika emblems and armbands. Skokie filed suit to prevent the marchers from displaying anything that would incite or promote hatred against persons of Jewish faith or ancestry.

The trial court enjoined the march, and the Illinois appellate court affirmed the injunction. The Illinois Supreme Court then refused to grant review of the case or to stay the injunction, effectively denying the Nazis the right to march. In *National Socialist Party of America v. Village of Skokie* (1977), the U.S. Supreme Court then held, in a 5–4 decision, that the Illinois Supreme Court's failure to provide for either appellate review or a stay of the injunction violated the First Amendment. The Court did not say that the Nazis had a constitutional right to march in Skokie, but that a "prior restraint" had been imposed that denied the Nazis appropriate procedural safeguards, such as swift appellate review. The case was remanded back to the Illinois appellate court, which this time limited the injunction to a prohibition on displaying the swastika. The Illinois Supreme Court went even further, holding that the entire injunction was invalid.

In an attempt to bypass the court's decision, Skokie legislators passed ordinances that prohibited the dissemination of any material within the Village of Skokie that promoted and intended to incite hatred against persons by reason of their race, national origin, or religion. The ordinances also prohibited anyone from engaging in a march or public demonstration as a member or on behalf of any political party while wearing a military-style uniform.

In response, the Nazis went to federal court to block enforcement of the ordinances. In *Village of Skokie v. National Socialist Party of America* (1978), the federal district court and the Court of Appeals for the Seventh Circuit both held the Skokie ordinances to be unconstitutional. Ironically, three days before the march was scheduled to occur, Frank Collin cancelled it, claiming that his purpose had simply been to establish his party's right to demonstrate in Skokie. Later that summer, Collin's Nazis held a one-hour rally in Chicago, where they were protected by four hundred police.

A series of recent court decisions have attempted to further clarify the constitutional protections on hate speech. In *R.A.V. v. City of St. Paul* (1992), the Supreme Court held that a cross burning on the lawn of a private residence constituted protected speech. The ruling was based on the principle that symbolic speech, such as cross burning, could not be restricted on the basis of its content. The Court here rejected a Minnesota ordinance that made it a crime to place on public or private property a "symbol, object, appellation, characterization or graffiti," including but not limited to a burning cross or Nazi swastika, that one has reasonable grounds to know will arouse "anger, alarm, or resentment in others on the basis of race, color, creed, religion, or gender."

In the Minnesota case, an individual had been charged with burning a cross inside a black family's yard. The Minnesota Supreme Court upheld the prosecution, distinguishing the cross-burning ordinance from the flag-burning statute that had been struck down in *Texas v. Johnson* because the Minnesota ordinance was limited to expressive conduct involving "fighting words," as defined in *Chaplinsky*, or incitement to "imminent lawless action," as defined in *Brandenburg*. In rejecting the ordinance, the majority claimed that a cross burner might be constitutionally prosecuted under other statutes, such as laws against trespass, arson, or destruction of property. Justice Byron White, who wrote a concurring opinion, nonetheless predicted that the decision "will surely confuse the lower courts."

Indeed, the courts are still sorting out the implications of *R.A.V. v. City of St. Paul*. In 1993, the Maryland Court of Appeals struck down a state law against cross burning, citing the Supreme Court's rulings that such acts qualify as protected speech under the First Amendment. The Maryland law, passed in 1966, had made it illegal to burn a cross on private property without permission of the landowner and notification of the fire department. Still, in 1994, the Supreme Court let stand the conviction of two Illinois men who burned a cross on the property of a white neighbor who had a black couple as guests. Here the prosecution had been based on federal civil rights laws prohibiting the use of fire to commit a felony and barring interference with housing rights. Since those laws addressed action rather than speech, the Court did not see them to be in conflict with *R.A.V. v. City of St. Paul*.

In 1995, the Court seemed to further complicate matters by overturning an Ohio court ruling that in 1993 had prevented the Ku Klux Klan from erecting a ten-foot cross on a public square in Columbus. In this case, the Court decided that the Klan's raising of the cross was a religious act deserving protection, not an expression of hate.

The degree to which society should tolerate such speech has also been tested on college campuses, where both freedom of speech and tolerance for dissent have traditionally been protected. In the late 1980s, government statistics showed a sharp increase in racial conflict and anti-Semitic incidents on American campuses. The continuing increase in such incidents threatened not only the educational process, but the socializing process that forms the basis for a stable and democratic society. Many called for controls and penalties on hate speech, precipitating a conflict between the desire for racial tolerance and the commitment to free speech. The speech and behavior codes eventually created on many campuses were criticized and even challenged in local courts.

University campuses have long been a testing ground for limits on hate speech, and campus speech codes have occasionally been tested in the courts. In 1975, a commission was formed at Yale University to consider how to deal with campus hate speech. With little fanfare, the commission, led by historian C. Vann Woodward, concluded that a university should not assume as its primary value "the fostering of friendship, solidarity, harmony, civility or mutual respect." The Woodward report strongly rejected the censorship or punishment of speech on the basis of its content or the motives of the speaker. Almost fifteen years later, this position was reaffirmed at Yale in a 1989 report, but by this time the social tensions on American campuses had infused the issue of hate speech with national political significance. A study released during 1989 documented racist incidents at 250 colleges and universities since the fall of 1986. Anti-Semitic violence was also on the rise on American campuses.

During this period of social tension on campuses, many universities adopted speech codes in an attempt to avoid conflict and foster an effective educational climate. The University of Michigan adopted a code that could discipline any student for "behavior, verbal or physical, that stigmatizes or victimizes an individual on the basis of race, ethnicity, religion, sex, sexual orientation, creed, national origin, ancestry, age, marital status, handicap or Vietnam-era veteran status." Within a few years, the University of Michigan code was struck down in the courts as an infringement on free speech. A similar fate befell the University of Wisconsin code, which banned speech that demeaned a person's race, religion, sexual orientation, disability, or ancestry. That code was ruled unconstitutionally broad by a federal district judge in 1991. In 1992, when the Supreme Court unanimously struck down a Minnesota ordinance prohibiting the display of symbols that might arouse "anger, alarm, or resentment in others on the basis of race, color, creed, religion or gender" (*R.A.V. v. City of St. Paul*), most universities concluded that their speech codes would not pass constitutional muster. "*R.A.V.* basically struck the death knell for collegiate speech codes," said Jack Roach, legal counsel for the University of Maryland. "I would say that it is literally impossible to draft a speech code that doesn't end up infringing on protected speech in some way" ("Universities Forced to Withdraw Speech Codes," *Diamondback*, September 24, 1992, p. 3).

Some universities have attempted to revise their speech codes to conform with the laws that apply to the broader society. In 1994, the University of Pennsylvania changed its code to ban only threats of physical harm, not mere insults. The change was introduced after the campus code was unsuccessfully applied to a student who called a group of black students "water buffaloes." Brown University changed its speech code by replacing the word "demeaning" with "threatening" and specifying that such conduct included, but was not limited to, threats based on race, religion, or gender. MIT administrators claim that their code already mirrors federal guidelines for antidiscrimination policies and therefore requires no change. Stanford University has maintained its speech code without change since its adoption in 1990, in large part because it has never prosecuted anyone under the code.

REFERENCE: Laurence R. Marcus, *Fighting Words: The Politics of Hateful Speech*, Westport, Praeger, 1996.

HELMS, JESSE A., 1921–   Jesse Helms is a Republican senator from North Carolina who has become known for his antiobscenity crusades. He has introduced more antiobscenity legislation than any other politician, regularly attaching such amendments to virtually any major bill. He also led the passage of the "dial-a-porn" amendment, which restricts access to sex-talk phone numbers, but he is best known for his amendments restricting funding for the National Endowment for the Arts (NEA). Under various Helms amendments, the NEA was prohibited from funding obscene or indecent art or art that denigrates religion. In addition, the Helms amendments require artists receiving grants from the NEA to pledge that they will not produce obscene art. Before coming to Congress, Helms served as city editor for the *Raleigh Times*, administrative aide for two North Carolina senators, and head of WRAL television and the Tobacco Radio Network.

REFERENCE: Ernest B. Furgurson, *Hard Right: The Rise of Jesse Helms*, New York, Norton, 1986.

HENTOFF, NAT, 1925–   Nat Hentoff is a prominent author and columnist whose work has focused on issues of intellectual freedom. He is a regular columnist for the *Village Voice*, and his syndicated column, "Sweet Land of Liberty," is carried in the *Washington Post* and other major newspapers. Hentoff first came to prominence as a jazz expert and writer for magazines like *Down Beat*, but his broader interests in social issues and intellectual freedom soon emerged in his writing. His highly acclaimed book *Our Children Are Dying* describes the plight of inner-city schools, and his text *The First Freedom* is a definitive look at freedom of expression. Hentoff has also written several novels for young adults, including *The Day They Came to Arrest the Book*, which examines the dangers of censorship.

Hentoff has opposed legislative restraints on free expression represented by the Flag Desecration Act, the anti-terrorism bill, and the telecommunications bill. He has recently appeared to turn his critical attention away from the traditional conservative threats to free speech in order to attack affirmative action, campus speech codes, and what has come to be known as "political correctness." Hentoff's new focus has brought him into occasional conflict with the national leadership of the American Civil Liberties Union.

REFERENCES: Nat Hentoff, *American Heroes: In and Out of School*, New York, Delacorte Press, 1987; Nat Hentoff, *The Day They Came to Arrest the Book*, New York, Delacorte Press, 1982.

HOMOSEXUALITY   Social pressures are always behind the changing winds of censorship, and these pressures increase with visibility. For centuries, homosexuals were an invisible subculture, quietly acknowledged and tolerated by polite society so long as they camouflaged their sexual orientation. But as homosexuals in increasing numbers have come out of the closet, they have become the object of political and social controversy, including censorship.

Religious conservatives frequently challenge library materials that "legitimize" homosexuality, and two books about homosexual families, *Daddy's Roommate* and *Heather Has Two Mommies*, have been more frequently challenged in schools and public libraries than any other titles during the 1990s. In several states, the conservative group Concerned Women for America lobbied for the removal of *Daddy's Roommate* and similar books from library shelves. Eventually, the group took direct action by charging out the titles and refusing to return them. In response, the books' publisher, Alyson Publications, offered free copies of the titles to the first five hundred libraries requesting them. The publisher said, "[I]t's a way for us to tell the fundamentalists that there's no way they're going to win this battle; that the harder they fight the harder we'll fight back to make sure that these books stay available" ("Oregonians to Vote on Statewide Antigay Measure," *Library Journal*, October 1, 1992, pp. 17–18).

A 1992 protest against the inclusion of *Daddy's Roommate* in the Springfield, Oregon, public library occurred shortly after a local charter amendment was passed prohibiting the city from "promoting, encouraging or facilitating" homosexuality. The amendment had been sponsored by the Oregon Citizens Alliance (OCA), a conservative group that took the position that voter approval of the amendment meant that the community opposed the public availability of books promoting homosexuality. The local American Civil Liberties Union vowed to sue if the book was excluded from the library on the basis of the charter amendment. The crisis was defused when the librarian said that she would judge the book on the basis of the same selection criteria as any other book, but the OCA raised the stakes when it subsequently sponsored a statewide constitutional amendment even more strongly worded than Springfield's local ordinance.

The new measure would have required local governments in Oregon, along with their educational institutions, to officially recognize homosexuality as "abnormal, wrong, unnatural, and perverse" and would have prevented them from "promoting, encouraging, or facilitating homosexuality." The Oregon Library Association (OLA) made a public statement warning of the threat to library collections and concluding, "The OLA is concerned that not only could valuable portions of the literature of libraries be eliminated, but also that library personnel could also be fired for being gay or lesbian. In fact, the broader implications of the measure are staggering—would public libraries be mandated to refuse service to homosexuals, would meeting rooms be made available to groups based on their sexual preference?" ("OLA Condemns Oregon's Proposed Constitutional Amendment," *PNLA Quarterly*, Spring 1992, p. 11).

After Oregon voters rejected the amendment in 1992, the OCA softened the wording of its proposal and tried again. The new measure, which banned the use of city or state funds to "promote or express approval of homosexuality," was no less a threat to libraries, and though it passed in fourteen Oregon communities, it was rejected in the statewide ballot on election day, 1994. Other antigay ballot initiatives went before the voters in a number of states. One organizer of the Oregon initiative returned to his former home in Idaho to form the Idaho Citizens Alliance (ICA), which placed a similar initiative on the Idaho ballot. After Idaho's attorney general said that the initiative "violates both freedom of expression and due process rights guaranteed by the United States Constitution and the Idaho Constitution," the ICA revised and resubmitted the initiative, emphasizing the need to protect children from homosexuality and homosexual literature. In a second opinion, the attorney general stated, "It is evident that while minors may not have the full panoply of First Amendment rights as do adults, certainly, when it comes to library reading materials, minors cannot be denied access to those materials for no other reason than that the state disagrees with the ideas expressed therein."

The Idaho Library Association (ILA) passed a resolution in 1993, unanimously reaffirmed at its 1994 membership meeting, stating that the initiative violated the First Amendment and threatened library employees as well. The ILA then began a concerted public relations campaign that was instrumental in the narrow defeat of the initiative on election day, November 8, 1994, the same day that Oregon's measure was defeated ("The Margin of Victory," *Library Journal*, September 1, 1995, pp. 136–39).

Meanwhile, in Colorado, a voter initiative approved a constitutional amendment that outlawed gay rights laws and barred the enactment of such laws in the future. The measure sparked a nationwide boycott of the state's tourism industry and led to the most important court challenge to antigay initiatives. The Colorado measure never took effect because state District Judge Jeffrey Bayless issued a preliminary injunction, citing a strong likelihood that it would be found unconstitutional. Indeed, the

Colorado Supreme Court subsequently ruled that it violated the Constitution by preventing homosexuals from "having an effective voice in government affairs." The ruling was appealed to the Supreme Court, which on May 21, 1996, struck down the Colorado amendment. In a 6–3 decision, the Court said that Colorado had no legitimate reason or rational basis for precluding all legislative, executive, or judicial action designed to protect people based on their sexual orientation.

President Clinton, who had publicly criticized all of the antigay initiatives, gave a restrained endorsement of the Court's decision. Clinton had earlier received criticism for his ambiguous handling of the issue of homosexuals in the military, an approach that proved to have First Amendment implications. In 1993, Clinton had reversed the outright ban on gays in the military, but only if gay servicemen stayed in the closet. What came to be known as the "don't ask, don't tell" policy said that the military would no longer ask recruits about their sexual orientation or engage in witch-hunts for homosexuals in the service, and, in turn, gay service personnel could remain in the military as long as they did not declare their sexual preference or engage in homosexual conduct. The policy was first challenged in court by a naval petty officer who was discharged after he declared his homosexuality on national television. In September 1993, a U.S. district judge in Los Angeles barred the discharge of the officer. An appeals court ruled that the Navy was wrong to discharge the serviceman, but said that the case did not apply to other military personnel. The Justice Department then let the deadline for further appeals pass, saying that the court's ruling concerned the discharge of just one serviceman under the military's old rules, leaving the "don't ask, don't tell" policy unaffected.

The first direct constitutional challenge to the "don't ask, don't tell" policy came in March 1995 when a lawsuit filed by the American Civil Liberties Union on behalf of six gay servicemen argued that the policy violated the free-speech and equal-protection clauses of the Constitution. On March 30, 1995, U.S. District Judge Eugene Nickerson said that the policy was unconstitutional because it allowed the government to guess about future conduct on the basis of what someone says. The effect of the policy, Nickerson concluded, was to force homosexuals either to lie about or conceal an important fact about themselves. In rejecting the government's arguments that maintaining secrecy about sexual orientation encouraged military cohesion, Nickerson said, "Common sense suggests that a policy of secrecy, indeed what might be called a policy of deception or dishonesty, will call unit cohesion into question" ("U.S. Court Rejects Pentagon Policy on Gays," *Washington Post*, March 31, 1995, p. A21). The Pentagon asked the Justice Department to appeal the decision and said that it would continue to apply the policy because the ruling applied only to the six plaintiffs in this case.

On July 1, 1996, the U.S. Court of Appeals for the Second Circuit found that Judge Nickerson had erred by basing his decision on a subsection of the policy without determining whether the full section containing the "don't ask, don't tell" prohibition was unlawful. Though Nickerson's earlier ruling had said that the First Amendment "will not countenance the proscription of the expression of an idea because others find the idea repugnant," the appeals court said that the government had demonstrated that the speech restriction "substantially furthers its important interest in preventing homosexual acts in the military," and it ordered Nickerson to consider arguments that the broader ban against homosexual activity is illegal ("Case on Military Gay Policy Sent Back for Wider Review," *Washington Post*, July 2, 1996, p. A22).

At the same time, another important test of the "don't ask, don't tell" policy was being considered by the courts. The case arose in 1995 when naval Lieutenant Paul Thomasson was discharged after he told his commanding officer that he was gay. The following year, the Thomasson case became the first constitutional challenge to the policy to reach a federal appellate court. Because Thomasson's performance record was never challenged, his lawyers contended that the policy unconstitutionally restricted his freedom of speech and discriminated against homosexuals. In arguing that it was speech, not conduct, that resulted in Thomasson's discharge, the defense declared, "This case is not about the ability or the readiness of homosexuals to serve in the U.S. military. It's not about conduct. This is a free speech issue" ("Appeals Court Hears Case of Discharged Gay Sailor," *Washington Post*, December 6, 1995, p. A16). The government argued that once someone states that he is a homosexual, it gives rise to apprehensions that compromise unit cohesion. In April 1996, a divided Fourth Circuit Appeals Court upheld the "don't ask, don't tell" policy, ruling that the navy was within its power when it discharged Thomasson for admitting that he was gay. The four dissenting judges wrote that Thomasson was being punished for nothing more than an expression of his state of mind, an expression that was not illegal, and an admitted fact that was not a ground for discharge. Thomasson appealed the appeals court ruling to the Supreme Court, alleging that the Navy violated his constitutional right to free speech by singling out his statements as proof of homosexuality.

One of the more interesting First Amendment cases to reach the Supreme Court in 1995 concerned the right of homosexuals to march in Boston's St. Patrick's Day parade. When the War Veterans Council of Boston organized the 1994 parade and refused to allow the Irish-American Gay, Lesbian and Bisexual Group of Boston to participate, the group sued, relying on a state public accommodations law. The War Veterans Council claimed a First Amendment right to hold a parade of its liking, but the Supreme Judicial Court of Massachusetts ruled that the organizers had no discernible expressive message entitling them to free-speech protection. Indeed, a trial court had previously ruled that the gay group had been rejected because of its "message." In response to the Massachusetts Supreme Judicial Court decision, the War Veterans Council cancelled the parade rather than let the gays participate.

The case, *Hurley v. Irish-American Gay, Lesbian and Bisexual Group of Boston* (1995), was appealed to the Supreme Court, which on June 19, 1995, delivered a unanimous 9–0 ruling allowing the parade sponsors to exclude gays. "The issue in this case is whether Massachusetts may require private citizens who organize a parade to include among the marchers a group imparting a message the organizers do not wish to convey," wrote Justice David Souter for the Court. "We hold that such a mandate violates the First Amendment." Souter specifically noted that gay marchers could in the future assert their own First Amendment rights, but that they had relied solely on a public accommodations law in this case.

REFERENCE: Lois Shawver, *And the Flag Was Still There: Straight People, Gay People, and Sexuality in the U.S. Military*, New York, Haworth Press, 1995.

HONORARIA   The Ethics Reform Act of 1989 was primarily aimed at Congress itself, but it contained little-noticed provisions affecting all federal employees. One provision stipulated that no employee in government service on or after January 1, 1991, would be able to receive an honorarium, defined as the payment of money or anything of value, for a speech, appearance, or article. There were to be no exceptions, even for speeches or writing totally unrelated to one's government job. For example, an employee could not be paid for a speech on a hobby, such as stamp collecting. The penalty for violation of this provision was a $10,000 fine or the amount of the compensation, whichever was greater.

A number of lawsuits were soon initiated challenging the honoraria ban on First Amendment grounds. In December 1990, a U.S. district court denied a request from two federal unions and the American Civil Liberties Union (ACLU) for an injunction. That ruling was appealed, and on December 15, 1991, Judge Clarence Thomas of the D.C. Circuit Court of Appeals refused to halt the ban on honoraria for federal employees. Thomas acknowledged that the law's long-term effects might be to "reduce or even eliminate the willingness of government employees to pursue certain remunerative First Amendment activities," but he said that this did not give courts the authority to suspend the law before a final ruling on its merits.

The ACLU and the employee unions claimed that the ban limited employees' free-speech rights and hindered them from pursuing secondary careers in areas unrelated to their work. Lower-level federal employees, in particular, said that they supplemented their salaries with writing or consulting fees, often on subjects that had nothing to do with their work.

On March 30, 1993, in *United States v. National Treasury Employees Union* (1993), the honoraria ban was struck down by the U.S. Court of Appeals for the D.C. Circuit on the grounds that it was an unconstitutional infringement on free speech. Circuit Court Judge Stephen F. Williams, who wrote the majority opinion, said that the law was overinclusive and too broad. He gave examples of individuals whose free-speech rights were being inappropriately restricted, including a Nuclear Regulatory Commission lawyer who writes on Russian history, a U.S. Postal Service employee who writes and speaks on the Quaker religion, a Labor Department lawyer who lectures on Judaism, a Health and Human Services employee who reviews art and music for local newspapers, and a civilian Navy electronics technician who writes on Civil War vessels. "It is clear that the ban reaches a lot of compensation that has no nexus to government work that could give rise to the slightest concern," said Williams. "The topics appear not to be such that the employee could have used information acquired in the course of his government work; there is no suggestion of any use of government time, word processors, paper or ink." The ruling affected approximately two million federal workers below the pay grade of GS-16, or $86,500 a year. The appeals court decision kept the honoraria ban intact for members of Congress, their staff, the judiciary, and senior executive-branch employees.

The only dissent on the three-judge panel came from Judge David B. Sentelle, who claimed that the honoraria ban placed "only a moderate burden on employees' First Amendment rights." A. Raymond Randolph, the third judge on the panel, disagreed, quoting the English essayist Samuel Johnson: "No man but a blockhead ever wrote, except for money" (Stephen Barr, "Court Strikes Down Honoraria Ban," *Washington Post*, March 31, 1993, p. A1).

The Justice Department did not immediately seek an emergency order staying the appeals court ruling, leading many to believe that the issue was resolved. But in January 1994, the Justice Department confirmed that it had authorized the filing of a petition asking the Supreme Court to reinstate the honoraria ban. The department continued to claim that an across-the-board ban was necessary to deter abuse of honoraria, but Stephen D. Potts, director of the Office of Government Ethics, denounced the ban, saying that the driving reason behind the administration's appeal was the belief that the Justice Department had an obligation to uphold any law Congress had passed. Many of the writers and lecturers who were affected expressed surprise that President Clinton, a former constitutional law professor, would support a law that had been found unconstitutional by nine of eleven federal judges who had considered it.

On February 2, 1994, the Clinton administration announced that it would not seek punishment for federal workers who accepted money for writing articles or giving speeches on subjects unrelated to their official duties until the Supreme Court had ruled on the issue. In a letter to the Office of Government Ethics, Assistant Attorney General Frank W. Hunger said that it would not punish any worker who received honoraria between September 28, 1993, and the date of a Supreme Court ruling on the issue.

In November 1994, the Supreme Court engaged in spirited oral arguments over the issue, with concerns being expressed that the 1989 ethics law banning honoraria was too broadly written and violated free-speech rights. Deputy Solicitor General Paul Bender told the justices that it would be an unreasonable administrative burden for the government to determine whether the subject of each speech or article was job related, and therefore a general ban was more practical. The attorney representing federal workers argued that administrative efficiency should not outweigh the free-speech rights of workers.

Finally, on February 22, 1995, the Court struck down the Ethics Reform Act of 1989. In a 6–3 ruling, the Court said that the honoraria ban breached the First Amendment rights of government employees, largely because it applied broadly to expression that had no connection to the workers' official duties. Justice John Paul Stevens, writing for the Court, said that a ban on payments for speech is effectively a ban on free expression, and that such a ban also impinges on the public's right to know. He acknowledged a government interest in avoiding the misuse of power through honoraria, but he said that the government had provided no evidence of misconduct related to honoraria in the vast rank and file of federal employees below grade GS-16.

The Court's ruling said that the honoraria ban was unconstitutional only as it applied to the mid- and low-level workers who had challenged it, leaving in place the ban for members of Congress and their staffs, federal judges, and top executive-branch officials. Despite the Court's ruling, some members of Congress and watchdog groups like Common Cause continue to express concern about conflicts of interest within government. Legislation is being considered to ban honoraria for any federal employees whose lectures or publications relate to their official duties. Other proposals would specify a salary level above which federal employees could not accept honoraria.

REFERENCE: Ian Morrison, "The Case for Minimal Regulation of Public Employee Free Speech: A Critical Analysis of the Federal Honoraria Ban Controversy," *Washington University Journal of Urban and Contemporary Law*, Summer 1995, pp. 141–81.

HOUSE UN-AMERICAN ACTIVITIES COMMITTEE   In 1934, Congress established the first House Committee to Investigate Un-American Activities. The committee drew little attention and expired in 1937, but was reestablished in 1937 as the House Special Committee on Un-American Activities. Chaired by the veteran anti-Communist Representative Martin Dies (D-Tex.) and generally known as the Dies Committee, it attacked all left-wing political thought, including President Franklin Roosevelt's New Deal. The Dies Committee used smear tactics, guilt by association, and a variety of extralegal tactics in an effort to destroy the progressive political structure in America. Witnesses summoned before the committee were attacked and insulted, were prevented from testifying in their defense, and were often denied counsel. Though the committee failed to convict a single witness, it had generally sympathetic press coverage and exercised a powerful influence on the American political process.

In 1939, the Dies Committee attacked not only the American Communist Party but liberal organizations like the American Civil Liberties Union, and many of these groups responded by purging their membership of "leftists." In 1940, the committee began an investigation of the motion-picture industry, calling many prominent stars as witnesses. All were exonerated.

After the resignation of Martin Dies, the committee, now known as the House Un-American Activities Committee (HUAC), continued under the joint leadership of Representative John S. Wood (D-Ga.) and Representative John Rankin (D-Miss.). HUAC maintained the Dies style, using innuendo and guilt by association, but unlike the Dies Committee, it succeeded in jailing some leaders of the Communist Party of the USA (CPUSA) for contempt of Congress. HUAC picked up where the Dies Committee left off with its investigation of the entertainment industry, and after the committee condemned a number of radio scripts for subversive content, the networks dismissed two of the commentators involved.

When the Wood-Rankin leadership of HUAC ended in 1946, the committee issued a directive alleging Communist infiltration of the government, and it demanded implementation of loyalty checks for all government employees. President Truman responded in 1947 by implementing loyalty oaths and issuing an executive order calling for an investigation into the loyalty of more than two million federal employees. Under these investigations, dismissible offenses included membership or sympathetic association with any group on a newly created list of subversive organizations. Though no one was proved guilty of subversion, 139 people were fined and 600 others resigned.

In 1947, Representative J. Parnell Thomas (R-N.J.) became chairman of HUAC, and Representative Richard Nixon (R-Calif.) became a prominent member after making a name for himself with public attacks on the "Red Menace." Informers like Elizabeth Bentley and Whittaker Chambers gained publicity for HUAC when they described a spy network within the government. In June 1947, Thomas charged that the National Labor Relations Board was promoting a Communist takeover of the motion-picture industry, but a subsequent investigation found no such conspiracy. The Hollywood establishment sided with HUAC, but a number of stars, including Katharine Hepburn, Humphrey Bogart, and Judy Garland, formed the Committee for the First Amendment to protest HUAC's tactics. Ten witnesses before the committee refused to answer questions. Called the "Hollywood Ten" by the press, they were found guilty of contempt, fined $1,000, and jailed for terms of six to twelve months. Despite their appeals, all served time in prison and were blacklisted upon their release.

One of the most successful functions of HUAC was its encouragement of blacklisting. In 1951, the motion-picture industry dutifully followed HUAC's demands by threatening to fire anyone who did not cooperate with the committee. Even the Screen Actors Guild and Artists Equity refused to defend "unfriendly" witnesses before HUAC. John Wayne became an active and effective HUAC supporter as head of the Motion Picture Alliance for the Preservation of American Ideals (MPAPAI).

After the 1952 presidential elections, Representative Harold N. Velde (R-Ill.) was appointed as the new HUAC chairman, but the nation was tiring of HUAC's witch-hunts. Velde resigned in 1954, and his successor, Representative Francis Walter (D-Pa.), oversaw a period of declining influence for HUAC. In 1959, former President Harry Truman called HUAC "the most un-American thing in the country today" (Jonathon Green, *The Encyclopedia of Censorship*, New York, Facts on File, 1990, p. 158). Nonetheless, HUAC stumbled through the 1960s, targeting civil rights and peace groups. HUAC's final hearings covered the 1966 urban riots and the demonstrations at the 1968 Democratic National Convention in Chicago. In February 1969, HUAC was disbanded and replaced by the House Internal Security Committee.

REFERENCES: Griffin Fariello, *Red Scare: Memories of the American Inquisition: An Oral History*, New York, Norton 1995; Kenneth O'Reilly, *Hoover and the Un-Americans: The FBI, HUAC, and the Red Menace*, Philadelphia, Temple University Press. 1983.

IMMIGRATION   The Immigration and Naturalization Act of 1952, usually called the McCarran-Walter Act, identified the following groups as ineligible to receive visas and excluded from admission to the United States: (1) aliens who advocated the economic, international, and governmental doctrines of world communism or the establishment in the United States of a totalitarian dictatorship; (2) aliens who wrote or published such doctrines. Under the McCarran-Walter Act, the State Department could exclude anyone whose presence was deemed "prejudicial to the public interest." It examined the politics of every person who entered the United States and kept a "lookout book" of some 50,000 names based on rumor and hearsay. Among the prominent individuals excluded under this statute were British comedian Charlie Chaplin, Italian playwright Dario Fo, Mexican novelist and ambassador Carlos Fuentes, English novelist Graham Greene, French film stars Yves Montand and Simone Signoret, and Nobel Prize winners Gabriel Garcia Marquez and Czeslaw Milosz. Even Pierre Trudeau was in the "lookout book" until he was elected prime minister of Canada. Nonetheless, the Supreme Court ruled in *Kleindienst v. Mandel* (1972) that such restrictions were not a violation of the First Amendment. The government could do this without a hearing by simply asserting that its decision was based on confidential information.

In 1989, Congress passed a law prohibiting the government from excluding individuals based on their beliefs or associations, and in 1990, an amendment to the immigration bill officially repealed the McCarran-Walter Act, though it retained some bothersome aspects of the act. For example, immigrants could still be excluded for mere membership in the Communist Party, and the representatives and officials of the Palestine Liberation Organization were also barred. Two general grounds for deportation, terrorism and foreign policy interests, were added, and both areas were defined broadly and vaguely. For example, under the 1990 law, the government could exclude or expel anyone whose presence posed "potentially serious adverse foreign policy consequences." The law also retained the McCarran-Walter Act's "confidential information" procedure to deny access to the evidence on which exclusion or expulsion was based.

During the 1990s, the spectre of terrorism replaced communism as the cover for xenophobic immigration policies, but there were indications that the courts would have no part of it. In 1995, the U.S. Court of Appeals for the Ninth Circuit issued a landmark opinion in *American Arab Anti-Discrimination Committee v. Reno* that clearly affirmed the constitutional rights of aliens. The case began in 1987 when agents of the FBI and the Immigration and Naturalization Service burst into the apartments of seven Palestinians and brought them, shackled hand and foot, before an immigration judge. The Justice Departments of Presidents Reagan, Bush, and Clinton attempted to deport these aliens for associating with the Popular Front for the Liberation of Palestine (PFLP), an alleged terrorist organization. In reality, the Palestinians had done nothing more than distribute a PFLP magazine and raise funds for various Palestinian causes that had no connection with terrorism. After almost nine years of appeals, their ordeal ended when the court ruled that "aliens who reside in this country are entitled to full due process protections." Judge Dorothy Nelson said for a unanimous panel: "The values underlying the First Amendment require the full applicability of First Amendment rights to the deportation setting. ... [T]his underlying principle is especially relevant to our attitude toward current immigrants who are a part of our community. The right of association is a basic constitutional right that lies at the foundation of a free society."

But even as the courts affirmed the right of all immigrants to speak and associate as freely as citizens, the government moved in the opposite direction. The Anti-Terrorism and Effective Death Penalty Act of 1996 made it a crime to support the lawful activities of any organization that the Secretary of State designates as "terrorist." The new bill once more makes ideology and association a condition for entering the United States. It removes the presumption of innocence for aliens under investigation, allows surveillance of individuals and groups on the basis of their beliefs and associations, and establishes a secret court that can deport persons convicted of no crime. All indications are that the spirit of McCarran-Walter is alive and well.

REFERENCE: David A. Liller, *The History of the Conflict between the McCarran-Walter Act of 1952 and First Amendment Freedoms*, Thesis (M.A.), University of South Florida, 1991.

INDECENCY   Within the hierarchy of censorable sexual expression, indecency would appear to be a lesser concern to society than is obscenity or pornography. Dictionary definitions are predictably vague, describing indecency as expression that is morally "indelicate or improper or offensive" or "tending" to be obscene. This imprecision relegated the censorship of "indecency" to fundamentalist challenges to public school literature until the federal government's relatively recent interest in protecting the public from indecency in art, broadcasting, and telecommunications.

American art has suffered censorship of sexually explicit materials for many years, but recently there has been a flurry of legislative action restricting indecent art. Much of this action has focused on controlling or defunding the National Endowment for the Arts (NEA). In 1990, Senator Jesse Helms (R-N.C.) introduced legislation barring NEA funding for any obscene or indecent works. In subsequent years, Congress specified that the NEA must consider decency in approving all grants, and NEA Chair John Frohnmayer resigned rather than become a "decency czar." Four artists then brought suit challenging the "general standards of decency" requirements in the NEA's reauthorizing legislation. The courts subsequently ruled that the decency provision was excessively vague and awarded damages to the four artists who had been denied grants. Nonetheless, Congress has continued to impose decency restrictions on NEA funding.

The federal government has been particularly aggressive in censoring "indecent" expression in broadcasting. In 1975, following a declaratory ruling against an "indecent" radio broadcast, the Federal Communications Commission clarified its position: "[T]he concept of 'indecent' is intimately connected with the exposure of children to language that describes, in terms patently offensive as measured by contemporary community standards for the broadcast medium, sexual or excretory activities and organs, at times of the day when there is a reasonable risk that children may be in the audience" (*Pacifica Foundation*, [975]).

During the 1980s and 1990s, the FCC has applied its definition of indecency repeatedly in regulating broadcast material. Though the courts have ruled that a twenty-four-hour ban on indecent programming is unconstitutional, the FCC's definition of "indecency" and its authority to impose reasonable regulation on such expression were upheld by the Supreme Court in *Federal Communications Commission v. Pacifica Foundation* (1978).

The most recent area in which the federal government has imposed decency controls is in telecommunications, particularly the Internet. Because the Internet is so new, its explosive growth caught government censors by surprise, leading many to conclude that cyberspace was impervious to censorship. The Communications Decency Act of 1995, eventually passed in 1996 as part of a broader telecommunications bill, ended the optimism in the on-line community. The bill extended criminal liability to anyone who makes available on a computer or other telecommunications device any "obscene, lewd, lascivious, filthy or indecent" communication. Penalties could be up to $250,000 in fines and two years in prison. *See also* ART; BROADCASTING; INTERNET.

REFERENCE: Stacy M. Tomlins, *FCC Indecency Regulation and the First Amendment: Conflict or Compatibility?* Thesis (M.A.), University of Maryland, College Park, 1991.

INFORMATION SECURITY OVERSIGHT OFFICE The Information Security Oversight Office (ISOO) was created in 1978 by President Jimmy Carter, and to this day it remains the overseer of federal and industrial secrecy. Its primary goal is to ensure the safeguarding of national security information by government and industry. In this regard, it oversees the federal government's massive information-classification system and its elaborate security-clearance program. Still, among its goals, ISOO lists holding "classification activity to the minimum necessary to protect the national security" and promoting "declassification and public access to information as soon as national security considerations permit."

ISOO's authority is derived from the presidential executive orders on national security information issued by virtually all Presidents since World War II. It reports annually to the President, who must approve the appointment of ISOO's director, Steven Garfinkel, who has served since the creation of ISOO in 1978. ISOO is responsible for overseeing the information-security programs of all executive-branch agencies that create or handle national security information (classified information). It monitors the information-security programs of approximately sixty-five executive-branch departments, independent agencies, and their major components. It develops, coordinates, and issues implementing directives and instructions regarding the current executive order on national security information and also reviews and approves the implementing regulations issued by executive-branch agencies.

ISOO maintains liaison with its agency counterparts and conducts on-site inspections and document reviews to monitor agency compliance. It also monitors each agency's security education program, developing and disseminating security education materials for government and industry. It receives and takes action on complaints, appeals, and suggestions from persons inside or outside the executive branch regarding the administration of the executive order on national security information.

Each year, ISOO gathers statistical data on each agency's information-security program and analyzes this data for inclusion in its annual report to the President. It also conducts special studies and convenes interagency meetings on matters relating to the information-security program.

ISOO was originally an administrative component of the General Services Administration (GSA), though it received its direction from the President through the National Security Council (NSC). In October 1994, ISOO was made a part of the Office of Management and Budget (OMB), but its policy and program direction remained in the hands of the NSC. The ISOO and its Director serve as a spokesperson to Congress, the media, special-interest groups, professional organizations, and the public. On November 17, 1995, ISOO became a component of the National Archives and Records Administration (NARA), and in March 1996, it relocated to the National Archives Building, 700 Pennsylvania Avenue, NW, Room 100, Washington, DC 20408.

REFERENCE: Information Security Oversight Office, *Report to the President*, annual.

INTERNET   Telecommunications, the transmission of information by wire, radio, optic, or infrared media, has been subject to its share of secrecy, censorship, and surveillance from its inception, but the emergence of the Internet signalled a telecommunications revolution with new forms of information control. The Internet is a system of linked computer networks, worldwide in scope, that greatly extends the reach of each participating system. Initially established by the U.S. Defense Department in the early 1970s, the Internet became a public fixture when thousands of corporate computer systems and commercial service providers joined it. By the mid-1990s, after the introduction of graphical user interfaces and expanded content, the Internet was serving over twenty million users through two million host computers, and a million new users were being added each month.

At first, the Internet seemed to be outside the control of traditional corporate and governmental authorities due to its direct form of communication combining the immediacy of telephone, the intimacy of mail, the graphics of television, and the social interaction of a community bulletin board. But by the early 1990s, new forms of restraint on Internet communication were emerging.

In 1990, Prodigy, one of the early commercial providers of Internet services, drew nationwide attention when it imposed content restrictions on the messages that could be posted on its electronic bulletin board. Prodigy claimed that it was curtailing public postings about suicide, crime, sex, or pregnancy, but Jerry Berman of the American Civil Liberties Union (ACLU) and Marc Rotenberg of Computer Professionals for Social Responsibility pointed out in the *New York Times* that controls were also imposed on messages considered contrary to Prodigy's corporate interests. When some of Prodigy's subscribers learned of a proposed rate increase, they posted public complaints on the Prodigy bulletin board. After Prodigy informed subscribers that they could no longer post public messages about

Prodigy's fee policy, the subscribers turned to the private electronic mail service to communicate their complaints to individuals and businesses. Prodigy responded by cancelling the protesters' memberships without notice, and it imposed a general ban on e-mail communications with merchants.

Prodigy claimed that it was not a common carrier required to carry all messages, and that there were other electronic forums available to satisfy the free-speech needs of its cancelled or curtailed subscribers, but there was wide concern that the emerging electronic networks would soon be carved up among private providers with no common-carrier obligations to free speech. Berman and Rotenberg concluded, "Prodigy's dispute with its subscribers shows why, to protect First Amendment rights in the electronic age, we need to press Congress to establish the infrastructure for an accessible public forum and electronic mail service operating under common carrier principles" ("Free Speech in an Electronic Age," *New York Times*, January 6, 1991, sec. 3, p. 13).

But by 1994, there were indications that common-carrier principles might not be the appropriate system for controlling the Internet. After Laurence Tribe relied on the First Amendment to successfully argue a case that allowed Bell Atlantic Corporation to offer video programming over its phone lines, many concluded that the telecommunications companies would be afforded the same free-speech opportunities and protections as newspapers. Previously, a Baby Bell was just a telephone company, a heavily regulated common carrier obliged to give equal access to all at government-approved rates. Now it would be treated more like a newspaper publisher or movie studio that happened to have wires running into homes and businesses. Comparable court rulings gave other Baby Bells similar freedoms, and though these rulings may be appealed all the way to the Supreme Court, they offered the possibility that the First Amendment, not antitrust laws or FCC rulings, would become the preeminent industrial policy of the information age.

In the meantime, however, recurring censorship incidents on the Internet suggested otherwise. A husband and wife in Tennessee were convicted of distributing pornography via their members-only computer bulletin board. A postal inspector had joined the Internet bulletin board under a false name in order to bring charges against the couple for transmitting obscenity through interstate phone lines. In California, two female junior-college students sued for sexual harassment in successfully silencing an on-line campus discussion group. Carnegie Mellon University banned all sexually oriented on-line discussion groups, though it later agreed to reinstate text-only communications. A University of Michigan student was indicted on federal criminal charges that he had used an Internet discussion group to threaten a fellow student.

In 1995, Senator James Exon (D-Nebr.) introduced a bill regulating electronic communications, amending an existing law against harassment, obscenity, or threats made by telephone and changing the word "telephone" to "telecommunications devices." The Exon bill extended criminal liability to anyone who makes available any "comment, request, suggestion, proposal, image or other communication" that is found "obscene, lewd, lascivious, filthy or indecent." The penalties under Exon's Communications Decency Act of 1995 included fines of up to $100,000 and two years in jail and applied even to privately exchanged messages between adults.

Current obscenity laws defer to local community standards, but how would communications on the Internet, which cross local and national boundaries at the touch of a button, be judged? Also, unlike phone and mail communication, Internet messages often have no "sender" in the traditional sense. Anyone in cyberspace can surf the world and download material without anyone's knowledge or assistance. A coalition of public interest groups, including the American Library Association (ALA) and the Electronic Frontier Foundation, submitted a joint letter to Senator Exon expressing concern that the bill posed a significant threat to freedom of speech and the free flow of information in cyberspace. It also raised questions about the right of government to control content on communications networks.

An electronic petition against the bill appeared on the Internet's World Wide Web and generated 56,000 signatures in two weeks. The text accompanying the on-line petition said, "The more people sign the petition, the more the government will get the message to back off the online community. We've been doing fine without censorship until now—let's show them we don't plan on allowing them to start now. If you value your freedoms— from your right to publicly post a message on a worldwide forum to your right to receive private email without the government censoring it—you need to take action NOW."

Senator Patrick Leahy (D-Vt.) urged an alternative approach. "Empowering parents to manage—with technology under their control—what the kids access over the Internet is far preferable to bills . . . that would criminalize users or deputize information-service providers as smut police," said Leahy. "[G]overnment regulation of the content of all computer and telephone communications, even private communications, in violation of the First Amendment is not the answer—it is merely a knee-jerk reponse" (Nat Hentoff, "The Senate's Cybercensors," Washington Post, July 1, 1995, p. A27)

Nonetheless, the bill, folded into a major telecommunications deregulation package, easily passed through committee and on to the full Senate. President Bill Clinton issued a go-slow request to the Senate, saying that there were important First Amendment issues that needed to be addressed before the legislation was rushed through, but in June 1995, the bill passed the full Senate by an overwhelming 84–16 vote. A Washington Post editorial immediately proclaimed that the bill represented genuine and sweeping censorship, which might well end up being overturned by the courts on First Amendment grounds, but not before creating paralysis and perhaps permanent damage to a uniquely promising technology.

Then, in a surprise development, House Speaker Newt Gingrich condemned the Communications Decency Act as a clear violation of free speech and the rights of adults to communicate with each other. Senator Exon responded by characterizing Gingrich as out of touch, but Jerry Berman, executive director of the Center for Democracy and Technology, applauded the Speaker's leadership.

While the political battle over cyberspace was proceeding, *Time* magazine's July 3, 1995, issue featured a sensationalized cover story, "Cyberporn," showing a terrified child and a headline, "A new study shows how pervasive and wild it really is." The study touted by *Time* had been done by an undergraduate student at Carnegie Mellon University and was later shown to be seriously flawed and possibly fraudulent. For example, the Carnegie Mellon study said that 83.5 percent of Internet content was pornographic, when in fact the most common measure was 0.5 percent. Nonetheless, the *Time* article generalized to a conclusion that kids should stay off the Internet. At the same time, the software industry announced packages designed to help parents police the on-line activity of their children. There was also work on a set of standards, called KidCode, that would signal Internet users when materials that they were requesting might be unsuitable for children.

By the end of June 1995, two members of the House of Representatives introduced new legislation, the Internet Freedom and Family Empowerment Act, aimed at encouraging the on-line industry to police itself. The sponsors of the House bill, Representives Christopher Cox (R-Calif.) and Ron Wyden (D-Oreg.), rejected the Senate bill, saying that they hoped instead to spur technologies that would help companies, parents, and schools to block out objectionable material from the Internet. Their legislation would also ensure that on-line companies could screen out obscene material without being held liable for every message transmitted over their systems. The New York Supreme Court had earlier ruled that Prodigy was liable for a slanderous statement transmitted on its system because the company's policy of screening out objectionable sexual material made it a "publisher," responsible for all of its transmissions.

The House amendment to the telecommunications bill passed by a 420–4 vote. Despite the considerable improvement over the Senate bill, the House bill nonetheless included an amendment that would make it a crime to use offensive terms about "sexual or excretory activities or organs" in computer communications with someone who is believed to be under eighteen years of age. Representative Wyden said, "This idea of a federal Internet-censorship army would make the Keystone Kops look like crackerjack crime fighters. Our view is that the private sector is in the best position to guard the portals of cyberspace and to protect our children" ("Internet Users

Relieved by House Measure's Provisions on Indecent Material," *Chronicle of Higher Education*, August 18, 1995, p. A20).

By the end of 1995, the congressional tide had turned against the moderates and free-speech advocates, moving back toward the hard-line provisions of the original Exon bill. House lawmakers agreed to apply to computer networks the existing sexual-content laws designed for broadcasting and telephone conversations. Like the earlier Senate bill, the House bill provided prison sentences and heavy fines for anyone who "knowingly" transmits obscene or indecent material to minors or to public areas of the Internet where minors might see it.

Ralph Reed, director of the Christian Coalition, was delighted with the heavy new restrictions, for which he had lobbied heavily. Barry Steinhardt of the ACLU declared, "Congress is making it ever more clear that we will have to turn to the courts to uphold free speech in the promising new medium of cyberspace." A spokesman for Prodigy complained that no one knew what the new decency standard meant, and he warned, "It's going to wind up in the courts and be there for years" ("Congress Nearing Passage of Rules Curbing On-Line Smut," *Washington Post*, December 7, 1995, p. A1).

The *Washington Post* said that the language eventually negotiated by the House and Senate conferees "combines some of the worst of a broad array of misguided restrictions on speech, none of them likely to protect children." Noting that the new provisions would make the Internet more tightly restricted than print, radio, or even television, the *Post* concluded: "The conferees should dump this disastrous legislation entirely and give the public—and Congress—more time to learn what this medium is about" ("Internet Mess: Return to Sender," *Washington Post*, December 15, 1995, p. A24).

Shortly before the passage of the final telecommunications bill, including the indecency provision, an international Internet incident arose that dramatized the danger of applying local community standards of decency on global cyberspace. CompuServe Inc., a major on-line provider, announced that it was blocking access to 200 "newsgroups" on the Internet in response to complaints by German authorities. Newsgroups, where computer users can post publicly available messages, offer discussion on everything from computer games to sexual practices, and the German authorities identified two hundred newsgroups that they said contained indecent material. CompuServe said that there was a real possibility of arrest if it did not comply with German demands, so it banned the newsgroups to all Americans as well.

Suddenly the borderless quality of the Internet appeared to be an international liability, not the great strength that had been claimed. Internet users were dismayed at CompuServe's willingness to censor massively on the basis of charges that had never been formally filed, much less proved in court. Among the items CompuServe chose to hide from its users were serious discussions about human rights, marriage, and the Internet censorship being planned by Congress.

On February 1, 1996, Congress overwhelmingly passed the Telecommunications Act of 1996, including what was called the Communications Decency Act, which imposed heavy criminal penalties for Internet indecency. The bill defined indecency as any communication "that, in context, depicts or describes, in terms patently offensive as measured by contemporary community standards, sexual or excretory activities or organs." In addition to the decency provision, the bill made it a crime, punishable by up to five years in jail and a maximum fine of $250,000, to electronically transmit or receive any information about ways to obtain and/or perform an abortion. This cyberspace gag rule was a resurrection of the 123-year-old Comstock Act, which had been used 80 years ago to arrest Margaret Sanger for distributing leaflets on birth control.

President Bill Clinton signed the full bill just a week after its passage, but many in Congress and elsewhere were uncomfortable. Senator Patrick Leahy (D-Vt.) said, "I am concerned this legislation places restrictions on the Internet that will come back and haunt us." He warned that quoting from literary classics on-line could result in criminal prosecution. "Imagine if the Whitney Museum . . . were dragged into court for permitting representations of Michelangelo's David to be looked at by kids."

An on-line publication, *American Reporter*, announced that it would publish an article intentionally laced with "indecent" language and would sue immediately after publication. "We want to move promptly to have this statute set aside as unconstitutional," said Randall Boe, attorney for the *American Reporter*. "The longer it's in place, the greater the harm to the Internet and to the First Amendment."

A group of public service organizations, including the ACLU and the Electronic Frontier Foundation, prepared their own lawsuit, *ACLU v. Reno* (1996), challenging the Internet indecency provisions on constitutional grounds. Chris Hansen, the ACLU's lead counsel in the case, said, "Our chances of success depend fundamentally on how the judges come to see the Internet—will they view it as analogous to the print medium, or to broadcasting? We argue that the Internet should be analyzed as another element of the public square, rather than a new variant of a broadcast medium. . . . If the judges understand that even though a computer monitor may resemble a television, the Internet has more in common structurally with the printing press, our chances of obtaining a preliminary injunction are strong" (*ACLU Spotlight*, Spring 1996, p. 3).

The Justice Department said that it would defend the indecency standard in the legislation and would continue to defend similar statutes against constitutional challenges so long as it could assert a defense consistent with the Supreme Court rulings in this area. On February 15, in response to the ACLU suit, U.S. District Judge Ronald Buckwalter blocked government enforcement of the Internet indecency provision. Buckwalter said that his order applied only to the ban on "indecent materials," not to the provision against "patently offensive" material. Civil liberties lawyers were somewhat confused by the ruling, since the words "patently offensive" appear within the bill's definition of "indecent materials." Still, the ACLU counsel said, "We are very glad that the judge did consider the free-speech rights of on-line users to be very important. While we have obtained a partial victory, the fight's not over." As provided in the telecommunications bill, the chief judge for the U.S.District Court for Eastern Pennsylvania named a three-judge panel to rule on the challenge to the indecency provision, after which the matter could be appealed directly to the Supreme Court.

The Clinton administration defended the indecency provision, claiming that it applied only to communications to minors, though the Justice Department had earlier written to Senator Patrick Leahy (D-Vt.) warning that the provision would "impose criminal sanctions on the transmission of constitutionally protected speech" and "threaten important First Amendment and privacy rights" ("Judge Blocks On-Line Smut Law Enforcement," *Washington Post*, February 16, 1996, p. B1). The plaintiffs argued that Congress had failed to consider the least restrictive means to block indecency from minors, which would be software designed for parental control of Internet access. Plaintiffs contended that the law as written would chill free speech on-line, including material with literary or educational value that dealt with issues such as sexuality, reproduction, human rights, and civil liberties.

On February 26, another group of organizations and businesses filed suit under the umbrella of the American Library Association (ALA). The suit, which for the first time included all the major on-line companies as well as the trade and professional associations of newspaper publishers, editors, and reporters, was filed in the same court as the ACLU suit and was combined with it. The draft ALA complaint maintained that the on-line medium in which people seek information differs from the broadcast model that gave rise to the indecency standard. The complaint noted: "The speech at issue in this case . . . does *not* include obscenity, child pornography, or other speech that lacks First Amendment protection even for adults."Comparing the Internet with a global library, the ALA's Judith Krug said that the decency provision narrowed the available materials "to what is suitable for the youngest child that uses the library." Kristi Hamick, a spokesperson for the conservative Family Research Council, said, "The American Library Association has long been known for its liberal bent and its pro-pornography views. To pretend that our nation would somehow end if there weren't hard- core pornography within a child's reach is not only disingenuous, it's uncivilized" ("Coalition to File Suit over Internet Rules," *Washington Post*, February 26, 1996, p. A4).

On June 12, 1996, the special three-judge panel addressing *ACLU v. Reno* declared that the Internet restrictions in the Communications Decency Act (CDA) violated the constitutional guarantee of free speech. Nearly half of the 215–page decision was devoted to what cyberspace is and how it works, and the opinions of the three judges showed a knowledge and respect for the Internet. Judge Stewart Dalzell wrote, "The Internet is a far more speech-enhancing medium than print, the village green, or the mails. Because it would necessarily affect the Internet itself, the C.D.A. would necessarily reduce the speech available for adults on the medium. This is a constitutionally intolerable result." Dalzell concluded: "Cutting through the acronyms and argot that littered the hearing testimony, the Internet may fairly be regarded as a never-ending world-wide conversation. The Government may not, through the C.D.A., interrupt that conversation. As the most participatory form of mass speech yet developed, the Internet deserves the highest protection from government intrusion. . . . Just as the strength of the Internet is chaos, so the strength of our liberty depends upon the chaos and cacophony of the unfettered speech the First Amendment protects. For these reasons, I without hesitation hold that the C.D.A. is unconstitutional on its face."

The opinion granted First Amendment protections to the Internet that are equal to, if not stronger than, those afforded to print material. The court accepted the plaintiffs' contention that parents could best protect their children from objectionable on-line material by using readily available software to screen Internet content. The availability of such tools, said the judges, meant that the CDA had failed to employ the least restrictive means to regulate speech, as required by the Constitution. Chief Judge Dolores K. Sloviter wrote, "Those responsible for minors undertake the primary obligation to prevent their exposure to such [indecent] material. Instead, in the C.D.A., Congress chose to place on the speakers the obligation of screening the material that would possibly offend some communities. Whether Congress's decision was a wise one is not at issue here. It was unquestionably a decision that placed the C.D.A. in serious conflict with our most cherished protection—the right to choose the material to which we would have access."

Judge Ronald Buckwalter wrote, "I believe that the challenged provisions are so vague as to violate both the First and Fifth Amendments. . . . In addition, I believe that technology as it currently exists . . . cannot provide a safe harbor for most speakers on the Internet, thus rendering the statute unconstitutional under a strict scrutiny analysis." Nonetheless, Judge Buckwalter left the door open for other legislative attempts to regulate the Internet, saying, "I believe it is too early in the development of this new medium to conclude that other attempts to regulate protected speech within the medium will fail a challenge. That is to say that I specifically do not find that any and all statutory regulation of protected speech on the Internet could not survive constitutional scrutiny."

Judge Dalzell took a different view, saying that the court's decision led to the conclusion that "Congress may not regulate indecency on the Internet at all." Legislators like Representative Richard White (R-Wash.), who had opposed the "decency" provision in the act, vowed to overhaul the legislation after the Supreme Court made a ruling. "That's when we go back to the drawing board and do something that works," said White. "The issue isn't going to go away."

It is commonly assumed that the issue will eventually require a Supreme Court ruling. Indeed, even before the panel's ruling, government lawyers had said that they would appeal any adverse decision to the Supreme Court, and after the decision, President Clinton said that he remained convinced that the Constitution allowed laws like the CDA to protect children from exposure to objectionable material. Senator James Exon (D-Nebr.), who had introduced the bill that became the CDA, said that he expected to win approval for the bill in the Supreme Court, but Laurence Tribe, a constitutional expert at the Harvard Law School, disagreed. He had argued the 1989 case before the Supreme Court in which the Court unanimously ruled that a federal ban on "indecent" telephone messages violated the constitutional right to free speech. The same principles, according to Tribe, applied with respect to the CDA. "The Internet is the telephone writ large," he said ("Ruling Declares Internet a Complex Medium That Will Be Hard to Regulate," *New York Times*, June 13, 1996, p. B10).

REFERENCE: Jana Varlejs, ed., *Safeguarding Electronic Information*, Jefferson, N.C., McFarland, 1996.

IRVINE, REED JOHN, 1922–   Reed Irvine is a cofounder of and major spokesperson for Accuracy in Media (AIM) and Accuracy in Academia, two conservative organizations that claim to be combatting "liberal bias" in the media and on campuses by challenging and attacking liberal ideas in those areas. Irvine, who helped found AIM in 1969, worked as an economist for the Federal Reserve System until the late 1970s. AIM's official publication, *The AIM Report*, culls examples of liberal bias from various news media, refuting and correcting such reports. AIM has sometimes been criticized for disinformation and McCarthyism because of its frequent characterization of liberal opponents as Communists. In 1981, AIM published the book *Target America: The Influence of Communist Propaganda on the U.S. Media*, by James L. Tyson.

Irvine and AIM have been particularly hard on any journalist who criticizes America's wars. For example, Irvine attacked Alexander Cockburn for suggesting that American bombardment of General Manual Noriega's headquarters caused homelessness in Panama; he characterized Peter Arnett's reporting from Baghdad as unpatriotic Iraqi propaganda; and he has accused a number of journalists, past and present, of being receptive to the Soviet slant on international stories during the Cold War years. In 1985, Irvine founded Accuracy in Academia and vowed to place members of the new organization in classrooms around the country to report on professors whose lectures showed a "liberal bias."

REFERENCE: Reed Irvine, *The News Manipulators: Why You Can't Trust the News*, Smithtown, Book Distributors, Inc., 1993.

J

JEFFRIES, LEONARD, 1937–   Dr. Leonard Jeffries is a former chairman of the Black Studies Department of City College, New York (CCNY), which is a part of the City University of New York (CUNY). Jeffries taught political science at CCNY in 1969 and later became the founding chairman of Black Studies at San Jose State University. He became an important figure within the black power movement and traveled frequently to Africa. In 1972, Jeffries became the first chairman of CCNY's Black Studies Department, a position he held continuously for the next two decades. Each time Jeffries was nominated for another term as chairman, the college president and the CUNY board of trustees routinely confirmed the nomination.

Then, on July 20, 1991, Jeffries delivered a controversial speech to the Empire State Black Arts and Cultural Festival in Albany, New York. The speech claimed that Jewish control of the slave trade, the motion-picture industry, and City College itself had contributed to the oppression of African Americans. The speech, described by a New York columnist as "pure Goebbels," led New York Governor Mario Cuomo to request that CUNY seek an appropriate punishment for Jeffries. New York Senator Alfonse D'Amato demanded Jeffries' resignation as chairman.

CUNY's chancellor, W. Ann Reynolds, issued a statement saying that she was shocked and deeply disturbed by the speech. Bernard Harleston, president of City College, said that the speech contained clear statements of bigotry and anti-Semitism, and he announced a thorough review of Jeffries' status as chairman. Despite the fact that the review concluded that

Jeffries was doing an adequate job as chairman, in October 1991, Harleston persuaded the CUNY board of trustees to reduce Jeffries' term as chairman to one year, rather than the normal three years. Harleston began searching for a replacement for Jeffries, and on July 1, 1992, Edmund Gordon, former chairman of African and Afro-American studies at Yale, was appointed as the new chairman of CCNY's Black Studies Department. No reason was given for the dismissal of Jeffries, who promptly filed suit challenging his removal.

In May 1993, a jury in federal district court decided that Jeffries' rights to free speech and due process had been violated when he was removed as chairman, and it awarded him $400,000 in damages. In *Jeffries v. Harleston* (1993), the jury concluded that Jeffries had been removed as a direct result of his Albany speech and subsequent criticism from Governor Cuomo and others.

After the jury's determination, Judge Kenneth Conboy reinstated Jeffries as chairman, saying that the administrators and trustees of the City University system had been dishonest and cowardly in their presentation of the case. Judge Conboy's opinion stated that the university's action against Jeffries was "constitutionally impermissible." State Attorney General Robert Abrams, whose office represented the university, criticized the decision and said that it would be appealed.

The appeals court subsequently affirmed the district court's ruling that CCNY had violated Jeffries' right to free speech, but the case was sent to the U.S. Supreme Court for examination. In November 1994, the Supreme Court remanded the case back to the appeals court for reconsideration in light of another case, *Waters v. Churchill*, which had been decided several months earlier. In that case, the court held that Cheryl Churchill, a public hospital nurse, could be fired for insubordination if her speech was genuinely disruptive of the workplace, rude to patients, and hostile to coworkers. In sending the Jeffries case back for retrial, the Supreme Court implied that Jeffries' speech might be similarly unprotected since he also was a public employee.

When the appeals court reexamined the Jeffries case in April 1995, it concluded that CCNY had acted legally when it demoted Jeffries. The appeals court thus set aside the earlier findings of a judge and jury that CCNY had violated Jeffries' free-speech rights. "We recognize that academic freedom is an important academic concern," wrote the appeals court. "Jeffries' academic freedom, however, has not been infringed here." The court said that City College had "made a substantial showing at trial that the decision to limit Jeffries' term was based upon a reasonable prediction" that the "speech would disrupt university operation."

Jeffries' chairmanship of the Black Studies Department ended on June 16, 1995, but he vowed to take his case back to the Supreme Court. On October 2, 1995, the Supreme Court turned back his effort to revive his First

Amendment lawsuit against CCNY, effectively ending the three-year legal battle.

Some have interpreted the outcome of the Jeffries case to bear narrowly on the right of a university to determine who is fit to serve in leadership positions, such as department chairmen, that represent the university to the public. Such an interpretation would protect the tenure of faculty members like Jeffries, no matter how objectionable their speech. However, some have interpreted the court's ruling to authorize public institutions to discipline employees generally for disruptive speech, an erosion of First Amendment protections.

REFERENCES: *Jeffries Appeal*, videocassette of TV show "Court TV," covering the appeal of Leonard Jeffries in the case of *City College of New York v. Leonard Jeffries*, New York, Courtroom Television Network, 1994; James Traub, "The Hearts and Minds of City College," *New Yorker*, June 7, 1993, pp. 42–53.

K

KRUG, JUDITH FINGERET, 1940–   Judith Krug has been director of the American Library Association's Office for Intellectual Freedom (OIF) since 1967. As the nation's premier organization fighting censorship in libraries, schools, and public institutions, the OIF publishes a *Newsletter* documenting censorship incidents around the country and recommends strategies for opposing such censorship. Krug also serves as executive director of the Freedom to Read Foundation, an organization dedicated to the protection of freedoms of speech and press, with special emphasis on the First Amendment rights of librarians and libraries. She is a frequent lecturer and guest speaker on radio and television, often representing the cause of intellectual freedom in nationally televised debates. She has frequently testified before Congress on pending legislation or problems relating to intellectual freedom. Among the honors and awards she has received are the Robert B. Downs Intellectual Freedom Award and the Carl Sandburg Freedom to Read Award.

REFERENCE: Judith Krug, Anne Levinson Penway, and Eve B. Burton, "Censorship in the Public Schools," in *Book Publishing and the First Amendment*, New York, Association of American Publishers, 1993.

L

LEAR, NORMAN MILTON, 1922–   Norman Lear is a successful television producer who used his media prominence to help create one of the nation's most influential intellectual freedom support groups, People for the American Way. Lear began his career as a comedy writer for television, and his immensely popular comedy series "All in the Family" broke new ground on TV with its candid and satirical look at racism, sexism, and homophobia. That series, which began in 1971, ran for fifteen seasons and was followed by other ground-breaking shows like "The Jeffersons" and "Sanford and Son."

In 1980, in response to the rising conservative backlash against civil liberties, Lear formed People for the American Way, which finances advertising campaigns in support of civil liberties, provides resources to similar-minded groups, and publishes studies and surveys on censorship and related issues. Its annual report, *Attacks on the Freedom to Learn*, is an authoritative summary of the major attempts to control freedom of expression in schools and libraries.

REFERENCE: *Norman Lear, Seminars at the Museum of Broadcasting: Mark Goodson Seminar Series, June 1986*, New York, the Museum of Broadcasting, 1987.

LEVIN, MICHAEL, 1940–   In 1987, Dr. Michael Levin, a professor of philosophy at the City College of New York (CCNY), made racist remarks that provoked students on the CCNY campus to picket his classes. In early 1988, Levin published an article criticizing the efforts to bring blacks into the educational mainstream. Levin espoused the racist view that high failure rates for blacks in college were inevitable because the average black is less intelligent than the average white. In response to Levin's opinions, the Faculty Senate passed a motion of censure that condemned Levin's "racist prejudices." CCNY then created separate sections of his courses for students who might have been offended by the views Levin expressed outside of class. In May 1990, CCNY's president, Bernard Harleston, formed an ad hoc committee to determine whether Levin's statements and those of another CCNY professor, Leonard Jeffries, went beyond the bounds of academic freedom. In September 1990, Levin filed suit in federal court against Harleston, the ad hoc committee, and CCNY's dean, asking that they be enjoined from infringing on his academic freedom and First Amendment rights.

The committee report, released in March 1991, rebuked both Levin and Jeffries for their statements about race, but said that disciplining either professor would undermine academic freedom and free speech. Nonetheless, Levin's suit proceeded, and a trial in May 1991 resulted in a ruling by Judge Kenneth Conboy that CCNY could not punish Levin for his views. According to the ruling, CCNY officials had violated Levin's rights to free speech and due process when they formed the ad hoc committee to investigate him, failed to discipline protesters, and established separate sections of his classes for students offended by his views. The ruling blocked the college from continuing the special sections of Levin's classes and from initiating discipline or investigation predicated solely upon his protected expression of ideas.

CCNY appealed Judge Conboy's ruling, but in June 1992, the Court of Appeals for the Second Circuit held that CCNY had abrogated Levin's right to free speech and due process. The three-judge panel declared, "It is the chilling effect on free speech that violates the First Amendment, and it is plain that an implicit threat can chill as forcibly as an explicit threat." No damages were sought or awarded, but Levin's lawyer said, "We think that this is a great victory for the First Amendment and a strong setback for the forces of political correctness" (Robert McFadden, "Court Finds a Violation of a Professor's Rights," *New York Times*, June, 9, 1992 p. B3).
REFERENCE: Michael Levin, "The Lessons of Hate," *New York Times*, September 26, 1991, p. A2.

LIBEL   Libel is a form of unprotected speech involving defamatory words that are written or broadcast. Defamation is defined in terms of injury to one's standing in the community, including damage to business, family, or social relationships.

As a defense against libel, a newspaper may claim that certain "hot news" must be disseminated without delay, preventing full investigation of the truth or falsity of a report. With the exception of the "hot news" category, a person or group must at least attempt to ascertain the truth of a statement before publishing or repeating it. Otherwise, under current libel laws, the person or group must demonstrate "reckless disregard" for the truth.

The historic 1964 Supreme Court decision in *New York Times Co. v. Sullivan* clarified the restraints on libelous speech by restricting legal recovery for libel. The case arose when the *Times* ran an advertisement by the Committee to Defend Martin Luther King that condemned Southern racism and the arrest of King in Alabama on trumped-up charges. An Alabama political official, L. B. Sullivan, sued the *Times* for libel and won a $500,000 judgment. The Supreme Court overturned the libel verdict, stating that a public official must prove that libelous words were published with either knowledge of or reckless disregard for their falsity. In his landmark opinion, Justice William Brennan established this standard for criticism of public officials in order to ensure "robust" debate on public issues.

The precedent established in the *Times* decision provided two standards for libel when it involves issues of public concern. The Court applied the "knowing or reckless" standard to libel of public figures, but the lesser standard of "negligence" when the libel concerned a private figure. A still more lenient standard for libelous speech was established when the victim was a private figure and the issues involved were of only private concern. *See also* DEFAMATION.

REFERENCES: Lois G. Forer, *A Chilling Effect: The Mounting Threat of Libel and Invasion of Privacy Actions to The First Amendment*, New York, Norton 1987; Theodore R. Kupferman, ed., *Defamation—Libel and Slander*, Westport, Meckler, 1990.

LIBERTY FEDERATION   The Liberty Federation was founded in 1979 as the Moral Majority by the Reverend Jerry Falwell. The federation has organizations in every state and a membership of over four million. Its primary purpose is to organize political conservatives and religious fundamentalists to oppose pornography, abortion, homosexual rights, and "liberal" political views. In this regard, it has endorsed and supported conservative political candidates representing the religious right. The activities of the federation are conducted through the ministries of the Reverend Jerry Falwell and local organizations.

The Liberty Federation is located at P.O. Box 190, Forest, VA 24551. Its president is Jerry C. Nims.

REFERENCE: John B. Harer, *Intellectual Freedom: A Reference Handbook*, Santa Barbara, ABC-CLIO, 1992.

LIBRARY AWARENESS PROGRAM   The Library Awareness Program and related FBI programs sought to recruit librarians around the country to restrict access to publicly available, unclassified scientific library collections and to report on those who tried to use them. Because controlling individual access to information inevitably requires surveillance, that unfortunate combination was played out in libraries around the country during the 1970s and 1980s. The FBI divided its library surveillance programs into two categories: proactive and reactive. The proactive programs followed no particular leads or suspects. They simply identified America's openly published scientific research as something to be protected from foreign eyes and sought to recruit librarians to gather "positive intelligence" about the scientific needs and interests of foreign nationals. The most infamous of the bureau's proactive programs was originated in New York City in 1973 and became known as the Library Awareness Program. When the *New York Times* broke the story of the Library Awareness Program in September 1987, there was considerable initial public anxiety about whether librarians really were checking on the reading habits of library patrons and reporting such information to the FBI. This impression was strengthened when a Freedom of Information Act (FOIA) request made public the transcript of a secret briefing given by the FBI to the National Commission on Libraries and Information Science (NCLIS), an official federal organization that supposedly represented the interests of libraries and librarians. The transcript revealed that NCLIS was not only secretly supporting the Library Awareness Program, but was contemptuous of librarians who opposed it.

The Library Awareness Program was an attack on both library confidentiality and open access to library information. Throughout the program, the FBI attempted to prevent foreign nationals, particularly Soviet citizens, from accessing unclassified scientific information. One of the more frequent targets of FBI control on access to unclassified library materials concerned information from the National Technical Information Service (NTIS). NTIS is a clearinghouse of unclassified government reports, and the index/database to these reports is held by most science libraries. The FBI decided that American libraries should not allow Soviet citizens access to NTIS. When librarians explained that there were no more restrictions on access to NTIS than on acess to any other unclassified library materials, the bureau floated a story that an executive order from President Jimmy Carter specifically prohibited Soviet access to NTIS. It was subsequently discovered that there was no such executive order, but the bureau continued a program of disinformation in an attempt to restrict access to NTIS through libraries.

Among the science libraries on which the FBI intruded were the library at the University of Maryland at College Park (UMCP), Columbia University's Math and Science Library, New York University's Courant Institute of Mathematical Sciences Library, the New York Public Library, and the science collections at numerous other academic and public libraries around the country. The FBI's visits to UMCP were part of the bureau's reactive, as opposed to proactive, program, under which FBI agents presumably followed specific leads about suspicious foreigners using science libraries. Librarians around the country had difficulty distinguishing between the reactive and proactive programs because the FBI agents behaved essentially the same in either case. At UMCP, the agents asked librarians to report on anyone with "a foreign-sounding name or foreign accent" who used the libraries. Such a characterization would fit the majority of students and faculty on most American campuses, yet librarians were asked to monitor reference questions and on-line literature searches, including searches of NTIS, in order to establish the subject interests of these suspicious foreigners. All of this surveillance was conducted despite the fact that the UMCP libraries contained no classified materials, and their collections were presumably open to anyone. When the university complained about the surveillance, an FBI representative claimed that the libraries should feel no obligation to protect the access and privacy rights of noncitizens.

Throughout the Library Awareness Program, the FBI characterized its critics as witting or unwitting dupes of the Soviet Union. Proceeding on that assumption, the bureau conducted a sixteen-month investigation of librarians who had openly opposed the Library Awareness Program. A secret 1989 FBI memo revealed that the bureau had investigated these librarians because it suspected them of participating in "an active measures campaign" to discredit the Library Awareness Program. The term "active measures" is intelligence jargon for foreign attempts to influence the public through disinformation, propaganda, or front groups.

Librarians were not the only group that spoke out against the Library Awareness Program. The American Association of University Professors approved a resolution in 1988 condemning the program as "an assault on the confidentiality of library records and a chill on the scholars' right to free access to libraries." The American Federation of Teachers (AFT) and numerous other organizations made similar statements. Representative Don Edwards (D-Calif.), himself a former FBI agent, said: "They think they can learn what the Russians are doing scientifically if they know what they are reading. But turning librarians into agents is terribly chilling. It's reminiscent of the domestic intelligence files the FBI kept for many years. I thought those bad old days were gone" (Ann Hagedorn, "FBI Recruits Librarians to Spy on 'Commie' Readers," *Wall Street Journal*, May 19, 1988, p. 32).

In response to the Library Awareness Program, communities around the country worked with librarians and local legislators to craft library confidentiality statutes that made it illegal for any librarian to reveal library records or patron inquiries to anyone without a court order. Most states have now passed such laws. Unfortunately, library confidentiality statutes affect the behavior only of librarians, not of federal agents, who remain free to intrude on American libraries.

REFERENCE: Herbert N. Foerstel, *Surveillance in the Stacks: The FBI's Library Awareness Program*, New York, Greenwood Press, 1991.

LYNN, BARRY, 1948–   Barry Lynn is a leading attorney for the American Civil Liberties Union (ACLU) and a prominent national spokesperson for the First Amendment. Lynn is an ordained minister in the United

Church of Christ who earned his master's degree in theology from Boston University and his law degree from Georgetown University. In addition to representing clients of the ACLU in several civil liberties and First Amendment cases, Lynn has lectured and published in support of ACLU positions. Lynn has been a vocal critic of the Attorney General's Commission on Pornography (the Meese Commission), and he was a contributor to *The Meese Commission Exposed*, published by the National Commission against Censorship. In 1987, Lynn received the Hugh M. Hefner First Amendment Award for leading the effort to inform the public about the flawed Meese Commission.

REFERENCE: Barry Lynn, *The Right to Religious Liberty: The Basic ACLU Guide to Religious Rights*, 2nd ed., Carbondale, Southern Illinois University Press, 1995.

McMASTERS, PAUL, 1942– Paul McMasters is a journalist with a lifelong commitment to free expression. As a reporter and editor, he made the First Amendment a primary professional obligation for himself and his colleagues. During his tenure as deputy editorial director of *USA Today*, he also served as a member of the Freedom of Information Committee of the American Society of Newspaper Editors.

In 1991, McMasters became executive director of the Freedom Forum First Amendment Center at Vanderbilt University. While running the center, he spearheaded a number of initiatives, including a fifty–state pilgrimage to alert the nation to the First Amendment threats on college campuses. He spoke of the erosion of academic freedoms, the proliferation of speech codes, the theft or burning of student newspapers, and the suppression of art and photo exhibits. McMasters warned that when such activities are tolerated by campus officials, the idea of an open society becomes a farce.

McMasters was particularly concerned with the suppression and censorship of campus newspapers, which he said should be a safe haven for free inquiry and expression. He warned that the threat to student journalists had real and tangible implications for the broader profession, because students will eventually take their places in U.S. newsrooms and "carry with them the prejudices, pressures and ideas they get on campus."

In 1995, after four years helping to establish the First Amendment Center, McMasters was appointed to fill a newly created position, First Amendment Ombudsman for the Freedom Forum in Arlington, Virginia. His primary duties as ombudsman involve representing the public interest on First Amendment issues that arise on Capitol Hill, in support of which McMasters does extensive research, writing, and speaking. His role as ombudsman is informational and educational, through contacts with members of Congress, the media, advocacy groups, and the public. Of particular concern are the all-too-frequent legislative attempts to compromise free-speech or free-press rights.

Throughout his career, McMasters has played a prominent role in the professional organizations of journalism. In 1993, he became president of the Society of Professional Journalists (SPJ) and its freedom of information chairman. In that capacity, he appointed a task force to reorganize the society's freedom of information (FOI) efforts. The new FOI structure called for all of the SPJ's FOI activities—the Legal Defense Fund, Project Sunshine, national legal counsel, and so on—to fall under the National FOI Committee. Under McMasters, the SPJ also created an endowment fund to provide additional resources for its local, state, and national FOI efforts.

As an active SPJ president, McMasters announced that the journalism profession and the First Amendment were under siege, and that the society's membership must confront those challenges. He then visited SPJ chapters in every state to promote free-press rights and responsibilities. McMasters described his mission as preaching the gospel of the First Amendment to "a choir that apparently has been missing a lot of practice and has forgotten the words." He expressed surprise at the number of journalists who did not appreciate their rights as guaranteed by the Constitution. "If we're ignorant about free-press values . . . , then we put a constitutional franchise in jeopardy," he said. "The press is the only profession . . . that is singled out for this responsibility in the Constitution" (Tony Case, "A Call to Arms," *Editor and Publisher*, October 30, 1993, p. 14). McMasters' term as SPJ president ended in the fall of 1994.

REFERENCE: Debra Hernandez, "First Amendment Ombudsman: Paul McMasters Fills the Role of New Freedom Forum Position," *Editor and Publisher*, December 16, 1995, pp. 11–12.

MILITARY CENSORSHIP   Press censorship by the American military has become so commonplace in the twentieth century that one is tempted to assume that it has always existed. On the contrary, Thomas Jefferson wrote in an 1813 letter: "The first misfortune of the Revolutionary War induced a motion to suppress or garble the account of it. It was rejected with indignation" (James Russell Wiggins, *Freedom or Secrecy*, New York, Oxford University Press, 1964, p. 94). Indeed, no substantial military censorship occurred in the subsequent War of 1812 or in the Mexican War (1846–48).

Perhaps because of the introduction of the telegraph system, the American Civil War saw the first widespread use of American military censorship. At first, the Union government proposed a voluntary newspaper-censorship system, but the government subsequently imposed a compulsory system that closely supervised the information transmitted by telegraph and suspended any newspaper, after the fact, that printed inappropriate military information. Military leaders were particularly suspicious of the press, and General William T. Sherman discouraged any communication with reporters, claiming that the Confederate government obtained more intelligence from Northern newspapers than through espionage.

During the Spanish-American War, naval censorship units were established in Key West, Florida, Washington, D.C., and New York City, through which the Navy exercised complete censorship control over cable communications. Similar naval censorship was imposed in 1914 at Veracruz following the U.S. intervention there, but the American entrance into World War I in 1917 brought a systematic use of military censorship heretofore unseen. A new propaganda and censorship agency, the Committee on Public Information, was created in Washington, authorized to check on the content of all printed material and motion pictures and recommend the removal of anything objectionable. The committee was paralleled by special bureaus in the Post Office, Justice Department, War Department, and State Department.

The Espionage Act of 1917 broadly prohibited publication of any information that might conceivably aid the enemy or interfere with American military operations or war production, making such publication punishable by up to twenty years in prison and a $10,000 fine. The Sedition Act of 1918 provided similar punishment for anyone criticizing the actions of the American government or its armed forces, even including such things as negative comments about the flag or the military uniform.

The American press censor in France with the American Expeditionary Force was soon replaced by a committee of regular Army officers and ex-journalists who had been commissioned as reserve officers. Near the end of World War I, this censorship committee approved for publication a United Press dispatch announcing a full armistice several days before the real one was signed. When the story proved to be premature, the censors severed contact between United Press and France, preventing any possibility for correction or explanation.

The control of visual images was particularly important in both world wars. During the entire period of American involvement in World War I, the government prohibited publication of any photographs of American dead. A similar prohibition was imposed during the first twenty-one months of American involvement in World War II. The censorship of visual images of World War II was more sophisticated than it had been in World War I. By late 1943, the American public was allowed to see selected pictures of American war dead, but the disturbing image of "emotionally wounded" Americans was kept invisible throughout the war and after. The War Department's Bureau of Public Relations (BPR) insisted on "complete silence" about "psychoneurotic" casualties throughout most of the war.

In 1941, when Japan's attack on Pearl Harbor drew America into World War II, the Secretary of the Navy formally requested the media to stop publishing military-related information without specific naval authorization. Both the Army and Navy had earlier announced plans to control the press in the event of a national emergency, and these plans were quickly put into effect. On December 8, 1941, FBI Director J. Edgar Hoover was given temporary censorship authority over all news and other telecommunications traffic in and out of the United States. President Roosevelt requested that the American press voluntarily accept the censorship guidelines published earlier by the Department of the Navy, and on December 18, pursuant to the War Powers Act, the President created a new Office of Censorship, with Byron Price as Director of Censorship.

The Office of Censorship provided voluntary guidelines for domestic news censorship, relying on persuasion and a censorship system, called the Code of Wartime Practices, that was created with the full cooperation of the media. The Office of War Information (OWI) was created in June 1942 to function as America's propaganda agency and liaison between the government and the press. It was the job of the OWI to picture America's war effort in the most positive light without destroying the government's credibility with the press and public, but the reluctance of government agencies and the military to provide accurate and timely information to the public caused constant friction between the OWI and the press.

In the Pacific theater, General Douglas MacArthur exercised almost dictatorial censorship over the press, and the Chief of Naval Operations, Admiral Ernest J. King, was equally hostile to the press. MacArthur's restrictive news policy used censorship for "image building," and the Navy had a policy of delaying bad news until it could be matched with stories of combat success. For example, news of the American naval defeat off Savo Island was withheld until almost nine weeks after the battle. U.S. naval censorship was rigidly imposed throughout the war, in part because it was a simple task to control news correspondents confined to warships. On the other hand, press censorship on the ground in Europe required different procedures. By the time American troops arrived in Great Britain in January 1942, a system of joint British/American censorship had already been negotiated for the European theater.

The U.S. military censorship group in London, initially made up of four American officers, was located with the British censors at the Ministry of Information. By October 1942, the American censorship group had grown to ten officers and an enlisted man, who were broken into teams and assigned to the separate invasion task forces. The censors actually went ashore with the landing troops in order to monitor the war correspondents who accompanied the first assault waves. According to the procedures established in the Code of Wartime Practices, all news reports were to be submitted in duplicate, one copy to public relations and one copy to the censors. The censorship process often held up press reports for a week or more, first at Gibraltar, then in Algiers, and finally in London, while the "official" military press releases were processed immediately through censorship to reach the home front well in advance of the actual news reports.

In North Africa, the American censors were more concerned about blocking political news than military information. The American State Department was opposed to General Charles de Gaulle's French government-in-exile, supporting instead General Henri Giraud, who was considered more cooperative with the Allies in North Africa. As a result, American military and diplomatic officials decided to censor all political news out of North Africa until the situation was resolved. Indeed, General Dwight Eisenhower imposed tight political censorship for six weeks, until a political arrangement was negotiated between de Gaulle and Giraud.

As D day approached, a Joint Press Censorship Group composed of American, British, and Canadian officers was created. These officers, along with prominent media and military figures like Edward R. Murrow and Brigadier General David Sarnoff, attended an indoctrination course from April 10 to April 21, 1944. By D day there were over five hundred combat correspondents in England, and many accompanied the Normandy invasion. Others landed with the paratroopers behind German lines. Press reports from bridgeheads ashore were routed to censorship units behind the lines by courier, radio, or carrier pigeon. Naval censorship was conducted aboard the two command vessels of the invasion fleet. In August 1944, when Allied armies entered Paris, a new censorship headquarters was established in the Hotel Scribe. When Paris was completely secured, London was officially designated as the "rear" censorship headquarters and Paris as the "main" headquarters.

On April 11, 1945, advancing American troops reached the western bank of the Elbe River, where they prepared to move on Berlin. Lieutenant General William Simpson, on orders from Generals Eisenhower and Bradley, halted the advance on Berlin in order to allow a joint liberation of the city by Allied forces. At the news conference announcing this action, Simpson ordered his press censor to prevent any press communication of the decision. This form of policy censorship under the guise of military security was repeated a month later at the time of the German surrender. Military censors withheld the news of the initial signing of the surrender documents until a second ceremony could be arranged in the Russian headquarters, symbolizing the unity of the Western Allies and the Soviets.

In 1950, when America entered the Korean War, television was still in its infancy, but newspaper, radio, and newsreel correspondents arrived with the troops. As with previous wartime censorship, a voluntary gentleman's agreement between the military and the press was attempted, but when stories about South Korean civil corruption, inferior American military equipment, and other bad news were published, field press censorship was imposed. All news copy or film had to be approved by the Eighth Army's censors, and the Air Force performed similar screening through its Korean public information office. Even then, military officials apparently felt that too much was being approved, because Tokyo headquarters decided to institute a censorship review of all news passed by the field censors. This multiple censorship system remained in effect until the spring of 1951, when the Far East Command relieved the Eighth Army of its censorship duties. On January 6, 1953, the Far East Command created a Joint Field Censorship Group, composed of military censorship personnel from the Army, Navy, and Air Force. The Chief Field Press Censor who headed the group controlled censorship in all United Nations and Far East commands and wielded it in a rigid and political manner. At the Department of Defense (DOD) level, military press censorship was overseen by the Assistant Secretary of Defense for Public Affairs. In August 1954, DOD issued a joint service manual entitled *Field Press Censorship* that was to be the official procedural document for military censorship during future "media security programs."

After the Korean War, each of the armed services began its own information-security planning. The Air Force created an Office of Information that reported directly to the Secretary of the Air Force. The Navy's Office of Information was headed by the Chief of Information, who was also the public affairs adviser to the Chief of Naval Operations. Neither the Air Force nor the Navy maintained a separate, manned press-censorship group, leaving the Army with the only well-defined media-censorship capability. For example, within an hour of President Kennedy's announcement of Soviet missiles in Cuba, the Army's field press-censorship units were partially mobilized. Indeed, contingency plans were developed that envisioned an active combat zone in southern Florida, with military press censorship on American soil for the first time since the Civil War. With the resolution of the Cuban missile crisis, these plans were scrapped.

By 1964, when American military involvement in Vietnam reached a massive level, the Pentagon had entered the censorship planning process. Once more, the press voluntarily observed the initial military censorship rules, but in Vietnam these voluntary regulations were more successful than in past military conflicts. In over four and one-half years of voluntary censorship involving approximately two thousand news-media representatives, only six security violations were of sufficient seriousness to cause the military to remove a reporter's DOD accreditation. This quite remarkable record of military-press cooperation has been explained in a variety of ways. The Vietnam War, lacking a clear purpose or goal, was destined to be unpopular regardless of how much news was censored. Also, because the military did not control civilian transportation in South Vietnam, news correspondents were free to fly into, out of, or around the country on civilian planes. Any reporter with a censored story could simply board a plane out of Vietnam and file the story elsewhere. Once a reporter was outside of military jurisdiction, the only possible punishment was the loss of DOD press accreditation (Theodore Kupferman, ed., *Censorship, Secrecy, Access, and Obscenity*, Westport, Meckler, 1990, pp. 260–75).

In Vietnam, reporters traveled with combat units, unescorted by military censors. What they observed directly was often contradicted by the official military briefings, called the daily "Saigon follies." Reporters ignored the characterizations of the war fed to them by higher military authority, acting instead on the information provided to them by the lower-ranking field officers they respected. There were very few breaches of military security caused by the reporting in Vietnam, but the stories sent back home, particularly the television footage, brought the brutal reality of war to an already-disenchanted public. In the depressing aftermath of America's first lost war, many in the military blamed the press. Indeed, General William Westmoreland characterized Vietnam as the first war in history lost in the columns of the *New York Times*. The Pentagon's continuing hostility toward the press was evident during America's brief 1983 invasion of the tiny island of Grenada, during which the press was kept in total isolation. Journalists who tried to gain access to the island by way of chartered boats were intercepted by the U.S. military and held for two days on a Navy ship. Soon thereafter, the Pentagon took formal action to ensure that the kind of uncontrolled press access allowed during the Vietnam War would not be repeated in future military campaigns. The DOD commissioned a study of military press coverage, to be overseen by Brigadier General Winant Sidle, who as the military's chief of public affairs in Vietnam had warned of a press "conspiracy." Sidle recommended the establishment of a "pool system" of controlled and supervised press access to military action, and in 1984, the Department of Defense Media Pool was formally created.

The first opportunity to implement the new pool system came with the 1989 invasion of Panama. The press-pool plane was five hours late for the invasion, held up in order to keep the press out of Panama City when U.S. troops arrived. When reporters were finally allowed into the capital city, military escorts barred them from firsthand observation of combat areas. The full flower of this new system of military press control was to emerge several years later during the planning of Operation Desert Storm in the Persian Gulf. Here the military made sure that the roving reporters tolerated during the Vietnam War would be avoided by implementing the system of press pools under tight military escort.

In the Gulf War, reporters were disturbed by the requirement that direct access to troops and combat areas be limited to small groups of reporters who would always be accompanied by official military escorts. These segregated press pools would then be expected to pass their news on to the full contingent of reporters. Journalists were also subject to DOD restrictions on the kinds of information that could be reported. Among the kinds of prohibited information were details of future operations, specific data on troop strengths or locations, specific information about downed or missing airplanes or ships, and information about operational weaknesses in the Allies' military forces. Such constraints were standard fare for reporters who had covered previous military campaigns, and they dutifully followed the guidelines. But the new system of information control also included a review process in which stories filed by pool reporters were examined by military officials prior to release. The review process did not provide for direct censorship because disputes between military officials and reporters were to be resolved by the reporter's news organization. Pete Williams, the Assistant Secretary of Defense for Public Affairs during the Gulf War, claimed that there was virtually no censorship of pool reports. Still, the frequent delays in the transmission of stories were a major complaint from reporters. On the home front, for the first time in memory, Americans saw messages such as "Cleared by U.S. Military" or "Cleared by Israeli Censors" or "Cleared by Iraqi Censors" on their television screens or newspapers.

The tight control on movement and access imposed by the pool system chafed the press. Sydney Schanberg, associate editor and columnist for *Newsday*, complained to a Senate committee, "The purpose of the government's system is to control and manipulate information, to sanitize and clean it up so that the war will sound more like a choir boy's picnic than the grungy thing that it is" (Steve Daley, "Journalists Getting Only a Piece of the Story, Lawmakers Told," *Chicago Tribune*, February 21, 1991, p. 5). Ron Nessen, journalist and former White House Press Secretary for President Gerald Ford, had covered the Vietnam War for NBC, and during the Gulf War he wistfully recalled: "In Vietnam there were no omnipresent military escorts. To get to the fighting, you got from the Caravelle Hotel to Tan Son Nhut airbase by taxi or in your rented jeep or on your motor scooter. . . . And when it was time to file, you simply transmitted the film, broadcast radio spots from the ancient PTT studios or telexed your copy directly to the home office. There were no censors" (Ron Nessen, "The Pentagon's Censors," *Washington Post*, January 12, 1991, p. A21).

In January 1991, a group of magazines, newspapers, radio stations, and individual writers brought suit in federal court challenging the Pentagon's restrictions on press coverage of the Gulf War. The defendants in the case were the Department of Defense, Secretary of Defense Richard Cheney, Assistant Secretary of Defense for Public Affairs Pete Williams, Chairman of the Joint Chiefs of Staff General Colin Powell, and President George Bush. Another suit was brought by the French news service Agence France-Presse, seeking access to the tightly controlled media pools. Both cases were assigned to federal District Court Judge Leonard B. Sand.

The American suit claimed that the press controls devised for the Gulf War could not be justified on security grounds. The suit sought an injunction against hindering members of the press in their coverage of U.S. combat forces or prohibiting the press from areas where U.S. forces were deployed or engaged in combat unless legitimate security reasons could be demonstrated. Before Judge Sand had an opportunity to consider the merits of the case, Iraq withdrew from Kuwait and the United States ended hostilities. Judge Sand consequently ruled that in the absence of hostilities, with press-pool restrictions no longer being enforced, the case was moot. The suit was therefore dismissed.

The Gulf War was considered by many in the press to be the worst-covered major U.S. conflict of the twentieth century, and there was broad consensus that the pool system had been inappropriately used by the government to control the news and shape American political opinion about the war. In the aftermath of the Gulf War, a group of news organizations appointed five senior reporters to begin discussions with Pete Williams in an attempt to regain the press freedoms that had been lost. After eight months of discussions, a statement of nine principles was issued to govern future combat reporting. Foremost among the principles was the understanding that pools were never again to be the standard means for covering military action, though they could still be used during the early phase of a conflict, or in remote areas, or during highly classified "special operations."

Under the new principles, the Pentagon could no longer prevent news organizations from operating battlefield communications systems. The final principle stated that the other eight would also apply to the continuing "national media pool." There was no mention of "security review" in the principles, but in separate statements, the news organizations vowed to challenge any attempt to reimpose such a review on reporters. The Pentagon, however, insisted that it must retain the option of imposing security review on news reports.

The journalists who negotiated the nine principles of press coverage with the Pentagon were quick to admit that they had no guarantees that heavy-handed controls would not be imposed during future conflicts. One of the journalists, Stanley W. Cloud, said, "Despite the shortcomings of the principles we introduced, I am confident that they have helped re-establish the most important principle of all: that the First Amendment is, if anything, even more valuable to this democracy in wartime than in peacetime" (Stanley W. Cloud, "Covering the Next War," *New York Times*, August 4, 1992, p. A19).

Just two years later, during the Pentagon's 1994 planning for an invasion of Haiti, it became clear that military censorship was still alive and well. White House and Pentagon officials met with representatives of the television networks and asked for an eight-hour broadcasting blackout. In addition, reporters in Haiti were to be restricted to their hotels until military commanders gave them permission to go to the fighting. Because the full-scale invasion was cancelled after successful negotiations with the Haitian junta, these controls were never imposed, but the *New York Times* commented, "It shows that the news-management policies that took root in the Reagan-Bush years and reached their full propagandistic flower during Operation Desert Storm are still in place at the Pentagon" ("Military Censorship Lives," *New York Times*, September 21, 1994, p. A22).

Exacerbating the growing power of military censorship is an extremely compliant American press. What has emerged in the 1990s is a disquieting gentleman's agreement between the Pentagon and the major news agencies to cooperate in packaging wartime news. According to Ben Bagdikian, media expert and former dean of the University of California's journalism school at Berkeley, "Historically, when clans, kingdoms, and nations have gone to war, whoever brought information to the public have been full-throated cheering squads for the home army. . . . [W]ith rare exceptions, the American mainstream news during combat has been much like the hired bards of medieval monarchs: when war has come, our journalists have become propagandists. . . . The military learned its own lesson from Vietnam: keep wars short and keep the news media completely controlled in the opening days of the engagement. By mandating total control of the initial image in a military action, the government can create the framework into which the public thereafter fits subsequent information" (John R. MacArthur, *Second Front: Censorship and Propaganda in the Gulf War*, New York, Hill and Wang, 1992, p. xi).

The result is not so much a sinister political conspiracy as it is a triumph for public relations. The infamous "baby-atrocity" story, which galvanized public opinion against Iraq prior to the Gulf War, is a good example. After the nation of Kuwait hired Hill and Knowlton (H & K), one of the largest and most politically connected public relations firms in America, to convince Congress and the public of Iraqi atrocities, a story was circulated that Iraqi soldiers had removed 312 Kuwaiti babies from their incubators, leaving them to die on hospital floors. The press repeated the story uncritically, and the congressional Human Rights Caucus held a televised hearing at which a fifteen-year-old girl identified only as "Nayirah" gave tearful testimony verifying the incubator story. Soon the story became a regular part of political speeches—President Bush told it five times—and it was used as the basis for United Nations approval of American military action against Iraq.

Only after the Gulf War had ended did the truth emerge. The entire baby-atrocity story was fabricated by H & K, which orchestrated the congressional hearings and coached the witnesses. The tearful young eyewitness turned out to be the daughter of Kuwait's ambassador to the United States. None of this deception seemed to bother the press. In fact, CBS News quickly hired General Norman Schwarzkopf to host its war documentaries and engaged General Tom Kelly, the Pentagon's military spokesman during the Gulf War, in its news division. NBC then hired Pete Williams, the enforcer for the Bush administration's censorship system, and Richard Haass, former National Security Council staff member. By hiring the architects of press control, the media had confused public relations, propaganda, and journalism.

The power of public relations to determine the media image, and hence public perception, of war was maximized early in 1992 when civil war raged in the former Yugoslavia. Croatians and Bosnian Muslims were each paying thirty thousand dollars a month to an American public relations firm, Ruder Finn, to sell their version of the war to the world. During 1992, Serbian "atrocities" were paraded on television and lamented in the press, with little attempt to verify details. A representative of Ruder Finn said, "It's not our job to investigate the facts given us by our employers." Author Florence Levinsohn wrote, "The use of an American public relations firm by the former republics of Yugoslavia reflected great sophistication—the recognition that paid agents from the West could do a better job than the governments themselves in influencing world opinion. . . . The American media and government are well used to dealing with public relations firms, and they would be much more likely to accept information as reliable coming from fellow Americans than from the government of the obscure and unknown Bosnia, for example" (Florence Levinsohn, *Belgrade: Among the Serbs*, Chicago, Ivan R. Dee, 1994, pp. 7, 312–13).

With Serbia demonized by a one-sided public relations and media blitz, Croatia, Germany's client state, armed and trained by the United States, was given a free hand in the Balkans. By 1995, the American press was virtually unanimous in supporting joint U.S.-NATO military action against Serbia and the subsequent Dayton Accords.

By 1996, new Pentagon guidelines prohibited reporters traveling with U.S. troops in Bosnia from quoting them without permission. Media groups criticized the new Pentagon policy, but an Army spokesman said that violators would find it more difficult to gain access to the troops. The tight guidelines were introduced after an American colonel was quoted as telling two black soldiers, "It'll be interesting to hear what you two see, because the Croatians are racist. . . . They kill people for the color of their skins." The story angered the Croatians and nearly cost the colonel his job ("Reporting Guidelines Tightened," *Washington Post*, May 11, 1996, p. A27).

REFERENCES: *Seeing through the Media: The Persian Gulf War*, edited by Susan Jeffords and Lauren Rabinovitz, New Brunswick, Rutgers University Press, 1994; Theodore R. Kupferman, ed., *Censorship, Secrecy, Access, and Obscenity*, Westport, Meckler, 1990.

MORALITY IN MEDIA   Founded in 1962, Morality in Media is an organization of citizens opposed to the spread of pornography. Begun as Operation Yorkville by Father Charles Coughlin, a member of the 1970 President's Commission on Pornography and Obscenity, the organization is supported by the Roman Catholic church. Morality in Media conducts public education campaigns about the dehumanizing effects of pornography and encourages individuals to lobby law-enforcement agencies to enforce obscenity laws. It also operates the National Obscenity Law Center, a clearinghouse of legal information and materials on obscenity for use by prosecutors and other members of the bar.

Morality in Media and its law center jointly publish the bimonthly *Obscenity Law Bulletin*, which examines legal issues, current obscenity prosecutions, and constitutional trends relating to obscenity. The organization also publishes *Morality in Media Newsletter*, a bimonthly summary of the group's activities. Joseph J. Reilly, Jr., is president of Morality in Media, which is located at 475 Riverside Drive, New York, NY 10115.

REFERENCE: Jonathon Green, *The Encyclopedia of Censorship*, New York, Facts on File, 1990.

MOSAIC THEORY   In 1982, President Ronald Reagan's Executive Order 12356, "National Security Information," introduced the notion of "mosaic theory," also known as "compilation" or "aggregate" theory, to justify the national security classification of information "either by itself or in the context of other information." This dubious theory claimed that harmless information could become dangerous, hence classifiable, if viewed in a particular context. In his 1984 directive NSDD-145, Reagan expanded upon his executive order by likening intelligence data to a mosaic, saying that innocuous bits of unclassified information "can reveal highly classified and other sensitive material when taken in the aggregate."

A 1986 Air Force report, *The Exploitation of Western Data Bases*, followed with the claim that "individual elements of non-sensitive scientific and technical information may, when combined with other non-sensitive information yield MCT [militarily critical technology]." The report even claimed that "nonsensitive" information could be aggregated to create "sensitive" information that could itself be aggregated to produce classified information. By this convoluted chain of reasoning, information twice removed from any level of classification could be declared secret.

The mosaic theory is directed at information that might in the future be created from existing unclassified information. Government officials appear to believe that it is possible to define this nonexistent body of information and limit public access to it. Unfortunately, even the more liberal executive order issued by President Clinton in 1995 retained the following explicit support for the mosaic theory:

Compilations of items of information which are individually unclassified may be classified if the compiled information reveals an additional association or relationship that:

1) meets the standards for classification under this order; and

2) is not otherwise revealed in the individual items of information. As used in this order, "compilation" means an aggregation of pre-existing unclassified items of information.

REFERENCE: Herbert N. Foerstel, *Secret Science: Federal Control of American Science and Technology*, Westport, Praeger, 1993.

MOTION PICTURES   Since the creation of motion pictures, there have been persistent attempts to censor or control their content. One of the earliest organized systems of control appeared in New York in 1909 when a voluntary citizens' committee was formed under the name of the National Board of Censorship, later called the National Board of Review. Despite its name, the Board was local, not national, in its authority. It reviewed the films to be shown in New York City and condemned those it considered unfit for public display. Local officials and the film industry were free to accept or reject its judgments.

In other states, binding controls or prohibitions were soon imposed. In 1911, Pennsylvania enacted a movie-censorship law, and Ohio and Kansas passed similar laws two years later. In 1916, a New York State censorship bill was passed, and only a veto by the governor prevented its implementation.

In 1918, the National Association of the Motion Picture Industry voted for self-censorship, adopting a code of standards which specified subjects and situations unacceptable for motion pictures. Among these were illicit love affairs, nakedness, and exotic dances. In 1922, an organization called the Motion Picture Producers and Distributors of America, later called the Motion Picture Association, was created to oversee the application of the code. Headed by President Harding's Postmaster General, Will H. Hays, the organization represented 80 percent of all producers, but its initial control over motion-picture content was ineffectual.

In 1930, the Hays Office, as it was called, introduced a new and more formal Motion Picture Code that included prohibitions on the presentations of illegal drug traffic, the use of liquor (except as required by the plot), miscegenation, white slavery, and profane or vulgar expression such as "hell," "damn," "Gawd," and "S.O.B." The Production Code Administrator had the authority to fine those members of the Motion Picture Association who violated the code's provisions, but it soon became clear that those movies that challenged the code's standards were inevitable box-office hits. As a result, states and counties began to create their own local censorship boards.

In 1934, the Roman Catholic Legion of Decency was formed, offering national support for the Hays Office code. "Humanly speaking," said Will Hays, "it was the moral force of the Catholic Church that gave the *coup de grace* to Code-breakers. And it was the concrete program of the Legion of Decency, quickly taken up by other groups, that spearheaded the public demand for Code enforcement." The Legion adopted a pledge that read: "I condemn indecent and immoral motion pictures, and those which glorify crime and criminals. I promise to do all that I can to strengthen public opinion against the production of indecent and immoral films, and to unite with all who protest against them. I acknowledge my obligation to form a right conscience about pictures that are dangerous to my moral life. As a member of the Legion of Decency, I pledge myself to remain away from them. I promise, further, to stay away altogether from places of amusement which show them as a matter of policy" (Avery Robert Dulles, *The Legion of Decency*, New York, America Press, 1956).

The Legion also developed its own rating system, using four categories: A-1, morally unobjectionable for general patronage; A-2, morally unobjectionable for adults; B, morally objectionable in part for all; and C, condemned. A fifth category, seldom used, was for films that were not morally offensive, but required the Legion's explanation to protect the uninformed against drawing false conclusions. The movie *Martin Luther* received this rating.

As the power of the Legion grew, an effective system of cooperation emerged among movie producers, the Code Administration, and the Legion. Because almost all theaters had been owned by the producers, only their films were widely shown, and the tight relationship between the producers, the Code Administration, and the Legion ensured a well-controlled content. Often, the Legion's objections to movies resulted in prerelease alteration of the film. Then, in 1950, this censorship system was shaken by a Supreme Court ruling that the ownership of theaters by motion-picture producers was a violation of antitrust laws. Almost overnight, the Supreme Court decision produced a rash of independent theaters that felt free to show films by any producer, with or without the approval of the Code Administration or the Legion. Films like *The Moon Is Blue*, *I Am a Camera*, and *The Man with the Golden Arm*, all of which were denied the code's seal of approval, were shown widely and were well received by the public.

In 1952, another court decision undercut the system of film censorship. The Italian film *The Miracle* was attacked by the Catholic church and banned in New York City and New York State. When the bans were challenged in court, the case went to the Supreme Court as *Joseph Burstyn, Inc. v. Wilson*, in which the Court ruled that motion pictures were under the protection of the guarantees of freedom of the press. In particular, the Court ruled that a movie cannot be banned on the charge of sacrilege, and the ban on *The Miracle* was lifted.

State courts also began to question local film-censorship laws. Courts in Kansas and Pennsylvania declared their motion-picture–censorship laws unconstitutional, and in Massachusetts, the courts overruled a law that prevented the showing of films on Sunday. The Massachusetts Supreme Court ruled that the law, which allowed the mayor to deny a license to show a film that was not in keeping with the character of the day, constituted a prior restraint on the freedoms and rights of the distributor, in violation of the First and Fourteenth Amendments.

When Geoff Shurlock was appointed director of the Production Code Administration in 1954, Hollywood producers considered him a godsend. Shurlock believed that unless the association dealt more flexibly with motion-picture producers, the code would soon be discarded as an irrelevancy. Shurlock oversaw a 1954 amendment to the code that removed taboos on miscegenation, liquor, and some profane words, but independent producers said that it was not enough.

Several movie producers, led by Samuel Goldwyn, began to demand that the Motion Picture Code be revised. One author of the code responded that this would be "tantamount to calling for a revision of the Ten Commandments." Nevertheless, a new code was published in December 1956. It began by stating three principles:

1. No picture shall be produced which will lower the moral standards of those who see it. Hence the sympathy of the audience shall never be thrown to the side of crime, wrong-doing, evil, or sin.
2. Correct standards of life, subject only to the requirements of drama and entertainment, shall be presented.
3. Law—divine, natural, or human—shall not be ridiculed, nor shall sympathy be created for its violation.

The new code removed all remaining taboos except nudity, sexual perversion, and venereal disease. Subjects like drug addiction, prostitution, and childbirth could now be treated "within the careful limits of good taste," but prohibitions were added on blasphemy, mercy killing, double entendre, physical violence, and insults to races, religions, and nationalities. Even the mention of the word "abortion" was specifically forbidden, as was any "inference" of sexual perversion. Ministers of religion were never to be portrayed as comic characters or villains, because "the attitude taken toward them may easily become the attitude taken toward religion in general."

The American Civil Liberties Union described the new code as more harsh than the old one, noting that classics like Dostoyevski's *Crime and Punishment*, Mozart's *Don Giovanni*, and Euripides' *Bacchae* would be barred from motion-picture theaters. Many film companies created subsidiaries as a way to avoid the code. Subsidiaries were exempt from the rules imposed on companies within the Motion Picture Association, and studios used them to distribute pictures that could not acquire the seal. In addition, most foreign-film importers bypassed the Production Code Administration.

Even the Legion of Decency seemed to be softening. Father Patrick Sullivan, the new executive secretary of the Legion, rejected the idea that "the Catholic conscience" should be used to control Hollywood production, and the Legion soon offered a revised and wholly voluntary pledge for its parishioners: "I promise to promote by word and deed what is morally and artistically good in motion picture entertainment. I promise to discourage indecent, immoral and unwholesome motion pictures, especially by my good example and always in a responsible and civic-minded manner" (Leonard J. Leff, *The Dame in the Kimono*, New York, Grove Weidenfeld, 1990, p. 233).

In the 1959 *Lady Chatterley's Lover* case (*Kingsley International Pictures Corp. v. The University of the State of New York*), the Supreme Court found a section of the New York censorship law unconstitutional. The Court ruled that the law prevented the exhibition of a movie simply because it advocated an idea, namely, that adultery under certain circumstances may be proper behavior. "[T]he First Amendment's basic guarantee is of freedom to advocate ideas," said the Court. "The State, quite simply, has thus struck at the heart of constitutionally protected liberty."

In 1968, the Supreme Court ruled on two cases affecting film censorship. In *Ginsberg v. New York*, the Court affirmed the government's right to protect minors from sexually graphic materials. However, in *Interstate Circuit v. Dallas*, the Court found a municipal censorship ordinance too vague to enforce. The conclusion drawn from this pair of cases was that if state laws were carefully crafted, they could be used to prevent minors from attending certain movies. Jack Valenti, president of the Motion Picture Associaton of America (MPAA), quickly convinced board members to adopt a classification system for movies. Many believed that Valenti's prompt response preempted state legislation that would have imposed heavy-handed classification.

The new ratings system began on November 1, 1968, and the men who had once enforced the Production Code now assumed responsibility for the Code and Rating Administration. The ratings were nominally voluntary, with relatively flexible guidelines. The G rating was for general audiences of all ages. The M rating was for adults and mature young people. (Within a few years the M rating was changed to PG, meaning parental guidance.) Movies rated as R were not to be viewed by persons under sixteen years of age unless they were accompanied by a parent or adult. The X rating meant that under no circumstances was a person under sixteen to be admitted to the theater. Such pictures were denied a seal.

Directors frequently found themselves carefully walking the thin line between R and X or PG and R. Aaron Stern, director of the Code and Rating Administration, told movie producers that they were allowed to show love scenes, "but as soon as you start to unbutton or unzip you must cut. Afterward, you can show the two in bed, clothed. Anything else and you are going out of the GP rating."

In 1974, Valenti replaced Stern with Richard Heffner, under whom the Code and Rating Administration was renamed the Classification and Rating Administration, signalling a loosening of restrictions. In the 1980s, Valenti created a new rating, PG-13, that was to be somewhere between PG and R. Still, there were frequent charges from the film industry that the need to produce films to fit a given rating was tantamount to censorship. In 1990, New York Supreme Court Justice Charles Ramos wrote an opinion describing the rating system as "censorship from within the industry rather than imposed from without, but censorship nonetheless." Justice Ramos concluded, "The rating of X is a stigma that relegates the film to limited advertising, distribution and income" (Robert Radnitz, "It's Time to Elimi-nate the Present Movie Rating System," *Los Angeles Times*, July 23, 1990, p. F5).

In 1990, the MPAA responded to its critics by replacing the X rating with a new NC-17 rating. In reality, the change was in name only, but it was intended to remove the taint of X. Among other things, the advertising ban on X-rated films imposed by major newspapers and television stations was to be lifted for NC-17 films. As it turned out, some video-rental companies refused to buy NC-17 movies, and some theater chains refused to show them.

There remain many critics of the current rating system. The ACLU calls it "arbitrary MPAA censorship," but the current chairman of the Ratings Administration board, Richard Mosk, insists that it is far more desirable than government-controlled censor boards. Mosk also defends the MPAA's long-standing policy of keeping the names of all ratings board members secret, claiming that an anonymous board enhances the integrity of the system. Critics continue to complain of secrecy and censorship.

REFERENCES: Leonard J. Leff, *The Dame in the Kimono: Hollywood, Censorship, and the Production Code from the 1920s to the 1960s*, New York, Grove and Weidenfeld, 1990; Frank Walsh, *Sin and Censorship: The Catholic Church and the Motion Picture Industry*, New Haven, Yale University Press, 1996.

NATIONAL CAMPAIGN FOR FREEDOM OF EXPRESSION   The National Campaign for Freedom of Expression (NCFE) is an education and advocacy network of artists, arts organizations, and the public founded to fight censorship and to protect and extend the First Amendment right to freedom of artistic expression. NCFE was formed in 1990 to empower artists and activists in the arts community to respond to attacks from right-wing political and religious groups. It initially mobilized in response to the controversies over artists Andres Serrano and Robert Mapplethorpe and the politically motivated denial of grants by the National Endowment for the Arts. It publishes an eight–page quarterly *Bulletin* and also communicates via a national computer information network, *ArtsWire*. It produces regional Free Expression Forums and provides speakers for conferences, lectures, debates, and symposia. It has also become a respected source of information and advocacy within the media, offering status reports on free expression to print, radio, and television reporters and providing training in media advocacy and political organizing to community activists.

In 1991, NCFE formed and now coordinates the Free Expression Network, a group of over forty national organizations that conducts congressional briefings and quarterly strategy meetings. It also offers pro bono legal counsel and support to artists and organizations in censorship cases, monitors legislation, and advises its constituency on how to lobby elected officials. NCFE maintains offices in Washington, D.C., and Seattle, Washington. David C. Mendoza serves as executive director.

REFERENCE: *Encyclopedia of Associations*, 31st ed., Detroit, Gale Research Co., 1996.

NATIONAL COALITION AGAINST CENSORSHIP The National Coalition against Censorship (NCAC), a federation of nonprofit public interest and professional organizations, including the Association of American Publishers, the American Library Association, the American Association of University Professors, the Authors League of America, and the American Civil Liberties Union, was organized to promote freedom of expression and to combat all forms of censorship. To this end, it conducts educational activities such as public meetings on the First Amendment, posts lists of banned books in bookstores, recruits authors of banned books to speak to community groups, supports lawsuits against book banning, and offers anticensorship films to television stations.

NCAC maintains a legal information center, the National Information Clearinghouse on Bookbanning Litigation in Public Schools, which provides censorship information to attorneys, the media, and organizations. It also encourages the involvement of other national organizations in cases, coordinates amicus briefs, and maintains an extensive library on First Amendment topics. NCAC publishes *Censorship News*, a quarterly journal which examines censorship cases in schools and libraries and current issues such as textbook censorship, creationism, and open access to information. NCAC's executive director is Leanne Katz. The organization is located at 2 West 64th Street, New York, NY 10023.

REFERENCES: National Coalition against Censorship, *The Meese Commission Exposed: Proceedings of a National Coalition against Censorship Public Briefing*, 1987; National Coalition against Censorship, *The Sex Panic: Women, Censorship and Pornography: A National Coalition against Censorship Conference Report*, 1993.

NATIONAL COMMITTEE AGAINST REPRESSIVE LEGISLATION The National Committee against Repressive Legislation (NCARL) was founded in 1969 with the initial goal of disbanding the House Un-American Activities Committee. Since then, it has worked to promote the First Amendment and oppose repressive laws and inquisitorial government activities, especially government surveillance. NCARL aims to reform federal criminal laws and control federal intelligence-gathering agencies. Toward this end, it has circulated petitions demanding that the FBI cease its violations of the First Amendment.

Publications by NCARL include *The Right to Know and Freedom to Act*, a bimonthly publication presenting articles on the protection of First Amendment rights, with particular emphasis on violations by the FBI and CIA. NCARL also produces *FBI Petition News*, which reports on the success of its petition drives. NCARL is located at 1313 West 8th Street, Suite 313, Los Angeles, CA 90017. Its chair is Ruth Calvin Emerson.

REFERENCE:Richard L. Criley, *The FBI v. the First Amendment*, Los Angeles, First Amendment Foundation, 1990.

NATIONAL SECURITY ARCHIVE The National Security Archive is a nonprofit research institute on international affairs that includes a library and archive of declassified U.S. documents obtained through the Freedom of Information Act (FOIA), a public interest law firm defending and expanding public access to government information through the FOIA, and an indexing and publishing house. It was founded in 1985 by a group of journalists and scholars, led by Scott Armstrong, who had obtained documentation from the U.S. government under the FOIA and sought a centralized repository for these materials. The archive has subsequently become the world's largest nongovernmental library of declassified documents. Currently located within the George Washington University's Gelman Library in Washington, D.C., the archive is designed to apply the latest in computer indexing technology to the massive amount of material already released by the U.S. government on international affairs, make the material accessible to researchers and the public, and build comprehensive collections of documents on topics of greatest interest to scholars and the public.

The archive's mainframe computer system hosts major databases of released documents, authority files of individuals and organizations in international affairs, and FOIA requests filed by archive staff members and outside requesters. The archive reading room is open to the public without charge and has welcomed visitors from across the United States and around the world. Archive staff are frequently called on to testify before Congress, lecture at universities, and appear on national broadcasts and media interviews on the subject of FOIA, free access to government information, and international affairs generally. The archive has published a sizable number of important scholarly works, including *El Salvador: The Making of U.S. Policy*, *The Iran-Contra Affair: The Making of a Scandal*, *The Cuban Missile Crisis*, *Presidential Directives on National Security from Truman to Clinton*, and *White House E-Mail*.

In the process of developing its extensive collections and publications, the archive has become the leading nonprofit user of the FOIA, inheriting more than two thousand requests from outside scholars who donated their documents and pending requests to the archive and initiating more than ten thousand other FOIA requests over the past decade. The archive's work has set new precedents under the FOIA, including more efficient procedures for document processing at the State Department, less burden on requesters to qualify for fee waivers, and the archival preservation of electronic information held by the government. This expertise in the use of the FOIA, as well as in archival and library practices, has brought delegations from countries around the world to learn from the archive's innovative model of nongovernmental institutional memory for formerly secret government documents. Thomas S. Blanton is the current executive director of the National Security Archive.

REFERENCES: National Security Council, *Presidential Directives on National Security from Truman to Clinton*, Alexandria, Chadwyck-Healey; Washington, National

Security Archive, 1994; Frankie Pelzman, "The National Security Archive: Keeping the Government Honest," *Wilson Library Bulletin*, May 1990, pp. 31–36.

NATIONAL SECURITY DECISION DIRECTIVES National security decision directives (NSDDs) are sometimes termed "secret laws." The Congressional Research Service has described them as "secret policy instruments, maintained in a security classification status," and it has warned, "National Security Decision Directives clearly pose a problem for a free and open society and bring the U.S. and all of us very close to one of the most dangerous condition[s] of authoritarian or totalitarian government, rule by secret law." A 1987 congressional analysis of NSDDs concluded, "Operational activities undertaken beyond the purview of the Congress foster a grave risk of the creation of an unaccountable shadow government—a development that would be inconsistent with the principles underlying our republic" (U.S. House of Representatives, *Computer Security Act of 1987: Report*, 100th Cong., 1st sess., Rpt. 100-153, pt. 2. pp. 31–32).

NSDDs have been issued through the National Security Council (NSC) by each President since Truman, but they do not appear in any register, even in unclassified form, since the NSC claims that even a list of the titles of NSDDs would be classified. They have no prescribed format or implementing procedures and are not revealed to Congress or the public except under arbitrary or accidental circumstances. Not even congressional intelligence committees have been allowed to review most NSDDs, nor are they told how many have been issued or what subjects they cover. President Ronald Reagan alone signed about three hundred NSDDs, though Congress and the public remain ignorant of most of them. President George Bush maintained total secrecy over all of his NSDDs.

REFERENCE: Christopher Simpson, *National Security Directives of the Reagan and Bush Administrations: the Declassified History of U.S. Political and Military Policy, 1981–1991*, Boulder, Westview Press, 1995.

NATIONAL SECURITY INFORMATION The U.S. government claims and exercises the right to restrict access to information concerning the nation's defense or its foreign relations, that is, military and diplomatic information. This "national security information" is kept from unauthorized personnel, including most American citizens, through a system of classification justified by the need to deny such information to foreign governments regarded as military or economic adversaries. National security information consists primarily of military operations, weapons technology, diplomatic and intelligence activities, and cryptology. The authority for the executive branch to keep such information secret from U.S. citizens has been assumed by most Presidents to be implicit in their executive responsibilities, which include the national defense and foreign relations. This authority has been upheld by Congress and by judicial decisions, including Supreme Court cases, which have also implicitly recognized the President's authority to classify information. Atomic secrets are controlled through the authorization of the Atomic Energy Act of 1954, as amended, but the classification of all other information is conducted under the authority of presidential executive orders.

Some form of governmental control of information has existed in the United States since the Continental Congress (1774–89), whose proceedings were kept secret. The Second Continental Congress established a Secret Committee and a Committee of Secret Correspondence (later known as the Committee for Foreign Affairs) to deal with the purchase of war materials and correspondence with friendly nations. The only mention of secrecy in the Constitution is in Article I, Section 5, which requires the House and Senate to publish their proceedings, "excepting such Parts as may in their Judgment require Secrecy." The Constitutional Convention provided for presidential secrecy in national security affairs, and Presidents since then have used their implied constitutional authority to control access to such information.

President George Washington designated some documents as secret or confidential as early as 1790, and broader governmental use of the terms "secret," "confidential," and "private" date back to the War of 1812. Still, despite the implied authority for executive secrecy, no official secrecy system had been created by the time of the Civil War. However, the Civil War saw the first significant use of government secrecy to protect military technology. In 1869, the Army issued an order restricting the availability of information on forts, the first peacetime governmental directive protecting national security information. In 1897, just prior to the Spanish-American War, the 1869 restrictions were expanded in scope, and the following year Congress enacted a statute establishing a penalty for violating any War Department regulations concerning forts or harbor-defense systems.

In 1911, Congress enacted the Defense Secrets Act, which imposed penalties on anyone who attempted to obtain information respecting the national defense without proper authorization. In 1912, the War Department provided regulations for marking certain documents as "confidential." Such documents were to be kept under lock, numbered and inventoried, and copied only by the issuing office. After the 1917 entry of the United States into World War I, the War Department adopted regulations establishing three classifications limiting access to documents. "Secret" limited the use or sight of a document to a confidential clerk; "confidential" restricted the document for use and knowledge to a necessary minimum number of persons; "for official use only" indicated that the document was not intended for the public or the press.

The Espionage Act of 1917 expanded the restrictions on access to national defense information beyond what was specified in the Defense Secrets Act of 1911. Like the 1911 act, it presumed the existence of national defense information, but provided few specifics on it. The Trading with the Enemy Act (1917) allowed the President to designate as secret any patents whose publication might assist the enemy or endanger the prosecution of the war. In 1921, Army regulations introduced a significant change in classifying documents, focusing on the contents of the documents rather than who was allowed to see them. "Secret" was to be applied to information "of great importance" whose protection was "of prime necessity." "Confidential" was to be applied to information "of less importance and of less secret nature."

In 1936, the Army adopted "secret," "confidential," and "restricted" as its three levels of classification, dropping the category "for official use only." New definitions for these terms broadened classifiable information to include nondefense information and implied the inclusion of foreign policy within the areas of control.

From World War II to date, virtually all U.S. government classification has been conducted under the authority of presidential executive orders (EOs). The first of these was Executive Order 8381, "Defining Certain Vital Military Naval Installations and Equipment," issued on March 22, 1940, by President Franklin Roosevelt. The Roosevelt order adopted the three classification levels then used by the military, secret, confidential, and restricted, and in September 1942, after the U.S. entry into World War II, the Office of War Information redefined those categories. "Secret" was applied to information whose disclosure "might endanger national security" or cause "serious injury to the Nation or any governmental activity." "Confidential" was applied to information whose disclosure would compromise the effectiveness of governmental activity in the prosecution of the war. "Restricted" was applied to information whose disclosure would compromise "administrative privacy." The classification system promulgated in EO 8381 was the first in American history to control information outside the military and defense areas.

On February 1, 1950, President Harry S. Truman issued EO 10104, "Defining Certain Vital Military and Naval Installations and Equipment as Requiring Protection against the General Dissemination of Information Relative Thereto." This new EO on classification was based on a 1938 defense-installation statute. The three classification levels used in the previous EO were maintained, but a fourth level, "top secret," was added.

On September 24, 1951, President Truman replaced his EO 10104 with EO 10290, "Regulations Establishing Minimum Standards for the Classification, Transmission, and Handling, by Departments and Agencies of the Executive Branch, of Official Information Which Requires Safeguarding in the Interest of the Security of the United States." In his new EO, President Truman cited no specific statutory authority other than "the authority vested in me by the Constitution and statutes, and as President of the United States." Classified information, referred to as "security information," was to be designated as either top secret, secret, confidential, or restricted. The top secret level was assigned to information whose disclosure "would or could cause exceptionally grave damage to the national security." The secret marking was assigned to information that required "extraordinary protection in the interest of national security." Confidential information would require "careful protection to prevent disclosures which might harm national security." Restricted information required "protection against unauthorized use or disclosure."

The most significant change introduced by EO 10290 was the imposition of the classification system on nonmilitary federal agencies. Until the promulgation of this order, classification was used almost exclusively for the protection of defense information. The new EO did provide for downgrading and declassification, both automatic and nonautomatic, as well as regular classification review. In an attempt to avoid excessive classification, EO 10290 stated that "security information shall be assigned its lowest security classification consistent with its proper protection."

In November 1953, President Dwight Eisenhower issued EO 10501, "Safeguarding Official Information in the Interests of the Defense of the United States." Like Truman's order before it, EO 10501 cited "the authority vested in me by the Constitution and statutes, and as President of the United States." The new EO eliminated the "restricted" classification level, specifying only "top secret," "secret," and "confidential," the three levels maintained by all EOs since then. In EO 10501, top secret was to be applied to "information or material the defense aspect of which is paramount, and the unauthorized disclosure of which could result in exceptionally grave damage to the Nation." The secret classification applied to "defense information or material the unauthorized disclosure of which could result in serious damage to the Nation." The confidential level was assigned to information whose disclosure "could be prejudicial to the defense interests of the Nation."

President Eisenhower's EO remained in effect for almost twenty years, although subsequent orders amended agency classification authority and declassification procedures. For example, President John Kennedy's EO 10964 identified classification groups to be downgraded at twelve-year intervals, downgraded at three-year intervals, or declassified altogether after twelve years.

On March 8, 1972, President Richard Nixon issued EO 11652, "Classification and Declassification of National Security Information." The authority cited was simply "the Constitution and Statutes of the United States," and subsequent EOs have cited the same authority. Under EO 11652, the decision to classify material as top secret was to be based on "whether its unauthorized disclosure could reasonably be expected to cause exceptionally grave damage to the national security." "Secret" information and "confidential" information were similarly defined in terms of whether their disclosure could "reasonably" be expected to cause "serious damage" or "damage" to the national security.

Nixon's order included a caution against inappropriate classification: "In no case shall information be classified in order to conceal inefficiency or administrative error, to prevent embarrassment to a person or department, to restrain competition or independent initiative, or to prevent for any other reason the release of information which does not require protection in the interest of national security." EO 11652 also included a "General Declassification Schedule" that provided for downgrading classified documents from top secret to secret and secret to confidential at two–year intervals. Confidential documents were to be fully declassified at a six–year interval. Documents could be exempted from these schedules, but if exempted material was requested, it would undergo a classification review after ten years had elapsed from its date of origin. Automatic declassification was specified for information or materials thirty years old or more unless they had been exempted.

President Jimmy Carter's EO 12065, "National Security Information," replaced the Nixon order on December 1, 1978, and set a new tone for the nation's secrecy system. The Carter order began by stating the need "to balance the public's interest in access to Government information with the need to protect certain national security information from disclosure." The Carter order retained the previous order's definitions of top secret and secret, but changed the criterion for confidential from "damage" to "identifiable damage" to national security. More important, it advised that if there was doubt about the level of classification to be assigned to a document, "the less restrictive designation should be used, or the information should not be classified."

The Carter order identified seven areas of information that were appropriate for classification: military plans, weapons, or operations; foreign government information; intelligence activities, sources, or methods; foreign relations or foreign activities of the United States; scientific, technological, or economic matters relating to the national security; U.S. government programs for safeguarding nuclear materials or facilities; or "other" categories determined by the President, a designee, or an agency head.

The Carter order specifically prohibited the classification of basic scientific research information not clearly related to national security. It also stated, "Classification may not be restored to documents already declassified and released to the public under this Order or prior Orders." In addition, EO 12065 stressed that declassification "shall be given emphasis comparable to that accorded classification."

President Ronald Reagan's EO 12356, "National Security Information," effective August 1, 1982, dramatically reversed the emphasis and tone of the Carter order. The definitions for top secret and secret remained unchanged, but the definition of confidential now required only "damage" rather than "identifiable damage" to the national security. More significant, the general guidelines for classification were changed to read: "If there is reasonable doubt about the need to classify information, it shall be safeguarded as if it were classified. . . . If there is reasonable doubt about the appropriate level of classification, it shall be safeguarded at the higher level of classification." Executive Order 12356 added three new categories of classifiable information: the vulnerabilities or capabilities of systems, installations, projects, or plans relating to the national security; cryptology; and confidential sources.

The Reagan order was also conspicuous for what it omitted. Notably absent was the statement in the Carter order that declassification would be given emphasis comparable to that accorded classification. Nor did EO 12356 include explicit statements on balancing the public's right to information access against the government's national security interests, as did EO 12065. The Carter order had also stated that "references to classified documents that do not disclose classified information may not be classified or used as a basis for classification." That statement was notably absent from EO 12356.

None of the declassification schedules promulgated in previous EOs were present in EO 12356, which simply stated, "Information shall be classified as long as required by national security considerations." In addition, the Reagan order stated that classified information "shall not be declassified automatically as a result of any unofficial publication or unauthorized disclosure in the United States or abroad of identical or similar information." Indeed, in contradiction to the Carter order, EO 12356 authorized the reclassification of information previously declassified and publicly disclosed if it was determined that the information required protection and "may be reasonably recovered."

The Reagan order significantly expanded the group of persons subject to sanctions for unauthorized disclosure of information to include government contractors, licensees, and grantees, not just government officers and employees. The order did contain a statement similar to the one in Nixon's order prohibiting the classification of information to conceal violations of law, inefficiency, or administrative error. It also repeated the statement from Carter's EO that basic scientific information not related to the national security should not be classified.

Executive Order 12356 found imaginative ways to extend the range of traditionally classified information. For example, it introduced the "mosaic theory," which justified the classification of information "either by itself or in the context of other information." Another innovative form of secrecy introduced by EO 12356 was the category of special access programs (SAPs), which imposed information controls beyond the level of Top Secret.

When President Bill Clinton came to the White House, there was hope for a loosening of Reagan's tight controls on government information. In April 1993, President Clinton issued Presidential Review Directive 29, calling for a reevaluation of the security- classification system and preparation of a new executive order that would address "the reality of the current, rather than the past, threat potential." The preliminary draft, dated August 31, 1993, recommended the elimination of the "confidential" level of classification and specified a maximum period of forty years during which documents might remain classified. The draft order also recommended that new "secret" documents be declassified within ten years and "top secret" documents within fifteen years.

A second draft of the Clinton order, dated November 10, 1993, reinstated the "confidential" level of classification but ordered steps to avoid excessive classification, to declassify information as quickly as possible, and to reduce the number of "special access programs." A third draft order in March 1994 embodied even more openness, but its recommendation that documents be automatically declassified within twenty-five years of their original classification aroused protests from the CIA.

Finally, on April 17, 1995, President Clinton issued EO 12958, "Classified National Security Information," which said in its introduction: "Protecting information critical to our Nation's security remains a priority. In recent years, however, dramatic changes have altered, although not eliminated, the national security threat that we confront. These changes provide a greater opportunity to emphasize our commitment to open Government."

Prominent among the provisions increasing access to government information was a ten-year limit on how long newly classified documents could remain classified unless it was determined that the release of the information could reasonably be expected to

1. reveal an intelligence source, method, or activity, or a cryptologic system or activity;
2. reveal information that would assist in the development or use of weapons of mass destruction;
3. reveal information that would impair the development or use of technology within a United States weapon system;
4. reveal United States military plans or national security emergency preparedness plans;
5. reveal foreign government information;
6. damage relations between the United States and a foreign government, reveal a confidential source, or seriously undermine diplomatic activities that were reasonably expected to be ongoing for a period greater than ten years;
7. impair the ability of United States government officials to protect the President, the Vice President, and other individuals for whom protection services, in the interest of national security, were authorized; or
8. violate a statute, treaty, or international agreement.

The other important provision in the Clinton order was the requirement that already-classified documents twenty-five years old or older be automatically declassified unless they fell within exemptions similar to those specified for newly classified material. Agencies were to be given until the year 2000 to find and set aside sensitive information that would still have to undergo the regular declassification review process, but everything else twenty-five years old or more would be automatically declassified.

The Clinton order retained the three classification categories (confidential, secret, and top secret) and their definitions from the Reagan executive order, but it required classifiers to justify what they classified and encouraged employees to challenge improper classification without fear of retribution. It established an appeals panel to hear challenges to classification and specified sanctions for overclassification.

REFERENCE: Arvin S. Quist, *Security Classification of Information*, Martin Marietta Technical Report K/CG-1077, 1989.

NONDISCLOSURE AGREEMENTS The federal government and some of its agencies have imposed nondisclosure, prepublication, and secrecy agreements on employees, preventing them from publishing or otherwise communicating on a wide variety of subjects. The Central Intelligence Agency (CIA) requires all employees to sign a prepublication agreement saying that they will not publish any information relating to the CIA's activities, or to intelligence activities generally, either during or after their term of employment without specific prior approval by the agency. In *Snepp v. United States* (1980) and *McGehee v. Casey* (1983), the Supreme Court ruled that the CIA's nondisclosure agreements did not represent an unconstitutional prior restraint.

The CIA also requires all employees to sign the following secrecy agreement:

I do solemnly swear that I will never divulge, publish or reveal either by word, conduct, or by any other means, any classified information, intelligence or knowledge except in the performance of my official duties and in accordance with the laws of the United States, unless specifically authorized in writing, in each case, by the Director of the Central Intelligence Agency or his authorized representatives.

Similarly, upon leaving the CIA, employees are required to solemnly swear:

I will never divulge, publish, or reveal by writing, word, conduct, or otherwise, any information relating to the national defense and security and particularly information of this nature relating to intelligence sources, methods and operations, and specifically Central Intelligence Agency operations, sources, methods, personnel, fiscal data, or security measures to anyone including but not limited to, any future governmental or private employer, private citizen, or other Government employee or official without the express written consent of the Director of Central Intelligence or his authorized representative. (Leon Hurwitz, *Historical Dictionary of Censorship in the United States*, Westport, Greenwood Press, 1985, pp. 48–49)

In *United States v. Marchetti* (1972) and *McGehee v. Casey* (1983), the Supreme Court ruled that these oaths did not violate the First Amendment.

Perhaps less well known than the CIA's nondisclosure agreements are broader restrictions imposed by national security decision directives (NSDDs). NSDD-84, issued by President Ronald Reagan in 1983, required that all government employees with access to sensitive compartmented information (SCI) submit to lifelong censorship of their publications and even their public speech. NSDD-84 provided for an SCI nondisclosure agreement and imposed restrictions on media contacts by government employees who had access to any classified information. The nondisclosure form required government employees to submit for security review "all materials, including works of fiction," that might relate to SCI, with such restraints to apply during the course of the employees' access to SCI "and at all times thereafter." All royalties or remunerations that result from any disclosure, publication, or revelation not consistent with the terms of the agreement are assigned to the U.S. government, and breach of the agreement may result in termination of security clearance or of employment, as well as criminal prosecution. Congress expressed its dismay at the heavy-handed restrictions of NSDD-84 when a group of Republican congressmen issued a report stating that (1) there was no serious problem of former government employees divulging SCI; (2) no compelling overriding governmental need for prior restraint had been established; and (3) the few instances of unauthorized disclosure did not justify the imposition of a lifelong censorship system.

In 1985, President Reagan issued NSDD-196, which like NSDD-84 was aimed at government employees with access to SCI, but here the restrictions, including prepublication review, extended all the way to cabinet officials. Secretary of State George Shultz angrily denounced NSDD-196, proclaiming, "The minute in this government that I am told that I am not trusted is the day that I leave." United Nations Ambassador Jeane Kirkpatrick refused to sign the prepublication agreement, claiming that "it binds you not to write, not even from unclassified material that may have come to you in the course of your work in the State Department. It is an extraordinary document. You could never write after signing it" (Stephen D. Katz, *Government Secrecy: Decisions without Democracy*, Washington, People the American Way, 1987, p.28).

The agent of NSDD-196's broad controls on expression was Standard Form 189, which pledged almost four million government employees not to disclose "classifiable" information. Federal employee unions challenged the constitutionality of SF 189, claiming that no one knew what "classifiable" information was. One plaintiff stated, "My interpretation was that if at any time I were to write or speak something that displeased the government, they would have the opportunity to declare the information classified and charge me with violating the agreement" (*Classified Information Nondisclosure Agreements*, Hearings before the Subcommittee on Post Office and Civil Service, House of Representatives, 100th Cong. 1st sess., October 15, 1987, p.8). In response to the suit, the government issued Standard Form 312, replacing the term "classifiable information" with the equally vague term "classified information marked and unmarked."

Traditionally, the President has claimed that executive agencies have the authority to impose nondisclosure agreements even when they conflict with existing law. In 1990, for the first time, a President failed to challenge the wording of an appropriations bill that affirmed the primacy of existing law over nondisclosure agreements. As a result of the new bill, before agencies may receive funding to implement or enforce nondisclosure agreements, the corresponding forms must be amended to specify that when their secrecy provisions conflict with statutory rights to free expression, these rights will prevail. These new requirements appeared in the October 22, 1990, *Federal Register*, though their practical effect remains untested (Herbert N. Foerstel, *Secret Science*, Westport, Praeger, 1993, pp. 34–37).

REFERENCE: U.S. House of Representatives, Committee on Post Office and Civil Service, Subcommittee on Human Resources, *Classified Information Nondisclosure Agreements: Hearing*, 100th Cong. 1st sess., October 15, 1987.

O

OBSCENITY   Obscenity is a legal term describing written or visual works that may be unprotected speech because they are judged to be immoral or inciting individuals to lust or depravity. The three main tests for obscenity that have been used in American courts are the *Hicklin* standard, the *Roth* standard (and its revision under the *Memoirs* standard), and the currently applied *Miller* standard. Established by the British courts in *Regina v. Hicklin* (1868), the *Hicklin* rule was also applied by U.S. courts until it was overturned in *Roth v. United States* (1957). Under the *Hicklin* rule, "The test of obscenity is whether the tendency of the matter charged as obscenity is to deprave and corrupt those whose minds are open to such immoral influences and into whose hands a publication of this sort may fall." A significant aspect of the *Hicklin* rule was that an entire publication could be ruled obscene even if only a single passage was identified as obscene.

The first major test of obscenity in American courts came in 1934 after James Joyce's *Ulysses*, a classic not widely known to the American public, was banned as obscene. When early installments of the book appeared in a scholarly journal, they were burned by the Post Office. A few years later, when five hundred copies of the full book were imported, they were also burned, and a court ruled that the book could not be published domestically. In 1930, a copy of the book sent to Random House was again seized as obscene, and in 1933, when the Treasury Department held up delivery of a copy to Alexander Lindey, he petitioned to permit *Ulysses* into the country for noncommercial purposes as a classic. The Treasury Department complied, but a subsequent request to remove the restraint on importation of the book for commercial purposes resulted in a widely followed court case, *United States v. One Book Entitled Ulysses* (1934).

In a memorable opinion, U.S. District Court Judge John M. Woolsey said that the literary reputation of *Ulysses* required that he consider the intent of the author. Woolsey wrote: "[I]n any case where a book is claimed to be obscene it must first be determined, whether the intent with which it was written was what is called . . . pornographic—that is, written for the purpose of exploiting obscenity." Woolsey concluded:

[I]n *Ulysses*, in spite of its unusual frankness, I do not detect anywhere the leer of the sensualist. . . . The meaning of the word *obscene* as legally defined by the Courts is: tending to stir the sex impulses or to lead to sexually impure and lustful thoughts.

Whether a particular book would tend to excite such impulses and thoughts must be tested by the Court's opinion as to its effect on a person with average sex instincts. . . . It is only with the normal person that the law is concerned. Such a test as I have described, therefore, is the only proper test of obscenity in the case of a book like *Ulysses*.

Upon Woolsey's judgment, *Ulysses* could now be admitted into the United States. Woolsey's decision was upheld in New York Second Circuit Court of Appeals by Judge Augustus N. Hand, who declared: "While any construction of the statute that will fit all cases is difficult, we believe that the proper test of whether a given book is obscene is its dominant effect. In applying this test, relevancy of the objectionable parts to the theme, the established reputation of the work in the estimation of approved critics, if the book is modern, and the verdict of the past, if it is ancient, are persuasive pieces of evidence; for works of art are not likely to sustain a high position with no better warrant for their existence than their obscene content."

The new standard for obscenity established in the *Ulysses* case was adopted in most federal and state courts, but since it was never reviewed by the Supreme Court, it was not universally accepted as the law of the land. In 1945, the Massachusetts Supreme Judicial Court ignored the *Ulysses* standard in banning Lillian Smith's *Strange Fruit*, a book about a relationship between a white boy and a black girl. Judge Stanley Qua, speaking for the court, rejected the notion that the intent of the author or the admiration of critics were relevant to an obscenity judgment. "In dealing with such a practical matter as the enforcement of the statute here involved," said Qua, "there is no room for the pleasing fancy that sincerity and art necessarily dispel obscenity."

Though the *Hicklin* rule remained the nearest thing to a national standard for judging obscenity, many states rejected it as archaic and extreme. In 1948, after Philadelphia police raided publishers and booksellers to seize a number of prominent books, including William Faulkner's *Sanctuary*, the ensuing court case showed the growing discomfort with the *Hicklin* rule.

In quashing the police department's censorship spree, Judge Curtis Bok said, "The criminal law is not in my opinion the *'custos morum'* of the king's subjects as *Regina v. Hicklin* states: it is only the custodian of the peace and good order that free men and women need for the shaping of their common destiny." Judge Bok went on to say of the *Hicklin* rule: "Strictly applied, this rule renders any book unsafe, since a moron could pervert to some sexual fantasy to which his mind is open the listings of a seed catalogue. Not even the Bible would be exempt" (Robert W. Haney, *Comstockery in America: Patterns of Censorship and Control*, New York, Da Capo Press 1974 [c.1960], pp. 27–30).

Clearly, circumstances were ripe for a revision of the *Hicklin* rule, and in 1957 the Supreme Court did just that. In *Roth v. United States* (1957), the Court examined a federal postal law that imposed fines and imprisonment on anyone who delivered or received any obscene, lewd, lascivious, or filthy book, or any other publication of an indecent character. Samuel Roth, a New York publisher and bookseller, was convicted of violating this federal law by mailing obscene advertising and an obscene book. His conviction was affirmed by the court of appeals and was then appealed to the Supreme Court, where it was considered jointly with the conviction of a California businessman, David Alberts, under a similar statute.

Speaking for the majority, Justice William Brennan upheld the convictions of Roth and Alberts, reiterating the legal tradition that obscenity is not within the area of constitutionally protected speech or press. While providing little insight into why sexual expression should fall outside the First Amendment, the Court did feel the need to examine and evaluate the various tests for obscenity. In an important footnote, the Court added, "A thing is obscene if, considered as a whole, its predominant appeal is to prurient interest, i.e. a shameful or morbid interest in nudity, sex, or excretion, and if it goes substantially beyond customary limits of candor in description or representation of such matters."

The Court was explicit in rejecting the *Hicklin* rule. "The early leading standard of obscenity allowed material to be judged merely by the effect of an isolated excerpt upon particularly susceptible persons. . . . Some American courts adopted this standard but later decisions have rejected it and substituted this test: whether to the average person, applying contemporary community standards, the dominant theme of the material taken as a whole appeals to prurient interest. The *Hicklin* test, judging obscenity by the effect of isolated passages upon the most susceptible persons, might well encompass material legitimately treating with sex, and so it must be rejected as unconstitutionally restrictive of the freedoms of speech and press."

Not all of the members of the Court were comfortable with the new *Roth* standard for judging obscenity. Justice John Marshall Harlan wrote: "The Court seems to assume that 'obscenity' is a peculiar *genus* of 'speech and press,' which is as distinct, recognizable, and classifiable as poison ivy is among other plants. . . . [T]here is a significant distinction between the definitions used in the prosecutions before us, and the American Law Institute formula. If the latter is the correct standard, as my Brother [William] Brennan . . . intimates, then these convictions should surely be reversed. Instead, the Court merely assimilates the various tests into one indiscriminate potpourri."

While the *Roth* and *Alberts* cases seemed to tighten the definition of obscenity, ambiguity remained, and the power of Congress to control the transmission of obscene materials was strengthened by the Court's ruling that the "clear and present danger" test, previously used to evaluate government attempts to suppress speech, need not be applied with respect to obscenity. Indeed, on the same day that the decision in *Roth* and *Alberts* was announced, the Court referred to those judgments in handing down a verdict in *Kingsley Books, Inc. v. Brown* (1957) that approved a prior restraint on the sale of fourteen allegedly obscene books that were subsequently destroyed. In *Kingsley Books*, Justice Felix Frankfurter reiterated the Court's view that the state may constitutionally convict its citizens for selling or displaying obscene materials, but he went further in approving an injunction against sale or distribution of such materials prior to criminal proceedings. Chief Justice Earl Warren dissented: "It is the manner of use that should determine obscenity. . . . To do otherwise is to impose a prior restraint and hence to violate the Constitution. Certainly in the absence of a prior judicial determination of illegal use, books, pictures and other objects of expression should not be destroyed. It savors too much of book burning."

In *A Book Named "John Cleland's Memoirs of a Woman of Pleasure" v. Attorney General of Massachusetts* (1966), the Court revised the *Roth* standard when it ruled that John Cleland's *Fanny Hill* was not obscene. In that decision, the Court defined material to be obscene if it met three requirements: "(1) that the dominant theme of the material as a whole appeals to a prurient interest in sex; (2) that the material is patently offensive because it affronts contemporary community standards relating to the description or representation of sexual matters; (3) that the material is utterly without redeeming social value."

Not until 1973 did the Supreme Court revisit obscenity in two cases that established the current principles of adjudication. The primary case, *Miller v. California* (1973), created the most important precedent and remains the theoretical basis for determining obscenity. *Miller* involved a conviction for mailing unsolicited sexually explicit material, and, as in *Roth*, the Court assumed with little argument that obscenity is unprotected speech. Yet it once more grappled with a definition of obscenity. Chief Justice Warren Burger, speaking for the majority, said that the criteria for identifying obscenity must be (*a*) whether the average person, applying contemporary community standards, would find that the work, taken as a whole, appeals to the prurient interest; (*b*) whether the work depicts or describes, in a patently offensive way, sexual conduct specifically defined by the applicable state law; and (c) whether the work, taken as a whole, lacks serious literary, artistic, political, or scientific value. The *Miller* decision required that obscenity laws impose specific standards and that these be limited to "representations or descriptions of ultimate sex acts, normal or perverted, actual or simulated" or "of masturbation, excretory functions and lewd exhibitions of the genitals."

REFERENCE: Edward DeGrazia, *Girls Lean Back Everywhere: The Law of Obscenity and the Assault on Genius*, London, Constable, 1992.

OFFICE FOR INTELLECTUAL FREEDOM (AMERICAN LIBRARY ASSOCIATION)   The Office for Intellectual Freedom (OIF) is the nation's foremost organization devoted to combatting censorship in schools and libraries. Under the direction of Judith Krug and a staff of six, it documents examples of censorship nationwide, compiling statistics and maintaining a database on censorship incidents. As a service of the American Library Association (ALA), the OIF provides assistance to libraries and librarians in the defense of intellectual freedom. It promotes the unrestricted use of library materials through a national program of public education, including publications, workshops, and lectures. It works closely with the ALA's Intellectual Freedom Committee to develop that organization's policies, and it also coordinates activities with the Freedom to Read Foundation and the ALA's Intellectual Freedom Roundtable interest group.

The OIF's *Newsletter on Intellectual Freedom* is a substantial and important bimonthly publication documenting specific instances of censorship of all forms of media, art, drama, and speech. Book reviews and in-depth articles on current intellectual freedom issues are also included. The OIF also publishes *Memorandum*, a bimonthly newsletter aimed at ALA committee members and other interested librarians. The OIF is located at 50 East Huron Street, Chicago, IL 60611.

REFERENCE: American Library Association, Office for Intellectual Freedom, *Office Accountability Report*, 1990.

OFFICE OF CENSORSHIP   The federal government's Office of Censorship was created during World War II to control the dissemination of military information, and it worked closely with the Office of War Information (OWI), which coordinated the flow of war-related words and images from government to public. President Roosevelt set up the Office of Censorship shortly after the attack on Pearl Harbor, giving it the power of mandatory censorship over all international communications not covered by military censorship and over domestic information originating from military installations and industrial facilities with military contracts. In addition, under Director Byron Price, the office was empowered to coordinate the "voluntary" self-censorship of American media.

The Office of Censorship was divided into a Press Division, a Broadcasting Division, an Administrative Division, a Technical Operations Division, an Office of the Chief Postal Censor, and an Office of the Chief Cable Censor. Its powers were very broad. The office banned publication of all photographs of the race riots that occurred on military bases in Louisiana, New Jersey, and elsewhere. It also instructed postal censors that no films or photographs depicting labor or class conflict should be allowed into the country from abroad. The office advised amateur photographers not to take pictures that could be of use to the enemy, such as photographs of coastlines or industrial facilities. The office even had the ability to deny filmmakers the export licenses essential for adequate profits if their films violated office guidelines.

Nonetheless, the office's most prominent and controversial function was the censorship of the mass media, within which its broad censorship of domestic information relied upon "voluntary" press and public compliance with the office's guidelines. Director Byron Price formed a Press Division consisting of editors and reporters from around the country, and on January 14, 1942, he promulgated the voluntary Code of Censorship for all newspapers, magazines, and periodicals. The censorship code was voluntary only in the sense that it was to be implemented by the nation's editors and reporters, using guidelines created, monitored, and administered centrally by the Office of Censorship.

Though the office kept an eye on military information in general, it was particularly concerned with atomic information. In concert with the Office of War Information and Military Intelligence, it sent a confidential note to all editors stating that nothing should be printed or broadcast about atomic energy, atomic fission, atom splitting, radioactive materials, cyclotrons, or a wide range of specified elements and their compounds. The directive, dated June 28, 1943, was mailed to two thousand daily newspapers and one thousand weeklies, as well as most radio stations. The media responded to the directive by placing a cap on atomic stories, but the Office of Censorship soon expressed its unhappiness with the level of media restraint. On July 27, 1943, the *Schenectady Gazette* was reprimanded for printing a letter to the editor that referred to U-235 as "the most potent stuff on earth." The *Gazette* assured the office that no such letter would be printed again.

Numerous minor violations of the "voluntary" code were quickly called to the attention of other newspapers and radio stations. A Westinghouse radio script about peacetime atom smashing was faulted, even though it did not violate the code's prohibition against wartime applications. The Office of Censorship complained to the International News Service (INS) about a story on an atomic scientist and his scholarly research. The office explained, "We are trying to lead the enemy to believe that we never think about such a thing. . . . Maybe that's silly, but maybe not."

Even fiction was controlled by the Office of Censorship. On April 11, 1944, the Army asked the office to determine whether an already-published detective novel, *The Last Secret*, had violated the censorship code. The novel contained a brief mention of atomic energy in the first chapter, and the office rebuked the publisher, Dial Press, stating that "when fiction incorporates factual information dealing with restricted subjects, it can give information on to the enemy as readily as any other form of published material."

Universities across the nation were also forced to restrict their routine communications. The Office of Censorship halted the distribution of Ohio State University's promotional booklet about its atomic research. The University of Illinois was reprimanded for a press release on atom smashing. Dr. S. C. Lind, dean of the University of Minnesota's Institute of Technology, was ordered to cancel his scheduled lectures and a planned article on atomic power. Lind responded by noting that atomic fission had been discovered in Germany, and that German scientists knew far more about it than he did. Nonetheless, the *Bulletin* of the Minnesota Federation of Engineering Societies was pressured to withhold publication of Lind's article until after the war.

On August 24, 1944, the *Minneapolis Tribune* printed an op-ed column by a former employee of the Office of Censorship, William Mylander. The article stated, "All known explosives are popgun affairs compared to the dreadful power sub-atomic energy might loose." The Office of Censorship immediately responded by ordering postal censors not to send that issue of the *Tribune* outside of the United States. Shortly thereafter, General Leslie Groves, head of the U.S. atomic bomb project, visited the head of the newspaper chain that owned the *Tribune*. No similar articles appeared in any of the chain's newspapers thereafter (Patrick S. Washburn, "The Office of Censorship's Attempt to Control Press Coverage of the Atomic Bomb during World War II," July 1988, ERIC document ED295201, pp. 7–16).

Even comic strips were subject to censorship. On April 14, 1945, the "Superman" comic strip showed the Man of Steel in a university physics lab, where an arrogant professor addressed Superman and assembled guests. "Gentlemen," said the professor, "the strange object before you is the cyclotron—popularly known as an 'atom smasher.' Are you still prepared to face this test, Mr. Superman?" When the Man of Steel agreed to the experiment, his horrified friends shouted, "No, Superman, wait! Even you can't do it!" ("Superman" [comic strip], *Washington Post*, April 14, 1945, 7B). The Office of Censorship wrote to the syndicate that distributed the comic strip, saying that any discussion of atomic energy should be discouraged for the remainder of the war. The comic strip's plot was promptly rewritten to eliminate any reference to atom smashing.

Even after the surrender of Germany in May 1945, the Office of Censorship continued to function. When a *Newsweek* story predicted the lifting of censorship restrictions on atomic energy, the Office wrote to *Newsweek* complaining that this was the first time that the censorship code had been revealed to the public. The Associated Press was similarly reprimanded.

When the American atomic bomb was first tested on July 16, 1945, in the desert near Alamogordo, New Mexico, the Army prepared a phony press release claiming that the blast was the result of an ammunition-dump explosion. But the bomb blast was visible for many miles, producing numerous eyewitnesses. The Office of Censorship asked the media to submit any personal accounts of the blast for approval before printing them. In most cases, the office decided not to censor these accounts, fearing that it would tip off the eyewitnesses and the press that this was something special. In any case, no account other than the Army's bogus press release could be sent outside the country.

On August 6, 1945, the White House announced that an atomic bomb had been dropped on Hiroshima. The Office of Censorship promptly sent a message on all wire services to editors and broadcasters rescinding the 1943 secrecy directive. The message nonetheless cautioned them to continue withholding information on U.S. uranium stocks, scientific processes, formulas, and the mechanics of the atomic bomb. The media were also asked to suppress information on the quality and quantity of production of the bombs, their physics, and future military use.

The Office of Censorship was quickly bombarded with requests to publish stories on the atom bomb. The *Philadelphia Bulletin* submitted an eyewitness account of the Alamogordo bomb test to the office for approval. The story described the dangers of radioactivity to the towns surrounding the bomb site. The office returned the story to the *Bulletin* with two-thirds of it deleted.

Even in the final week of the war, the Office of Censorship continued to suppress stories. Finally, on August 14, 1945, the day of the Japanese surrender, General Groves thanked the Office of Censorship for its effective service, and on the following day, Byron Price, the Director of Censorship, announced the closing of the office and the end of the Code of Wartime Practices (Patrick S. Washburn, "The Office of Censorship's Attempt to Control Press Coverage of the Atomic Bomb during World War II," July 1988, ERIC document ED295201, pp. 45–53).

REFERENCE: *History of the Office of Censorship*, 1977, 3 microfilm reels in the National Archives.

O'LEARY, HAZEL R., 1937–   Prior to her appointment by President Clinton as the nation's seventh Secretary of Energy, Hazel O'Leary had served as president of the natural gas subsidiary for Northern States Power, a $2-billion utility company. She had earlier been a presidential appointee in the Department of Energy (DOE) during the Carter administration and in the Federal Energy Administration under President Ford. Before that, she had served as an Assistant Attorney General and an Assistant Prosecutor for the state of New Jersey.

When Hazel O'Leary assumed her duties as Secretary of Energy on January 22, 1993, she began rebuilding the DOE for the post–Cold War environment. She took steps to shift the agency's focus to industrial competitiveness, energy resources, environmental quality, science and technology, and national security. Budgets for nuclear weapons and commercial nuclear power were reduced. But what characterized her first year most was her commitment to open government and the dismantling of DOE's long legacy of secrecy.

In December 1993, Secretary O'Leary began the process of declassifying fifty years of Cold War secrecy about the U.S. nuclear weapons programs, including 204 underground nuclear tests that had been kept secret from the American public. During the first two years of her tenure alone, the Department of Energy declassified two million pages of documents and began plans in 1996 for review of an additional one hundred million pages for possible declassification.

O'Leary also opened up the files on a dark period in U.S. history involving radiation experiments performed on American citizens, many without their consent. O'Leary revealed evidence that federal researchers over the past fifty years had deliberately exposed up to eight hundred American citizens to radiation in Cold War–era experiments. She recommended financial compensation for the victims and established a toll-free "human experimentation hotline" to help identify them. During the first week, more than two thousand callers alleged that they had participated in these nuclear experiments, and O'Leary acknowledged that government secrecy in the past might have hidden the true extent of such experiments.

O'Leary created an Office of Human Radiation Experiments within DOE to investigate the extent of such experiments on Americans. In February 1995, that office released a report stating that the forerunners of the DOE had conducted 154 Cold War radiation experiments involving nine thousand people, including prisoners, mental patients, and children.

O'Leary announced, "We are moving from being a closed and secretive department to one that is open, responsive to the public and able to deal with our customers across the country." She said that her "Openness Initiative" would not only earn the public trust, but would save public dollars as well. She announced that during the first year these initiatives had reduced DOE's annual security costs from $1.2 billion to $993 million. Still, many federal bureaucrats, including some within her own department, thought that she was revealing too many government secrets. "During the Cold War, I would have been arrested for what I said," she admitted (Mary McGrory, "O'Leary's Energy Is Felt," *Washington Post*, December 14, 1993, p. A2). Indeed, Cold War scientists like Edward Teller, the "father of the hydrogen bomb," warned that O'Leary's declassification plans would provoke public hysteria, but President Clinton supported her efforts to open government files. In a 1994 public mailing, Thomas Blanton, executive director of the National Security Archive, applauded O'Leary "for her efforts to change the culture of secrecy at DOE and encourage broader public debate about the costs and consequences of nuclear weapons. If the

Clinton Administration as a whole matches her efforts, perhaps then we really will be able to declare the end of the Cold War."

In late 1995, Republican lawmakers who pressed for the dismantling of the Energy Department attacked O'Leary to bolster their case. First, she was criticized for hiring a private firm to rate coverage of her department by news reporters. Then she was faulted for costly overseas travels. But through it all, O'Leary remained steadfast in her insistence on an open department. In February 1996, she released a report titled "Plutonium, the First 50 Years" that provided the first complete account of the location and amount of all forms of plutonium stockpiled at U.S. government facilities. With this report, the United States became the first country to reveal such details, and O'Leary said that it was done in the hope of encouraging other nuclear powers to do the same. She said that she also intended the disclosures to produce better-informed public debate on how to safeguard plutonium stockpiles. At her press conference announcing the release of the unprecedented report, O'Leary also revealed a plan to relax the department's rules for automatically classifying most nuclear information. Such information, characterized as "born classified," would henceforth require specific justification before it could be classified.

REFERENCE: U.S. Department of Energy, *Secretary of Energy O'Leary's Brown Bag Lunch*, March 26, 1996, videocassette.

PATENT SECRECY   World War I spawned a wide range of legislation restricting any expression contrary to the war effort. Among these legislative initiatives was congressional authorization for the Patent and Trademark Office (PTO) to withhold patents considered important to national defense. Though this program of patent secrecy applied only for the duration of World War I, it was reinstituted shortly before the U.S. entry into World War II. Only during the Cold War, with the enactment of the Patent Secrecy Act of 1951, was permanent peacetime authority to suppress private patents introduced.

The Invention Secrecy Act of 1951 authorizes the federal government to prohibit the publication of any invention when its disclosure would threaten national security. In such cases, the inventor would normally be allowed to sue the government for "just compensation" for the loss of his intellectual property, but if the act of compensation would disclose military secrets, even this option could be denied to the inventor. The court is authorized to hold secret hearings on such patents, and if the judge believes that the risk of disclosure of national security information is great, he may dismiss the suit altogether.

The various defense agencies of the federal government supply the PTO with "fields of interest" lists to assist in determining when a patent secrecy order should be applied. The primary guidance document for this process is the classified Patent Security Category Review List, but a variety of supplementary documents from the export-control regulations are used as well. In its initial screening, the PTO refers any patents that "might be detrimental" to national security to appropriate defense agencies, which make the controlling decision on secrecy. The PTO issues the secrecy order, but its role is only ministerial, responsive to the will of the defense agencies.

A secrecy order withholds the grant of a patent, orders that the invention be kept secret, restricts filings of foreign applications, and prevents related technical data in the patent application from being disclosed. Patent applications relating to atomic energy are considered particularly sensitive, and the Department of Energy has separate authority under the Atomic Energy Act to review all such patents.

Once a secrecy order has been issued, the associated patent application is suspended. Violation of a secrecy order results in criminal penalties and loss of private rights to the invention. The applicant may appeal upon payment of a fee.

Patent secrecy orders were formerly issued for the duration of an "emergency," the definition of which was left entirely to the President. For example, President Truman declared a national emergency in 1950 that would have remained in effect to this day if Congress had not passed a bill in 1978 terminating all existing "emergencies" as they affected patent secrecy orders. The Patent Office was thereafter required to apply the peacetime provisions of the Patent Secrecy Act, including annual review of all secrecy orders, though these reviews usually result in renewals of the secrecy orders.

In recent years, three specialized secrecy orders have been established to handle different sensitivity levels. The type 1 secrecy order applies to both private and government-owned inventions and is used to prevent publication of any unclassified patent information that is export controlled. The type 1 secrecy orders are based upon the Department of Defense Authorization Act of 1984, which granted the DOD authority to withhold from public disclosure unclassified technical data relating to militarily critical information or space technology.

The type 2 secrecy orders are applied to patent applications containing technical data that are either classified or "classifiable." The term "classifiable" here designates privately owned unclassified information that could warrant classification if a government interest existed. One concern about type 2 secrecy orders is that they specify a level of secrecy without the classification authority, declassification instructions, or page markings, creating substantial difficulties in classifying related subject matter. Also, in the absence of any indication of which portions of the document are classified or classifiable, the entire patent application must be treated as classified.

Type 3 secrecy orders cover privately owned "classifiable" technology. They are imposed upon patent applications that contain technical data that might have been classified if the government did have a property interest in the invention. Such patents cannot be placed under a type 2 secrecy order because of the verified absence of any government property interest.

It should be noted that all three types of patent secrecy orders can cover unclassified information. Indeed, types 1 and 3 cover only unclassified information, while type 2 covers both unclassified and classified information. The Patent Office admits that the vast majority of secrecy orders are being imposed on unclassified information, and the total numbers of secrecy orders have reached all-time record highs.

Congress, the business community, and the general public have begun to ask why the desire of defense agencies to impose peacetime secrecy should outweigh the First Amendment rights of private inventors to publish and market their inventions. Why is privately owned information considered to be under the control of the government simply because it is contained in a patent application? The Office of Technology Assessment explains: "Imposition of a secrecy order can be avoided simply by not seeking a patent. . . . Nevertheless, imposition of a secrecy order does operate as a restriction on traditional freedom of scientific communication. This authority must therefore be considered as part of the total burden on the exercise of free speech" (Herbert N. Foerstel, *Secret Science*, Westport, Praeger, 1993, p. 171).

REFERENCE: Ellis Mount and Wilda B. Newman, *Top Secret/Trade Secret: Accessing and Safeguarding Restricted Information*, Washington, New Republic Books, 1977.

PENTAGON PAPERS   In two companion cases, *New York Times Co. v. United States* and *United States v. Washington Post Co.* (1971), the Supreme Court ruled that the government had not justified its attempt at prior restraint of publication of *The Pentagon Papers*, a classified Pentagon study of the history of U.S. involvement in Vietnam. The *Papers*, formally titled *History of United States Decision-making Process on Viet Nam Policy*, contained no secret documents, but the Nixon administration claimed that publication would harm the national interest. The *New York Times* had published excerpts of the *Papers* in June 1971, but was halted by a restraining order from a federal appeals court. A similar process occurred when the *Washington Post* attempted to publish the *Papers*. The Supreme Court's decision allowed both newspapers to proceed with publication.

The Court's ruling was contained in a brief per curiam decision, with several justices adding concurring opinions. Justice Hugo Black, joined by Justice William Douglas, wrote: "I believe that every moment's continuance of the injunctions against these newspapers amounts to a flagrant, indefensible, and continuing violation of the First Amendment. . . . Now, for the first time in the 182 years since the founding of the Republic, the federal courts are asked to hold that the First Amendment does not mean what it says, but rather means that the Government can halt the publication of current news of vital importance to the people of this country. . . . Both the history and language of the First Amendment support the view that the press must be left free to publish news, whatever the source, without censorship, injunctions, or prior restraints." The joint opinion concluded, "In revealing the workings of government that led to the Vietnam war, the newspapers nobly did precisely that which the Founders hoped and trusted they would do. . . . To find that the President has 'inherent power' to halt the publication of news by resort to the courts would wipe out the First Amendment and destroy the fundamental liberty and security of the very people the Government hopes to make 'secure.' "

Justice William Brennan's concurring opinion stated, "The chief purpose of the First Amendment's guarantee is to prevent previous restraints upon publication. Thus, only governmental allegation and proof that publication must inevitably, directly, and immediately cause the occurrence of an event kindred to imperiling the safety of a transport already at sea can support even the issuance of an interim restraining order."

Today, there are few who defend Nixon's attempt to suppress the *Papers*. Even former Solicitor General Irwin Griswold, who argued the government's case against publication, has admitted, "I have never seen any trace of a threat to the national security from the publication. Indeed, I have never even seen it suggested that there was such an actual threat" ("Issues Larger than Lives," *Washington Post*, February 17, 1989, p. A2).

REFERENCES: D. J. Herda, *New York Times v. United States: National Security and Censorship*, Hillside, Enslow Publishers, 1994; Sanford J. Ungar, *The Papers and the Papers: An Account of the Legal and Political Battle over the Pentagon Papers*, New York, Notable Trials Library, 1989.

PEOPLE FOR THE AMERICAN WAY   People for the American Way is a public interest organization that promotes pluralism, freedom of expression, and religious diversity as fundamental American values. The organization was formed in 1980 by the prominent television producer Norman Lear to counter the growing political influence of the Moral Majority and its leader, Jerry Falwell, and it uses mass-media campaigns to oppose such conservative and religious fundamentalist groups. People for the American Way has about 300,000 members, including religious, business, media, and labor figures committed to reaffirming the traditional American values of pluralism, diversity, and freedom of expression and religion. It provides support to groups and individuals facing challenges to their First Amendment rights and produces educational materials and seminars on related issues. It maintains a speakers bureau, conducts research, and distributes information on issues such as censorship, school prayer, and access to abortion clinics.

John H. Buchanan, a former Republican congressman, and Arthur J. Kropp succeeded Lear as presidents of the organization. Kropp, who became president in 1987, achieved a high profile in the defeat of Supreme Court nominee Robert H. Bork. After Kropp's death in 1995, he was succeeded by former representative Thomas H. Andrews (D-Maine), a liberal with a long background in community organizing. Andrews pledged that People for the American Way would mount a national effort to reclaim the nation from those conservative organizations and political candidates that would compromise Americans' rights for political gain.

People for the American Way is located at 2000 M Street, NW, Suite 400, Washington, DC 20036. Its primary publication is the PFAW *Forum*, a quarterly newsletter of the organization's activities and positions. The organization also publishes the annual *Attacks on the Freedom to Learn*, an important summary and analyses of censorship incidents nationwide.
REFERENCE: Leon Hurwitz, *Historical Dictionary of Censorship in the United States*, Westport, Greenwood Press, 1985.

POLITICALLY CORRECT   The term "politically correct" or "PC" emerged in the 1980s as a sarcastic characterization of the attitudes and language expected of a good citizen in the modern multicultural society. In reaction to the painfully wrought changes of the civil rights era, the conservative rebellion, personified by Ronald Reagan, rejected the preachiness of liberal do-gooders, including the suggestion that American society was racist, sexist, or otherwise socially flawed. Conservative politicians effectively marketed national pride and traditionalism, calling for a celebration of American preeminence, both economic and social. The liberal language of group tolerance and self-criticism was increasingly regarded as, at best, an unnecessary irritant and, at worst, censorious subversion.

In this new social climate, what had appeared to be growing tolerance was now portrayed as a self-conscious sham, within which the common language of civility had been accepted only under duress. Much of the liberal vocabulary of social accommodation became the object of scorn. Racial semantics were a particularly inviting target. The use of "native American" instead of "Indian" was ridiculed as PC, as was the semantic evolution from "colored" to "Negro" to "black" to "African American." Feminist vocabulary, such as the use of "Ms.," was lampooned as PC, as was any restraint on the traditionally crude but good-natured sexual vocabulary of American males. The emerging class of "angry white males," which came to dominate politics in the 1990s, would no longer be intimidated by labels like "sexist" or "racist."

In his 1991 commencement address at the University of Michigan, President George Bush weighed in against the evils of PC. "Although the movement arises from the laudable desire to sweep away the debris of racism and sexism and hatred, it replaces old prejudice with new ones," said Bush. "It declares certain topics off-limits, certain expressions off-limits, even certain gestures off-limits. . . . In their own Orwellian way, crusades that demand correct behavior crush diversity in the name of diversity" ("President Assails Silencing of Unpopular Views," *Washington Post*, May 5, 1991, p. A8).

The "multicultural" movement in education and scholarship was soon identified as a major source of "politically correct" doctrine, fomented by the liberalism of university campuses. In April 1994, a conservative group of college students calling themselves the First Amendment Coalition met at Harvard University to plot strategy to "liberate" classrooms and campuses around the country from PC. The coalition issued "The Cambridge Declaration," which opposed ideological conformity, speech codes, favored status groups (i.e.. affirmative action), and curriculum bias against Western traditions and American institutions. Critics said that the coalition was a tool of large corporations and wealthy families who funneled money to conservative groups that hoped to reverse the gains made by blacks, women, and homosexuals. But such revelations did not change the fact that much of the American public was no longer comfortable with the language of the civil rights era.

Campus speech codes were the most publicized example of politically correct controls on expression. The dramatic increase in racial conflict and anti-Semitic incidents on campuses in the late 1980s led many universities to develop codes and penalties to discourage hate speech, but such controls were unpopular and were eventually challenged in the courts. In the early 1990s, when the courts ruled that speech codes at the Universities of Michigan and Wisconsin were unconstitutional infringements on free speech, most other campuses abandoned their codes.

It turned out that there were numerous other "PC" speech codes scattered throughout America's corporate and government structure. In late 1993, it was revealed that the *Los Angeles Times* had prepared a nineteen–page style sheet titled "Guidelines on Ethnic, Racial, Sexual, and Other Identification," and that document was quickly dubbed the "PC Language List." The in-house document advised reporters to avoid the use of words like "babe," "biddy," "bra-burner," "hick," "hillbilly," "queer," and "white trash." Some staff at the *Times* complained that the new guidelines came too close to banning words, but Deputy Managing Editor Terry Schwadron insisted, "This is not about political correctness. It's about being accurate and being fair" ("Fighting Words at L.A. Times," *Washington Post*, December 18, 1993, p. D1). The national press was, of course, quick to pick up the story and ridicule the *Times*, though a few reporters did mention that national newspapers have always had style manuals that address the same semantic issues as did the "PC Language List."

Other investigative reporters soon discovered the taint of PC in less liberal bastions than the campus and the media. It was revealed that since 1965 the FBI had included in its background checks on judicial candidates an examination of any words they might have uttered reflecting "potential bias or prejudice." Such procedures were subsequently expanded to include other federal positions influencing policy or personnel, but now the bureau extended its concern to offensive statements about "any class of citizens."

In 1987, the terms "politically correct" and "political correctness" appeared 9 times in the *Washington Post*. In 1994 alone, these two terms were used 292 times in the *Post*, and the usage counts held at roughly that level into 1996. Columnist Donna Britt has described PC as "journalism's most over-used, under-examined catchword." As the public relations aspects of the campaign against political correctness gained momentum in the press, a number of ironic contradictions emerged. Because the characterization "politically correct" had always been pejorative, it soon became highly incorrect to be politically correct. Any language that sounded socially conscious, or just liberal, was inappropriate. Even the word "liberal" became tainted, and from the time of the 1988 election campaigns, the press began referring to it as the "L-word."

Columnist and language maven William Safire defined PC in his political dictionary as "conforming to liberal or far-left thought on sexual, racial, cultural or environmental issues." Novelist Saul Bellow defined political correctness as "free speech without debate," an effort to delegitimize expressions of "implicit racism and sexism." When Bellow and other conservative intellectuals claimed that the origins of PC lay in Marxism, one could sense a post–Cold War cultural Red Scare in the offing (Jefferson Morley, "A P.C. Guide to Political Correctness," *Washington Post*, January 15, 1995, p. C1).

Despite conservative complaints that PC was a form of censorship, the charge of PC was itself increasingly applied to silence speech critical of the American government or its history. In the 1990s, a number of important museum exhibitions were attacked, cancelled, or bowdlerized under the charge that they were unflattering to the nation and therefore "politically correct." In 1991, the Smithsonian's National Museum of American Art produced an exhibit, "The American West," that made the mistake of accompanying well-known nineteenth-century paintings of the American frontier with wall texts that challenged the traditionally glorious image of the "old West." Conservative columnists like Charles Krautenhammer complained that the exhibit's wall texts were PC, and the *Washington Post* attacked the show as "the Smithsonian Institution's first politically correct art exhibit." Claiming that such thought was surfacing just as global communism crumbled, the *Post* ridiculed the Smithsonian as the heir of the 1960s, seeing only conflict and oppression. Politicians on Capitol Hill joined the chorus, complaining that the exhibit stained the glory of America's westward expansion.

A few years later, when the Smithsonian's Air and Space Museum attempted to assemble an exhibit marking the fiftieth anniversary of the dropping of the atomic bomb on Hiroshima, congressional conservatives intervened. Once more, the complaint was that by including photos and commentary on the devastation wrought by the bomb, the exhibit cast doubt on the good judgment of the American government in dropping it. At a news conference in January 1995, Representative Peter Blute (R-Mass.)

said, "[W]e think there are some troubling questions in regard to the Smithsonian, not just with this Enola Gay exhibit but over the past 10 years or so, getting into areas of revisionist history and political correctness." Because of its alleged record of PC, Blute said that the House would hold hearings to review the Smithsonian's $300-million funding ("Air and Space Director under Fire," *Washington Post*, January 20, 1995, p. D1).

Within a week, eighty-one members of Congress joined veterans' groups in calling for the cancellation of the exhibit and the firing of Director Martin Harwit. Senate Majority Leader Bob Dole joined the call for hearings on the Smithsonian, and House Speaker Newt Gingrich named Representative Sam Johnson (R-Tex.), a harsh critic of the exhibit, as a new regent for the Smithsonian. Complaining of "a certain political correctness seeping in and distorting and prejudicing the Smithsonian's exhibits," Gingrich said that the *Enola Gay* exhibit would be dramatically pared down to "one which every American, and frankly, every citizen of the planet, can be proud of" ("A Pared-down Enola Gay," *Washington Post*, January 28, 1995, p. D3).

Smithsonian Secretary Michael Heyman promptly scrapped the exhibit, replacing it with a drastically reduced display consisting of the plane that dropped the bomb, minimal text, and a video about its crew. The exhibit catalog of text and photos, already publicly advertised, was to be withdrawn. Nonetheless, the American Legion insisted that congressional hearings should proceed as planned, and the Smithsonian was pressured to alter or censor its other exhibits. In order to avoid further controversy, Smithsonian Secretary Michael Heyman postponed an exhibit on the Vietnam War and announced that he would revise an exhibition titled "Science in American Life" because its inclusion of scientific failures had been criticized as "politically correct." Planning for the National Museum of the American Indian was also said to be in jeopardy. Shortly thereafter, Martin Harwit, the beleaguered Director of the Air and Space Museum, resigned, citing the furor over the A-bomb exhibit.

By this time, the definition of PC had taken on a new focus: unpatriotic or un-American speech. In 1994, the *Wall Street Journal* had clearly espoused this new interpretation in an editorial attacking a State Department report that dared "to expose human rights abuses *within* the United States." The emphasis on "within" was added by the *Journal* to demonstrate its incredulity over any official suggestion that America might be less than perfect. "The document," said the *Journal*, "is a PC view of U.S. history as found only on campuses or among Smithsonian curators." The *Journal* concluded, "Political correctness was once merely the bane of campus life. Now, incredibly, it has been enshrined as official U.S. policy" ("The State of PC," *Wall Street Journal*, September 15, 1994, p. A14).

In May 1995, when the Senate hearings on the Smithsonian began, Rules and Administration Committee chairman Ted Stevens (R-Alaska) declared that the Smithsonian was not authorized to grapple with contentious issues. To demonstrate the dangers of allowing the Smithsonian to stray into such forbidden areas, Stevens said that the hearings would scrutinize "the revisionist and 'politically correct' bias" in Smithsonian exhibits.

Two long-term advantages to this seemingly endless public flap can be seen. First, heavy-handed attempts by liberals to impose tolerance and civility through restrictions on protected speech have been discouraged. Second, political conservatives, long identified with censorship in literature, films, and the arts, have embraced the First Amendment. This may have been done for short-term political gain, but the positive momentum may be difficult to reverse.

REFERENCES: *Are You Politically Correct? Debating America's Cultural Standards*, edited by Francis J. Beckwith and Michael E. Bauman, Buffalo, Prometheus Books, 1993; James F. Garner, *Once upon a More Enlightened Time: More Politically Correct Bedtime Stories*, London, Simon and Schuster, 1995.

PORNOGRAPHY   Most Americans believe that they can recognize pornography when they see it, but they have trouble defining it. The word "pornography" is derived from the Greek *pornographos*, meaning writing about harlots. The early dictionary definitions are circular, leading from pornography to obscenity to prurient to indecent to lascivious to lewd and back again (see the *Oxford English Dictionary*). The *American Heritage Dictionary (AHD)* defined "pornography" as "written, graphic, or other forms of communication intended to invite lascivious feelings." The *AHD* definition of "lascivious" was: "1. Of or characterized by lust; lewd; lecherous. 2. Exciting sexual desires." The word "lewd" was then defined as "Licentious; lustful," and "licentious" was defined as "lacking moral discipline or sexual restraint." *AHD* then defined "lust" as "sexual craving, especially excessive or unrestrained." Finally, "lechery" was defined as "excessive indulgence in sexual activity." To summarize *AHD*'s chain of meaning, pornography would appear to be any form of communication intended to arouse excessive sexual desire and morally undisciplined craving.

The confusion between pornography, erotica, and obscenity continues to plague dictionaries and society at large. *Webster's Third New International Dictionary of the English Language* (1981) defines "erotica" as "literary or artistic items having an erotic theme," "pornography" as "a portrayal of erotic behavior designed to cause sexual excitement," and "obscene" as "abhorrent to morality or virtue: stressing or revelling in the lewd or lustful." The language in these definitions becomes successively stronger, but the meanings remain essentially the same. The Random House unabridged dictionary (1987) has even more difficulty distinguishing between these terms. It defines "pornography" as "obscene writings, drawings, photographs or the like, especially those having little or no artistic merit," while "obscene" is characterized as "offensive to morality or decency" and "causing uncontrolled sexual desire." Clearly, Random House makes no distinction between pornography and obscenity, but it distinguishes both sharply from erotica.

In practice, these semantic convolutions are of little significance, for the courts have chosen to distinguish obscenity from all else. The major criteria used by the courts in distinguishing pornography from obscenity are whether it has some "serious literary, artistic, political, or scientific value" and whether a "reasonable person" in the community would consider it acceptable. Obscene communication has long been regarded by the courts as receiving no constitutional protection. This was affirmed in *Roth v. United States,* 354 U.S. 476, 485 (1957), where the Supreme Court held that "obscenity is not within the area of constitutionally protected speech or press." Subsequent court decisions have fine-tuned the definition of obscenity, but obscene speech remains without constitutional protection. We may therefore conclude that within the law, pornography is anything that promotes sexual arousal but retains constitutional protection as determined by the courts. *See also* EROTICA; INDECENCY; OBSCENITY.

REFERENCES: *Pornography and Censorship,* edited by David Copp and Susan Wendell, Buffalo, Prometheus Books, 1983; Roger Shattuck, *Forbidden Knowledge: From Prometheus to Pornography,* New York, St. Martin's Press, 1996.

POSTAL REGULATIONS   Virtually all federal convictions for obscenity have rested upon postal regulations. The regulation against mailing obscenity, originally passed in 1865, made it a crime to mail "an obscene book . . . or other publication of a vulgar and indecent character." When it was codified in 1873 as the Comstock Act, the regulation added the words "lewd" and "lascivious." Located in Title 18, Section 1461, of the *U.S. Code,* the regulation currently says that the U.S. mail will not carry any "obscene, lewd, lascivious, filthy book, pamphlet, picture, print, or other publication of a vulgar or indecent character" or "any letter upon the envelope of which, or postal card upon which scurrilous epithets may have been written or printed, or disloyal devices printed or engraved." The penalty for the first offense is not more than $5,000 or not more than five years in prison or both; for each subsequent offense, the penalty is $10,000 or ten years or both. In addition, advertisements that of and by themselves do not fall under any of the specified categories are nonetheless prohibited if they contain information on where and how to obtain any "obscene," "filthy," or "vulgar" material. The materials addressed in this regulation must be judged obscene by the judicial process before any penalties may be imposed.

There are a number of postal regulations that have been ruled unconstitutional restraints on protected speech. Title 39, Section 3001, of the *U.S. Code* stated that "any unsolicited advertisement of matter which is designed, adapted, or intended for preventing conception is non-mailable matter," with penalties for violation identical to the penalties for mailing obscene matter. In *Bolger v. Youngs Drug Products Corporation* (1983), the Supreme Court ruled this regulation to be an unconstitutional restriction on the free flow of truthful commercial information.

Postal regulations have also restricted the communication of political information. Section 305(a) of the Postal Service and Federal Employeees Salary Act of 1962 said that unsealed material printed in a foreign country and determined by the Secretary of the Treasury to be "communist political propaganda" should be detained by the Postmaster General and delivered only upon the addressee's specific request. Material received by subscription or otherwise determined to be desired by the addressee was exempt from these provisions, as was mail addressed to government agencies or educational institutions or mail sent pursuant to international cultural agreements. Nonetheless, the Supreme Court ruled in *Lamont v. Postmaster General* (1965) that the entire process was unconstitutional because it required the addressee to take positive action before he could exercise his First Amendment rights.

REFERENCE: James C.N. Paul and Murray L. Schwartz, *Federal Censorship: Obscenity in the Mail*, New York, Free Press of Glencoe, 1961.

PRESIDENT'S COMMISSION ON OBSCENITY AND PORNOGRAPHY

The President's Commission on Obscenity and Pornography was established in 1969 and required to report to the President and to Congress its findings and recommendations. Commission Chairman William B. Lockhart convened the first meeting at the University of Indiana's Kinsey Institute, where the members viewed classic pornographic movies. After President Nixon appointed Charles H. Keating, founder of Citizens for Decent Literature, to the commission, Keating made clear that he considered Chairman Lockhart to be soft on smut.

After a year of research and deliberation, the commission issued recommendations that called for (1) a massive national sexual education effort; (2) open discussion of the issues relating to obscenity and pornography; (3) development of citizens' organizations at the local, regional, and national levels to aid in the implementation of the commission's recommendations through persuasion rather than coercion or censorship; (4) the repeal of federal, state, and local laws prohibiting the sale, exhibition, or distribution of sexual materials to consenting adults; and (5) an end to governmental interference with the full freedom of adults to read, obtain, or view whatever such materials they wish. The commission said that empirical investigation provided no evidence that exposure to explicit sexual materials plays a significant role in causing crime, delinquency, sexual or nonsexual deviancy, or severe emotional disturbances. The commission concluded that parents should be free to make their own conclusions regarding the suitability of explicit sexual material for their children, and it advocated legislation to assist parents in controlling such access.

Keating opposed the commission's recommendations and requested a court order to bar publication of the final report, and President Nixon called the recommendations "morally bankrupt." Nixon distanced himself from the commission by pointing out that President Johnson had appointed most of its members, and Vice President Agnew used the report to criticize liberals and the "permissive society."

REFERENCE: Lane V. Sunderland, *Obscenity: The Court, the Congress, and the President's Commission*, Washington, American Enterprise Institute for Public Policy Research, 1975.

PRESS   Among the free speech protections embodied in the First Amendment to the American Constitution is the prohibition of any federal law "abridging the freedom of speech, or of the press." The extent to which the press is protected, or even privileged, by this brief statement has always been a point of contention. At the very least, the First Amendment embodies the English common-law protection against prior restraint of speech or publication, but certain forms of unprotected speech, such as libel or obscenity, are grounds for punishment after publication.

In 1833, the Supreme Court ruled in *Barron v. Baltimore* that the Bill of Rights applied solely to the federal government, allowing state prosecutions for licentious publications. Thomas Cooley, a nineteenth century authority on the Constitution, wrote that the First Amendment guarantees "a right to freely utter and published whatever the citizen may please, and be protected against any responsibility for so doing, except so far as such publications, from their blasphemy, obscenity, or scandalous character, may be a public offense, or as by their falsehood and malice they may injuriously affect the standing, reputation, or pecuniary interests of individuals" (Thomas Cooley, *A Treatise on the Constitutional Limitations*, vol. 2, Boston, Little, Brown and Co., 1868, p. 886).

The Press has always led the way in the struggle for access to government information. By 1950, the atmosphere of national security paranoia and government information control had mobilized the press for the first organized campaign in support of the public's right to know. James S. Pope of the American Society of Newspaper Editors (ASNE) warned of the growing tension between government and the press. "This is a conflict as old as government and news of government," said Pope. "But the conflict has gone far beyond the simple ceremonial. Only recently have most editors begun to realize that these familiar little guerilla skirmishes now are part of a broad-scale offensive against freedom of information—against the basic principle of a citizen's right to know, so that he may govern himself" (James S. Pope, "The Suppression of News," *Atlantic Monthly*, July 1951, p. 50).

As chairman of the ASNE's Freedom of Information Committee, Pope made that group into an effective national voice for the public's right to know. The ASNE responded by retaining Harold Cross, one of the top newspaper lawyers in the country and counsel for the New York *Herald Tribune*, to prepare a report on federal, state, and municipal information policies and practices. Cross's scholarly and comprehensive report, published in 1953 under the title *The People's Right to Know*, confirmed the fears of newspapermen around the country that basic government information was being systematically denied to them and thus to the American people.

Newpapermen like Kent Cooper, who spent forty-five years with the Associated Press and retired as its Executive Director in 1950, increased the pressure against government secrecy and disinformation. In fact, Cooper first coined the phrase "Right to Know," and in his 1956 book of the same name he wrote, "American newspapers do have the constitutional right to print. That is the so-called freedom of the press. But they cannot properly serve the people if governments suppress the news. To have that which the people are entitled to is a concept which long ago I first defined as 'the Right to Know.' "

In 1955, after repeated complaints from newsmen and newspaper organizations that the news was being suppressed by American officials, Representative John Moss (D-Calif.), head of the House Government Information Committee, initiated a formal inquiry of government sources, asking them to disclose whether information from government sources was sufficiently available to inform the people on the activity of their government. The work of the Moss Committee, as it was called, eventually led to the Freedom of Information Act (FOIA). Despite a number of strengthening amendments, the FOIA remained inadequate to serve the broad needs of the people to know the workings of their government. To accomplish that goal, the press continued to rely on the courts, as it had done through most of this century.

In early cases like *Schenck v. United States* (1919), *Frohwerk v. United States* (1919), *Abrams v. United States* (1919), and *Gitlow v. New York* (1925), the Supreme Court had approved heavy-handed restraints on unpatriotic publications. A landmark turning point in the Court's support for freedom of the press came in *Near v. Minnesota* (1931), when the Court ruled that even if published accusations of official corruption led some individuals to use violence as a means of redress, governmental prior restraint of such publications was unconstitutional. A similar judgment in *New York Times Co. v. Sullivan* (1964) said that criticism of offical conduct "does not lose its constitutional protection merely because it is effective criticism and hence diminishes . . . official reputations."

In *New York Times Co. v. United States* (1971), the Court upheld the right of the *Times* to publish the *Pentagon Papers*, a classified study of the Vietnam War that embarrassed government officials. In recent years, individul journalists have brought suit against Presidents Reagan, Bush, and Clinton to prevent the White House from destroying the electronic records of the National Security Council and the White House. Journalists have gone to court to broaden press access to military operations during the Grenada invasion and the Gulf War. Through both aggressive reporting and litigation, the press continues to play the vanguard role in securing the people's right to know.

REFERENCE: Charles S. Steinberg, *The Information Establishment: Our Government and the Media*, New York, Hastings House Publishers, 1980.

PRIOR RESTRAINT   American jurisprudence has a particular antipathy for any legal action to suppress speech prior to its expression, rather than punishing it on the basis of what was said. This view was strongly influenced by British common law. The English jurist William Blackstone, regarded by the framers of the Constitution as the preeminent authority on common law, believed that speech or publication may not be censored in advance, but anyone publishing "improper, mischievous, or illegal" speech could suffer severe consequences after the fact.

The First Amendment to the U.S. Constitution embodied the common-law rejection of prior restraint, and though it went even farther than Blackstone in its general tolerance for free speech, it was not absolute. The Supreme Court has usually held that prior restraints violate the First Amendment (*Near v. Minnesota ex rel. Olson* [1931]), but prior restraint does not apply if there has already been a judicial determination that the expression in question is unprotected. Also, the Court has approved prior restraint of certain national security information (e.g., sailing dates of troop ships) during wartime, the dissemination of political information on military bases (*Greer v. Spock* [1976]), and the publications of current and former CIA agents, especially under prepublication review agreements (*Snepp v. United States* [1980] and *McGehee v. Casey* [1983]).

Perhaps the most famous failed attempt at prior restraint occurred in the 1971 *Pentagon Papers* case, when the Supreme Court ruled that the government had not justified its attempt at prior restraint of a classified Pentagon study of the Vietnam War. The most recent rejection of prior restraint occurred in March 1996, when the Sixth U.S. Circuit Court of Appeals reversed a controversial order barring *Business Week* from publishing sealed court documents. That First Amendment dispute began when a U.S. district judge ordered *Business Week*, just hours before deadline, not to publish the documents. After the appeals court reversal, a *Washington Post* editorial observed that court attempts to stop publication of any material are rare and have never been approved by the U.S. Supreme Court. While acknowledging that journalists and media owners who publish in violation of court orders can be punished after the fact, the *Post* noted that they could only be prevented from publishing in an extremely narrow class of cases where the national interest would be seriously and irreparably jeopardized. The *Post* concluded that if the government were allowed routinely to censor the press by prior restraint, "voters could be kept in the dark, reformers denied a platform and incumbents protected from charges of corruption or incompetence. . . . In the *Business Week* case, the court was dealing with standard litigation filings and, as the court found, 'the private litigants' interest in protecting their vanity or their commercial self-interest simply does not qualify as grounds for imposing a prior restraint' " ("Goodbye to

a Gag Order," *Washington Post*, March 8, 1996, p. A20). *See also* PENTAGON PAPERS.
REFERENCE: Michael C. Soper, *The Progressive Case and Its Impact on the Doctrine of Prior Restraint*, Thesis (M.A.), University of Maryland, College Park, 1984.

PRISON REGULATIONS   The question of what First Amendment rights are retained by those in prison has been examined a number of times by the courts. In *Procunier v. Martinez* (1974), the Supreme Court ruled that a group of California prison regulations constituted censorship of protected expression in violation of the First Amendment. The regulations defined the receiving of mail as a privilege rather than a right and allowed the suspension of individual mail privileges if letters complained unduly, magnified grievances, or expressed "inflammatory political, racial, religious, or other views or beliefs." In declaring the regulations void for vagueness, the Court said that they failed to provide minimum procedural safeguards against arbitrary censorship of inmate correspondence.

Generally, the courts have upheld prison regulations restricting free expression if they appear to serve the interest of order and discipline. A regulation allowing wardens to open letters to prisoners from their attorneys was upheld by the Supreme Court in *Wolff, Warden v. McDonnell* (1974). In ruling that this practice was a proper attempt to prevent contraband, the Court said that prison officials could require that letters from attorneys be clearly identified and that such letters could be opened and searched in the presence of inmates.

The Bureau of Prisons has a regulation that allows inmates to receive hardcover books only directly from publishers, book clubs, or bookstores. In addition, the regulation authorizes the warden of each prison to inspect incoming publications and censor those he regards as detrimental to the security, good order, or discipline of the institution. In *Bell, Attorney General v. Wolfish* (1979), the Supreme Court upheld this regulation as a permissible restriction on the First Amendment rights of inmates.

Another regulation contained in Policy Statement 1220.1A of the federal Bureau of Prisons states: "Press representatives will not be permitted to interview individual inmates. This rule shall apply even where the inmate requests or seeks an interview. However, any conversation may be permitted with inmates whose identity is not to be made public, if it is limited to the discussion of institutional facilities, programs or activities." In *Saxbe v. Washington Post Co.* (1974) and *Pell v. Procunier* (1974) the Supreme Court upheld this regulation, ruling that a prison is not a forum or public place and that the First Amendment does not therefore guarantee the press a constitutional right of special access to prisons or inmates.

The prison regulation that has most recently concerned First Amendment advocates is the one that prevents an inmate from acting as a reporter, publishing under a byline, or receiving compensation for any communication with the news media. In 1988, when Peter Sussman, editor of the *San*

Francisco Chronicle's "Sunday Punch," published an article on prison conditions submitted by Dannie Martin, an inmate at California's Lompoc Prison, Martin was thrown in "the hole" for violating the regulation. The prison had been aware of Martin's bylined articles for the *Chronicle* for two years, and Sussman claimed that Martin was punished for the content of the article, a violation of the First Amendment. The courts, however, gave wide latitude to prison authorities to restrict a convict's rights to free expression. *See also* SUSSMAN, PETER.

REFERENCE: Leon Hurwitz, *Historical Dictionary of Censorship in the United States,* Westport, Greenwood Press, 1985.

REPORTERS COMMITTEE FOR FREEDOM OF THE PRESS

The Reporters Committee for Freedom of the Press was founded in 1970 to protect the First Amendment rights of journalists in all media. It has been either the plaintiff or friend of the court in every major case affecting the First Amendment rights of reporters and editors since 1972, and it provides free legal advice to members of the press whenever their rights are challenged. It also conducts research on shield laws and how the subpoenaing of reporters' notes compromises their subsequent ability to work with confidential sources.

The Reporters Committee publishes the quarterly *News Media and the Law*, which reports on cases and legislation affecting the rights of reporters, editors, and broadcasters and provides information on the activities of the committee. Its *News Media Update* is a biweekly report on current events. The organization is located at 1735 I Street, NW, Suite 504, Washington, DC 20006. Its executive director is Jane E. Kirtley.

REFERENCE: *Encyclopedia of Associations*, 31st ed., Detroit, Gale Research Co., 1996.

ROBERTSON, PAT, 1930–   Pat Robertson is a prominent televangelist who founded the Christian Broadcasting Network (CBN), created the religious television show "The 700 Club," and ran for the presidency of the United States in 1988. His conservative politics determine the programming on his network, which features news and analysis on topics such as abortion, pornography, and the occult. In 1981, he founded the Freedom Council to recruit Christians for political action in support of conservative causes. In addition, Robertson's National Legal Foundation (NLF) has supported numerous challenges to textbooks and library materials in schools around the country. Robertson's NLF initiated the 1989 legal controversy surrounding the *Impressions* textbook series, which was banned in many schools because of charges that it promoted "secular humanism."

REFERENCE: John B. Donovan, *Pat Robertson: The Authorized Biography*, New York, Macmillan, 1988.

SEDITION   Sedition has been defined as the act of raising a commotion in a state, short of insurrection. It has also been described as exciting discontent against the government or resistance to lawful authority. Courts have sometimes regarded such action as tending to treason without an overt act. Historically, virtually all behavior characterized by the government as "seditious" has been speech, publication, or expression critical of the government, and the common term for such inappropriate criticism of authority has been "seditious libel."

The crime of seditious libel emerged in seventeenth-century Europe when royal infallibility found itself publicly questioned by the growing ranks of political and religious pamphleteers. The first prominent application of this doctrine in the United States came in 1735 in the trial of New York printer John Peter Zenger. Zenger was merely the printer for the *New York Weekly Journal*, which had published a series of unsigned satirical attacks on the corrupt and tyrannical New York governor, William Cosby. But when Governor Cosby ordered copies of the *Journal* impounded and burned, Zenger was indicted and charged with "seditious libel."

Zenger's lawyer was Andrew Hamilton, who insisted that a jury of one's peers should judge the criminality of the publication. Hamilton argued that truth was a defense against the charge of seditious libel. This may seem obvious, but the English law from which the American tradition of seditious libel is drawn was governed by the maxim "The greater the truth, the greater the libel." The prosecutor in the Zenger case asserted that the defamation of an official, whether true or false, deserved especially severe punishment because it occasioned both a breach of the peace and a scandal injuring the government. In claiming that libel against the state was an offense against the laws of God, the prosecutor quoted the biblical injunction "Thou shalt not speak evil of the ruler of the People" (*Acts* 23:5 and *Exodus* 22:28).

Though the judge had been handpicked by Cosby, Hamilton had no trouble convincing the jurors that Zenger's paper had accurately described the Cosby administration under which they all suffered. It took the jury only a few minutes to render a verdict of not guilty. Zenger's victory was celebrated throughout the colonies and widely disseminated in the book *A Brief Narrative of the Case and Tryal of John Peter Zenger, Printer of the New York Weekly Journal*. Though the acquittal was accepted as part of the new colonial culture, it never became formal legal precedent.

The framing of the American Constitution and the adoption of the First Amendment subsequently gave rise to speculation about the validity of the doctrine of seditious libel. Though the Constitution did not expressly reject the doctrine, many scholars concluded that the First Amendment made prosecution for criticism of the government forever impossible in the United States of America. Nonetheless, one of the earliest acts of congressional repression was the Sedition Act of 1798, which criminalized any "scandalous" publication about the federal government or the President. This act was used by the Federalists to marginalize their political rivals and to suppress the egalitarian sentiments spreading from revolutionary France. The Sedition Act expired within two years, but the seeds of its legitimacy had been planted. In *People v. Croswell* (1803) for instance, Republicans prosecuted a Federalist editor for seditious libel against President Jefferson.

The next major application of the doctrine of seditious libel did not occur until the Civil War, when it was exercised by the executive branch rather than Congress. President Abraham Lincoln used his heavy hand as commander-in-chief to suspend the writ of habeas corpus, throwing thousands of dissenters and suspected "dangerous" men into military prisons without charges and without a trial. Thus, without statutory authority, precedent was established for the prosecution of seditious libel whenever the executive claimed the need to protect national security.

The great Red Menace during and following World War I brought the next wave of federal repression of dissent. Two months after America entered the war, Congress passed the Espionage Act of 1917 in an attempt to shore up support for the war and to punish those who spoke against it. Among the act's provisions were fines and imprisonment for anyone conveying false reports or statements with the intent to interfere with the American military effort, promoting the success of its enemies, or causing insubordination, disloyalty, mutiny, or refusal to serve in the military service.

Congress quickly moved beyond these provisions, passing a series of amendments prohibiting a broad category of "disloyal" speech. These amendments, commonly referred to as the Sedition Act of 1918, added such offenses as "saying or doing anything with intent to obstruct the sale of United States bonds" and "uttering, printing, writing, or publishing any disloyal, profane, scurrilous, or abusive language, or language intended to cause contempt, scorn, contumely or disrepute as regards the form of government of the United States" or upon the Constitution, the flag, or the uniform of the Army or Navy. The Sedition Act not only prohibited these and many other acts of expression, but criminalized the advocacy, teaching, defending, or suggesting of any such expression.

As excessive and outrageous as these prohibitions seem, they were actually enforced, resulting in thousands of prosecutions and nine hundred convictions. Indeed, the most disturbing aspect of this period was the role played by the Supreme Court, which responded to public hysteria by accommodating repression and legitimizing the doctrine of seditious libel. In a trilogy of cases, all decided in 1919, Justice Oliver Wendell Holmes spoke for the Court in upholding the punishment of defendants whose political expression represented no threat of force or physical violence against the state. The first of these cases to reach the Supreme Court was *Schenck v. United States* (1919), in which Justice Holmes announced the "clear and present danger" test for unprotected speech. Though that phrase later became a reasonable basis for protecting dissent, Holmes applied the test in *Schenck* to arbitrarily silence unpatriotic speech.

Charles Schenck, a member of the Philadelphia Socialist Party, had mailed leaflets to men who had passed their draft exams, urging them to resist conscription. The leaflets characterized the war as a capitalist conspiracy engineered by Wall Street and argued that conscription was unconstitutional. Justice Holmes admitted that in "ordinary times," Schenck's words would be protected by the First Amendment, but he said that these were not ordinary times. Holmes used a homespun analogy: "The most stringent protection of free speech would not protect a man in falsely shouting fire in a theater, and causing a panic." Holmes said that the judgment in *Schenck* would turn on whether the words and circumstances in question created "a clear and present danger that they will bring about the substantive evils that Congress has a right to prevent." Holmes argued that Congress had the power to outlaw the act of obstructing the draft, and therefore it had the power to punish words that produced the same effect. In fact, Holmes went so far as to say that even if the words did not produce the effect, they could be punished if they were "intended" or had a "tendency" to produce the effect. Thus *Schenck* silenced political expression not because of a "clear and present danger," but because of poor intentions and bad tendencies.

Within a few days of the *Schenck* decision, two similar cases, *Frohwerk v. United States* and *Debs v. United States*, applied the same heavy-handed restraint on unpatriotic speech. *Frohwerk* involved a series of articles published in a tiny German-language newspaper in Missouri. The articles criticized the war effort, saying that it was a monumental error to send American troops to fight in Europe. The author asked rhetorically whether Americans could fault a draftee for considering his self-preservation first. For writing the articles, Frohwerk was convicted under the Espionage Act and sentenced to a fine and ten years in prison. The case was reviewed by the Supreme Court, where Justice Holmes, writing for a unanimous Court, affirmed the conviction. Frohwerk's articles had actually condemned anti-war riots and violence, but Holmes claimed that Frohwerk's choice of words conveyed an "innuendo" of a different kind. Holmes reiterated his view in *Schenck* that "words of persuasion" can constitute obstruction of the draft.

Eugene Debs suffered the same fate as Frohwerk. Debs had risen to prominence as a labor leader in the 1890s and had gone on to found the Socialist Party of America. He became the Socialist Party's candidate for President four times between 1900 and 1920, receiving his highest vote total of almost one million while he was in prison for seditious libel.

On June 16, 1918, Debs had given a speech in Canton, Ohio, in which he praised three comrades who had been imprisoned for aiding and abetting resistance to the draft. For this speech, he was himself charged with violation of the Espionage Act of 1917. At his trial, he addressed the jury himself, admitting that he abhorred war, but insisting that he had said nothing worthy of punishment. Debs was found guilty and sentenced to two concurrent ten-year prison sentences.

The case was appealed to the Supreme Court, where Justice Holmes, again writing for a unanimous Court, affirmed Debs's conviction. Holmes stated that "one purpose of the speech, whether incidental or not does not matter, was to oppose not only war in general but this war," and the effect of the speech was therefore to obstruct recruiting. For this, Debs went to prison, where he remained until he was released on a presidential order in 1921. His citizenship was never restored.

Although Justice Holmes never explicitly repudiated his opinions in the somewhat hysterical Red Menace trilogy, his dissent just a few months later in *Abrams v. United States* (1919) showed a more composed tolerance for dissent. The issue in *Abrams* was an amendment to the Espionage Act of 1917 that made it a crime to advocate the curtailment of munitions production. Abrams received a twenty-year jail sentence for printing and distributing a leaflet urging a strike.

The majority of the Court upheld the statute and conviction, but in his dissent, Holmes insisted that the statute should be strictly construed and that Abrams could be punished only on a showing of specific intent. Holmes ridiculed the idea that Abrams's "silly leaflet" represented a threat to the government's war effort and said that Abrams's only crime was criticism of the war, expression protected by the First Amendment. Holmes was quite explicit in declaring that the First Amendment outlawed seditious libel, and he warned, "[W]e should be eternally vigilant against attempts to check the expression of opinions that we loathe and believe to be fraught with death, unless they so immediately threaten interference with the lawful and pressing purposes of the law that an immediate check is required to save the country."

In 1925, another Holmes dissent repudiated the doctrine of seditious libel. In *Gitlow v. New York* (1925), Holmes rejected the majority's finding that a left-wing leaflet represented "direct incitement." In a dramatic statement of the right to dissent, Holmes wrote, "Every idea is an incitement. . . . If in the long run the beliefs expressed in proletarian dictatorship are destined to be accepted by the dominant forces in the community, the only meaning of free speech is that they should be given their chance and have their way."

Two years later, Justice Louis Brandeis offered a concurring opinion in *Whitney v. California* (1927) that many regard as the definitive statement on the right to dissent. Brandeis paid tribute to the founding fathers, who "believed that freedom to think as you will and to speak as you think are means indispensable to the discovery and spread of political truth; that without free speech and assembly discussion would be futile; that with them, discussion affords ordinarily adequate protection against the dissemination of noxious doctrine."

In *Near v. Minnesota ex rel. Olson* (1931), the Court examined a Minnesota statute that criminalized the publication of "malicious, scandalous, and defamatory" newspapers. The Court conceded the state's authority to enforce the primary requirements of decency, but it placed the criticism of public officials outside the "indecencies" subject to censorship. Even if published accusations of official corruption led some individuals to use violence as a means of redress, governmental prior restraint on such expression was unconstitutional. The judgment in *Near* thus argued strongly against the doctrine of seditious libel.

Following a period of relative political calm and judicial tolerance for dissent, the McCarthy era of the 1950s proved that the doctrine of seditious libel was alive and well. In *Dennis v. United States* (1951), the Supreme Court sustained the convictions of twelve Communist Party members for conspiracy to violate the Smith Act, a constitutionally dubious statute that made it a crime to help organize any group of persons "who teach, advocate, or encourage the overthrow or destruction of any government in the United States by force or violence." The defendants in *Dennis* had organized individuals to teach Marxism-Leninism from standard works such as *The Communist Manifesto*. Though none of the individuals involved had ever advocated any specific acts of violence, the indictment charged that their group was working toward the violent overthrow of the government. Writing for the Court, Justice Fred Vinson analyzed the constitutional issues in a way reminiscent of the *Schenck-Debs-Frohwerk* trilogy, stating, "That it is within the power of Congress to protect the Government . . . from armed rebellion is a proposition which requires little discussion." After declaring, "Speech is not an absolute," Vinson concluded, "To those who would paralyze our government in the face of impending threat by encasing it in a semantic straitjacket we must reply that all concepts are relative." As in the earlier Red Menace cases, the Court concluded in *Dennis* that "the inflammable nature of world conditions" required the suppression of certain forms of ideological speech.

By the end of the 1950s, American society had repudiated Senator McCarthy and his outrages, and the Court seemed to regain its composure. In *New York Times Co. v. Sullivan* (1964), the Court repudiated seditious libel in terms of damages. *Sullivan* involved an advertisement in the *New York Times* that solicited contributions to Martin Luther King's civil rights campaign. The ad complained of police brutality and implied public misconduct on the part of Sullivan, the police chief in Montgomery, Alabama. It was found libelous under a state statute, and the jury returned a $500,000 damage award against the Times Company.

The Supreme Court struck down the award, stating that criticism of official conduct "does not lose its constitutional protection merely because it is effective criticism and hence diminishes . . . official reputations." The Court expressed a commitment to uninhibited and robust debate on public issues, even if it included unpleasantly sharp attacks on government and public officials. It even went so far as to take a swipe at the Sedition Act of 1798, saying that though the act had never been tested in the Supreme Court, "the attack upon its validity has carried the day in the court of history." Treating the Alabama statute as a seditious libel law, the Court concluded that it was no less constitutionally offensive because it provided only for civil, rather than criminal, penalties.

In 1971, the famous *Pentagon Papers* case reassessed the doctrine of seditious libel. In *New York Times Co. v. United States* (1971), the Court upheld the right of the *Washington Post* and the *New York Times* to publish classified documents on the Vietnam War that were embarrassing to the government. The Court's per curiam opinion rested upon *Near*'s rejection of prior restraints, but Justice Douglas's concurring opinion cited *Sullivan* in declaring that the dominant purpose of the First Amendment was to prevent the use of seditious libel to punish expression embarrassing to the powers that be. Justice Black's concurring opinion expressed a similar view, describing the historic aim of the First Amendment as protection of the press "so that it could bare the secrets of government and inform the people." The *Pentagon Papers* decision was a heavy blow to the doctrine of seditious libel because the Court protected the disclosure of secrets that it acknowledged would shatter public confidence in the government. Justice Byron White, for example, said that the newspapers' disclosures had damaged public interests, but he concurred nonetheless.

In *United States v. Progressive* (1979), the government attempted to impose a prior restraint on publication of an article that would allegedly reveal

America's ultimate secret: the hydrogen bomb. In reality, the article was written by a political journalist with no knowledge of science, whose purpose was only to criticize and expose a secrecy bureaucracy that maintained public ignorance about the nuclear weapons establishment. The oddity here was the government's claim that the advanced physics of nuclear fusion was revealed by a layman journalist, Howard Morland, who relied primarily on the *Encyclopedia Americana* and his freshman textbook from college. The government seemed less concerned with the actual information disclosed in Morland's article than with the appearance of a compromised security apparatus. The issue at hand was the concept of "born classified," the notion that virtually all nuclear information becomes classified the moment it is conceived, without the need for any government action to identify and mark it as classified.

Morland's article, "The H-Bomb Secret," was submitted in 1979 to *The Progressive*, a popular political magazine, with the intention of stimulating public debate and understanding of the nuclear weapons industry while showing that the secrecy surrounding the bomb was a sham. Morland explained in his introduction that he had written his article without access to classified materials and that his purpose was to show that nuclear secrecy contributed to a political climate within which the nuclear establishment could conduct business without public scrutiny.

In the process of researching his article in the encyclopedia, magazine articles, textbooks, and interviews, Morland realized that there was no secret at all, and that anyone could piece together a basic explanation of the workings of the hydrogen bomb. After Morland submitted a draft of his article to *The Progressive*, the editor sent it to several reviewers to check for accuracy. Without the magazine's knowledge or consent, one of the reviewers sent the article to the Department of Energy for security screening. Secretary of Energy James Schlesinger took the article to Attorney General Griffin Bell, complaining that it could help foreign nations to build thermonuclear weapons.

Shortly before the deadline for *The Progressive*'s April 1979 issue, DOE's general counsel called the magazine's editor, warning that unless he withdrew Morland's article, the government would prevent the publication of the entire issue. The DOE offered to rewrite the article to make it suitable for publication, but it would not identify the "secret" parts of the article. After consulting with *The Progressive*'s staff, the magazine's attorney notified DOE that they intended to publish the article without changes.

On March 9, 1979, Federal Judge Robert Warren issued a temporary restraining order that he characterized as "the first instance of prior restraint against a publication in this fashion in the history of this country." Though he had not bothered to read the article, he said that he did not want to give the hydrogen bomb to foreign dictators like Idi Amin. A few days later, Judge Warren issued a preliminary injunction barring Morland and *The Progressive* from publishing or otherwise communicating any of the "restricted data" in the article. Warren admitted that his order would "curtail defendants' First Amendment rights in a drastic and substantial fashion" and "infringe upon our right to know and be informed as well." Nonetheless, he justified his injunction on national security grounds.

Most of the press and the scientific community saw the injunction for what it was. The *New York Times* editorialized: "What the Government really aims to protect is a system of secrecy, which it seeks now to extend to the thought and discussion of scientists and writers outside Government." *In These Times* commented, "The Government's attempt to prohibit publication by *The Progressive* of a story on 'The H-bomb Secret' has less to do with anxiety over nuclear weapons proliferation than over the proliferation of legitimate information about the nuclear weapons industry among the American people" (Herbert N. Foerstel, *Secret Science*, Westport, Praeger, 1993, pp. 85–86).

During Morland's trial, even the most trivial scientific statements were censored. Not only was the *Encyclopedia Americana* article on the hydrogen bomb treated as secret, but the affidavits by which it was introduced were secret and the court's opinion about these "secrets" was secret. The court insisted that Morland's undergraduate physics textbook be kept secret until he erased his underlining. Morland tried to explain, to no avail, that he had done the underlining as a freshman preparing for an exam.

The affidavits for the government were led by statements from the Secretaries of State, Defense, and Energy, while all affidavits for the defense came from physicists, who were unanimous in stating that all information in Morland's article was readily available from countless unclassified public sources. The rationale for Judge Warren's injunction began to unravel when an ACLU investigator found highly technical H-bomb reports on the open shelves of the public library at Los Alamos. The government tried to claim that the documents must have been declassified by mistake, but many in the Justice Department wanted to drop the case at this point. Soon, other publications were discovered that contained the same information found in Morland's article.

A "nuclear hobbyist" named Charles Hansen then organized a nationwide "H-bomb Design Contest," with the winning entry defined as the first design to be classified secret by the DOE. Hansen also wrote a lengthy letter to Senator Charles Percy (R-Ill.) in which he summarized the technical data from Morland's article and other sources. On September 16, 1979, Hansen's letter was published in a Madison, Wisconsin, newspaper. The next day, the Justice Department announced that it would seek dismissal of its case against *The Progressive*, and the appeals court vacated Judge Warren's injunction. Morland's original article appeared without alteration in the November 1979 issue of *The Progressive*.

From the beginning, the attorneys for *The Progressive* had considered their case to be a strong one that would demonstrate that the secrecy provisions of the Atomic Energy Act were unconstitutional. After Judge

Warren's injunction was vacated, *The Progressive* asked the court to open the records of the case to the public, since they had been censored throughout the trial. Unfortunately, the Justice Department immediately moved to declare the case "moot," maintaining the trial's secrecy and leaving no formal legal judgment on the constitutionality of the government's action.

In 1980, the Court once more upheld restraint on expression critical of the government, this time under the cloak of contract law. In *Snepp v. United States*, the Court considered the enforceability of an agreement signed by Frank Snepp, a former CIA official, not to publish any information relating to the agency or its activities generally, either during or after his term of employment, without prior approval by the agency. After leaving his post as a CIA officer in Vietnam, Snepp published *Decent Interval*, a book exposing malfeasance, dishonesty, and corruption in the Agency. The CIA did not challenge Snepp's claim that his book revealed no classified information, but it sued him for violating the secrecy agreement. A trial court concluded that the book had caused the government "irreparable harm and loss" and imposed a constructive trust on Snepp's profits from the book as well as an injunction prohibiting him from speaking or writing about the CIA without the agency's permission for the rest of his life. The appellate court upheld much of this judgment, though it set aside the constructive trust as an unwarranted restraint on Snepp's First Amendment right to publish unclassified information.

The Supreme Court, in an unprecedented decision, reinstated the constructive trust and affirmed the injunction on Snepp's speech and publications, all without even hearing oral arguments or taking briefs on the issues. A $140,000 fine was imposed on Snepp, and he was required forever more to obtain the permission of the CIA before criticizing it. Except for a passing footnote, the Court ignored the First Amendment.

Amazingly, the Court added that Snepp would have been subject to sanctions even if he had not signed the secrecy agreement. The legitimacy of the Court's initial claim that it was simply enforcing a contract was further undermined by the CIA's unwillingness to enforce similar agreements against other government officials. Dozens of former CIA employees have published books about the CIA without submitting their manuscripts to the censors. Only Snepp and Victor Marchetti, strident critics of the agency, have been prosecuted. Indeed, the CIA admitted in congressional hearings that it had selectively enforced the prepublication review requirement to silence its critics.

CIA Director Stansfield Turner, allowed by the trial court to testify without cross-examination by the defense, claimed that Snepp's book and others like it had caused the CIA to lose face abroad. Because Snepp's attorneys were not allowed to challenge Turner's claim, the Supreme Court referred to his testimony as "undisputed evidence" of "irreparable harm." Though the government offered no evidence of harm to anything other than the CIA's reputation, the Court said that the government had a compelling interest in protecting the "appearance of confidentiality." In a chilling footnote, the Court declared, "The problem is to ensure *in advance*, and by proper procedures, that information detrimental to national interest is not published." By affirming the government's authority to criminalize injury to its reputation, the Court squarely supported the doctrine of seditious libel.

Following *Snepp* came the case of Philip Agee, an agent who resigned from the CIA and proceeded to criticize and discredit the agency. Agee characterized the CIA as a "sinister secret police force" and sought to expose the nature and size of CIA infiltration, foreign and domestic. Like Snepp, Agee had signed a secrecy oath, but unlike Snepp, he had revealed classified information, primarily in foreign publications. Eventually, the Secretary of State revoked Agee's passport, claiming that his activities were likely to cause serious damage to the national security or foreign policy of the United States.

Agee's passport was revoked despite the fact that his disclosures had violated no federal statutes and his activities had never before been cited as grounds for passport revocation. Agee brought suit, claiming that the revocation violated his First Amendment right to criticize the government. Both the trial and appellate courts agreed that the executive action was unauthorized, and the State Department was ordered to reinstate Agee's passport.

The appellate decision had been issued over the aggressive dissent of Judge George E. MacKinnon, who depicted Agee as a traitor and collaborator with terrorists. In an unprecedented action, MacKinnon appended to his opinion a lengthy statement of Agee's allegedly illegal conduct and a draft indictment of grand-jury charges against him. When the case reached the Supreme Court as *Haig v. Agee* (1981), Chief Justice Warren Burger used MacKinnon's framework in writing the majority opinion, which reversed the lower-court opinions and dismissed all constitutional claims. Burger leaned particularly hard on Agee's efforts to expose the identities of CIA employees abroad, characterizing such activity as solicitation of murder. The Court offered no evidence of a causal link between Agee's activities and violence against CIA agents, relying solely on vague references to terrorist attacks. Justice Burger echoed *Schenck* in claiming that Agee's speech was "clearly not protected by the Constitution" because its purpose of obstructing intelligence operations represented an immediate danger to national security.

In recent years, the doctrine of seditious libel has been most prominently applied to prosecute flag desecration. In 1989, the Supreme Court ruled in *Texas v. Johnson* that burning the American flag as an expression of disagreement or contempt for the government was political speech protected by the First Amendment. In writing the majority opinion, Justice William Brennan noted that whether Johnson's treatment of the flag violated the Texas law depended on the communicative impact of his expressive conduct. The

Texas regulation was therefore content based and unconstitutional. Chief Justice William Rehnquist's dissent expressed the view that because millions of Americans regard the flag "with almost mystical reverence," an attack on the flag was a sacrilegious attack on America's national heritage that could not be countenanced.

Before the *Johnson* decision, there had been a succession of state prosecutions and convictions for flag desecration. Convictions were frequently affirmed or reversed based on the vehemence of the desecration. To speak ill of the flag was usually protected; to alter the appearance of the flag or inappropriately display it was sometimes protected speech; to burn or destroy the flag as political protest was almost always punishable.

After *Johnson*, Congress passed the Flag Protection Act, a carefully crafted attempt to pass constitutional muster, but the Court, with Brennan again writing the majority opinion, ruled that the act was unconstitutional. The Court's rulings in 1989 and 1990 recognized that the flag was a symbol with a political meaning, and that regulations to control that meaning and guarantee a positive message were unconstitutional. By concluding that attacks on the flag, because of their political nature, must therefore be protected, the Court took another step in freeing citizens to criticize their government and governors. *See also* FLAG DESECRATION.

REFERENCE: Patrick S. Washburn, *A Question of Sedition: The Federal Government's Investigation of the Black Press during World War II*, New York, Oxford University Press, 1986.

SENSITIVE BUT UNCLASSIFIED INFORMATION   An initially secret 1982 government report, *The Exploitation of Western Data Bases*, claimed popular acceptance for protecting unclassified information on privacy or proprietary grounds, but admitted, "The case for withholding unclassified information which is 'militarily critical' is not as readily accepted, partly because the 'unclassified but sensitive' designator sounds like a contradiction in terms." Nonetheless, in 1984, President Ronald Reagan quietly signed National Security Decision Directive 145 (NSDD-145), officially designating a category of information called "sensitive but unclassified."

The NSDD-145 Steering Group recommended restricting access to any information that might adversely affect federal government interests, but the precise determination of what was "sensitive" was initially left to agency heads. Enforcement authority for NSDD-145 was assigned to the highly secretive National Security Agency (NSA), whose authority was extended to include "all computers and communications security for the Federal Government and private industry . . . including non–national security sensitive information."

National Security Adviser John Poindexter subsequently defined "sensitive but unclassified" information in dangerously broad terms, including "information the disclosure, loss, misuse, alteration, or destruction of which would adversely affect national security or other Federal government interests. . . . Other government interests are those related, but not limited, to the wide range of government or government-derived economic, human, financial, industrial, agricultural, technological, and law enforcement information, as well as the privacy or confidentiality of personal or commercial proprietary information provided to the U.S. Government by its citizens." Upon considering Poindexter's broad list of government interests, the Office of Technology Assessment concluded, "It now appears that the definition of 'sensitive' could be applied to almost any information, or at least a very broad range of information, even if it is already published or available."

Congress expressed its concern about NSDD-145's assignment of military control over "sensitive" information by passing the Computer Security Act of 1987, which made the civilian National Institute of Standards and Technology (NIST), rather than the NSA, responsible for unclassified information in government computers. The act also somewhat narrowed NSDD-145's definition of "sensitive" information by specifying that nothing in the act shall be construed to authorize any federal agency "to limit, restrict, regulate, or control the collection, maintenance, disclosure, use, transfer, or sale of any information . . . that is—(A) privately owned information; (B) discloseable under section 552 of Title 5, United States Code, or other law requiring or authorizing the public disclosure of information; or (C) public domain information." The Computer Security Act softened, but did not reverse, the repressive intent of NSDD-145, which has never been rescinded (Herbert N. Foerstel, *Secret Science: Federal Control of American Science and Technology*, Westport, Praeger, 1993, pp. 143–49).

REFERENCE: National Commission on Libraries and Information Science, *Hearing on Sensitive but Not Classified Information*, 1988.

SENSITIVE COMPARTMENTED INFORMATION Sensitive compartmented information (SCI) is the most highly guarded subset of the ultrasecret special access programs. In 1976, George Bush, then Director of the Central Intelligence Agency, issued a directive titled "Minimum Personnel Security Standards and Procedures for Access to Sensitive Compartmented Information," in which he defined SCI to include "all information and materials bearing special community controls indicating restricted handling within present and future intelligence collection programs and their end products for which community systems of compartmentation have been or will be formally established." The directive's detailed secrecy provisions applied to "all United States Government civilian and military personnel, consultants, contractors, employees of contractors, and other individuals who require access to Sensitive Compartmented Information."

President Reagan's 1983 National Security Decision Directive 84 required that all government employees with access to SCI submit to lifelong censorship of their publications and even their public speech.

Because unauthorized disclosure of SCI was said to cause "irreparable injury to the United States," those signing the SCI Nondisclosure Agreement acknowledged that "by being granted access to SCI, special confidence and trust shall be placed in me by the United States Government." By their signature, government employees agreed to submit for security review "all materials, including works of fiction," that might relate to SCI. Any royalties or benefits that might result from such publications would be assigned to the U.S. government. Breach of the Agreement could result in termination of employment and/or criminal prosecution. *See also* NATIONAL SECURITY INFORMATION; SPECIAL ACCESS PROGRAMS.

REFERENCE: U.S. Director of Central Intelligence, *Minimum Personnel Security Standards and Procedures Governing Eligibility for Access to Sensitive Compartmented Information*, Washington, The Director, 1984.

SHIELD LAWS A variety of laws have been enacted at the state level to protect the confidentiality of journalists' sources from legislative, judicial, or other official interrogation. These "shield laws" attempt to provide a "newsman's privilege" which does not exist in common law or in the Constitution. Reporters have been subpoenaed and even incarcerated for refusing to reveal their sources. Their claim is that the protection of news sources is essential to the journalistic process. There is indeed some empirical evidence that in the absence of this privilege, investigative reporting suffers from the chilled atmosphere between reporters and their sources. On the other hand, opponents of this privilege claim that it can compromise the search for truth in the administration of justice.

The American press has a long history of protecting the confidentiality of its sources. In 1722, Benjamin Franklin's half-brother refused to tell the government the name of the author of an article in his newspaper, and he was consequently imprisoned for a month. In 1848, during the secret Senate debate on the treaty to end the Mexican-American War, a reporter for the *New York Herald* obtained a draft of the treaty and related documents. The Senate subpoenaed the reporter, who was jailed for contempt of Congress after refusing to reveal his source.

America's first shield law was enacted in Maryland in 1896, but it remained unique until the 1930s, when seven other states enacted shield laws. By 1972, eighteen states had passed such legislation. In 1958, the federal judiciary first considered the question of a constitutional "newsman's privilege" during a libel action by actress Judy Garland, who sought to discover the source of a columnist's allegedly defamatory statements about her. In *Garland v. Torre* (1958), the court recognized a qualified privilege for the columnist, up to the point where the identity of the source went to the "heart of the plaintiff's claim." In the years following *Garland*, most courts refused to acknowledge a reporter's privilege, and in *Branzburg v. Hayes* (1972), the Court held that reporters have no constitutional right to refuse to appear before a grand jury or to refuse to answer relevant questions during a grand-jury investigation. The 5–4 decision in *Branzburg* left many aspects of the issue unresolved, but the majority opinion emphasized that Congress or state legislatures were not precluded from enacting shield laws, nor were state courts prevented from construing state constitutions to recognize a journalist's privilege.

Indeed, shortly after the *Branzburg* decision, eight more states enacted shield laws, bringing to twenty-six the number of states providing some protection for the confidentiality of reporters' sources. As such legislation proliferated, concerns arose about their conflict with the separation of powers doctrine. In fact, some states reviewed their shield laws and either narrowed them or judged them unconstitutional.

The debate over shield laws has weighed the public's interest in full news coverage against the need for effective law enforcement and administration of justice. The form of the particular shield statute has been central to the debate at the state level. A "qualified" statute leaves within the courts the authority to deny a reporter's privilege if the litigant can demonstrate that disclosure of the source outweighs the public's interest in the free flow of news. Such a statute is unlikely to be challenged as a violation of the separation of powers doctrine. But the "absolute" statutes passed by some states either absolve the reporter of any obligation to reveal sources or remove the court's contempt powers in such cases. These statutes do raise serious separation of powers questions (Theodore Kupferman, *Censorship, Secrecy, Access, and Obscenity*, Westport, Meckler, 1990, pp. 133–47).

In *Cohen v. Cowles Media Co.* (1991), the Supreme Court rendered an important judgment concerning confidential sources when it ruled that promises of confidentiality by a reporter are legally enforceable contracts. This put a new twist on shield laws by saying that not only did reporters have the right to withhold the name of a confidential source, but they could be sued if they did otherwise. *Cohen v. Cowles Media Co.* dealt with a political leak to two Minneapolis newspapers during the 1982 Minnesota gubernatorial race. The papers promised confidentiality to Cohen, a political worker associated with the Republican candidate, but subsequently revealed his name in their stories, resulting in Cohen's firing. In response to Cohen's suit, the newspapers claimed that treating the confidentiality agreement as an enforceable contract infringed upon the First Amendment rights of the press to fully report truthful information about a matter of public significance.

The Supreme Court's majority opinion, written by Justice Byron White, stated: "Respondents and amici argue that permitting Cohen to maintain a cause of action for promissory estoppel will inhibit truthful reporting because news organizations will have legal incentives not to disclose a confidential source's identity even when that person's identity is itself newsworthy. . . . But if this is the case, it is no more than the incidental, and constitutionally insignificant, consequence of applying to the press a generally applicable law that requires those who make certain kinds of promises to keep them."

REFERENCES: Theodore R. Kupferman, ed., *Censorship, Secrecy, Access, and Obscenity*, Westport, Meckler, 1990; Nickerson B. Miles, *The Chilling Effect and Confidentiality: A Study of Post-Branzburg Press-Source Relationships*, Thesis (M.A.), University of Maryland, College Park, 1976.

SMITH ACT The Aliens Registration Act, generally known as the Smith Act, enacted in 1940 and amended in 1948, states that anyone who "knowingly or willfully advocates, abets, advises, or teaches the duty, necessity, desirability, or propriety of overthrowing or destroying the government of the United States" or any of its states, districts, possessions, or subdivisions by force or violence shall be fined not more than $10,000 or imprisoned not more than ten years, or both, and shall be ineligible for employment by the U.S. government for the next five years. The statute applies very broadly to any person who "prints, publishes, edits, issues, circulates, sells, distributes, or publicly displays any written or printed matter advocating, advising, or teaching" such actions. The penalties also apply to any person who "organizes or helps or attempts to organize any society, group, or assembly of persons who teach, advocate, or encourage" such actions or is affiliated with such a group.

The validity of the Smith Act was upheld in *Dennis v. United States* (1951), in which the Supreme Court ruled that Congress could limit speech and press activities aimed at the violent overthrow of the government. The act has not been used since 1957, when the Court in *Yates v. United States* overturned the conviction of fourteen Communists, saying that the act could not prohibit mere advocacy or teaching of prohibited activities. Only the urging of imminent action representing a clear and present danger could be punished.

REFERENCES: Michal R. Belknap, *Cold War Political Justice: The Smith Act, the Communist Party, and American Civil Liberties*, Westport, Greenwood Press, 1977; Don R. Pember, *The Smith Act as a Restraint on the Press*, Austin, Association for Education in Journalism, 1969.

SPECIAL ACCESS PROGRAMS Special Access Programs (SAPs) are a broad category of ultrasecret information controls defined in 1982 by President Ronald Reagan's Executive Order 12356. Section 4.2 of EO 12356 states: "Agency heads . . . may create special . . . programs to control access, distribution and protection of particularly sensitive information classified pursuant to this Order or predecessor orders. Such programs may be created or continued only at the written direction of these agency heads." SAPs imposed controls beyond those required for access to the standard levels of classified information, confidential, secret, and top secret.

Until recently, the Stealth Bomber was a special access program. SAPs not only hide information from the public, but often from Congress and executive-branch agencies as well. Even the Information Security Oversight Office, the agency that oversees America's entire secrecy system, has had limited authority over SAPs.

Special access programs have fallen out of favor since the Reagan administration and currently exist in considerably reduced numbers. President Clinton's 1995 Executive Order 12958 said that only the Secretaries of State, Defense, and Energy and the Director of the Central Intelligence Agency could create a special access program unless otherwise authorized by the President. More important, the order stated,

These officials shall keep the number of these programs at an absolute minimum, and shall establish them only upon a specific finding that:

1) the vulnerability of, or threat to, specific information is exceptional; and
2) the normal criteria for determining eligibility for access applicable to information classified at the same level are not deemed sufficient to protect the information from unauthorized disclosure; or
3) the program is required by statute.

The Clinton order limited the number of persons who could have access to SAPs, required a system of accounting for them, and made them subject to oversight by the Information Security Oversight Office. Within six months after the effective date of the Clinton order, agency heads were required to review all existing SAPs and terminate any special access programs that did not clearly meet the provisions of this order.
REFERENCE: U.S. General Accounting Office, *DOD Special Access Programs: Administrative Due Process Not Provided When Access Is Denied or Revoked*, Washington, D.C., General Accounting Office, 1993.

STERN, HOWARD, 1954– Howard Stern is the most controversial radio personality of the 1990s, with an audience of about fifteen million listeners and the largest amount of Federal Communications Commission fines for "indecency" ever incurred by a radio show. Because the Stern show often includes scatological and sexual satire, it has been a principal target in the FCC's war against indecency. Between April 1987 and August 1993 alone, the stations carrying the "Howard Stern Show" incurred nearly $1.3 million worth of fines.

The FCC's August 1993 fine of $73,750 against a Las Vegas station was levied after just one listener complained about nine segments of Stern broadcasts between November 1992 and January 1993. Four other stations in New York, Philadelphia, Baltimore, and Washington, D.C., belonging to Infinity Broadcasting, were quickly fined $125,000 each for carrying the same programming as the Las Vegas station. In December 1992, the FCC had taken similar action, fining a Los Angeles station $105,000 for Stern broadcasts and following with a $600,000 fine against Infinity.

Greater Media, the parent company of the Los Angeles station, said that the FCC had applied a narrow interpretation of "contemporary community standards" to define indecency, inappropriate to the broad listener community for the Stern show. Greater Media also challenged the size of the fine and the FCC's claim that children could be adversely impacted by the Stern show. A research survey of the listener market for the Stern show determined that virtually no unsupervised children were exposed to the Stern show in the Los Angeles metropolitan area. Greater Media concluded that these findings undermined the commission's presumption that censorship of the Stern program was needed or welcome to help parents protect their children.

Infinity, a New York–based company that is the largest radio-station owner in the nation, has argued that Stern's on-air raunchiness is constitutionally protected speech, but the company does its best to avoid the FCC's wrath. Stern's contract specifically prohibits him from using any of the "seven dirty words" made famous by comedian George Carlin, or from reading the FCC's definition of "indecency" on the air. Infinity President Mel Karmazin said that his stations were attempting to conform to the FCC's rules, but that he wanted to know what the "speed limit" was.

In August 1993, Evergreen Media's WLUP in Chicago dropped the Stern show, saying that it had made a business decision to avoid having to defend indecency complaints against Howard Stern. WLUP said that the large fines against stations carrying the Stern show posed an unacceptable risk. General Manager Larry Wert said that Evergreen was particularly concerned about license renewals and FCC approval to purchase additional stations.

In November 1993, the African American Business Association (AABA) filed a petition with the FCC, complaining of "racist" comments on the "Howard Stern Show" and asking that the FCC deny Infinity's pending purchase of a Washington station and revoke Infinity's license to operate another Washington station that carried the Stern show. Infinity President Mel Karmazin said that it was absurd to characterize the Stern show as racist when it actually used parody as a way to point out how wrong racism was.

The FCC's attempts to muzzle Howard Stern have gone beyond the imposition of fines to include threats to revoke Infinity's broadcast license and to disapprove its purchase of three new stations. This has held up the largest acquisition package in the history of FM radio, all because of objections to Stern. One FCC commissioner said, "It seems that if we allow them to buy additional stations, we're condoning Stern" ("FCC Targets Employer of Radio 'Shock Jock,'" *Washington Post*, January 1, 1994, p. B1). When the FCC's apparent decision to delay approval of the Infinity acquisitions was announced in the *New York Times*, the company's stock declined sharply.

A January 1994 *Washington Post* editorial warned that the FCC's action represented a dangerous use of the government's licensing and regulatory powers to force a part of the press to alter its editorial content. The *Post* said: "What the commission has been doing—and the possibility that it could still move to wreck a $170 million purchase because of what Howard Stern says on the air—is censorship. . . . Censorship is arbitrary, and Congress should start thinking hard about getting government out of it" ("The Howard Stern Case," *Washington Post*, January 15, 1994, p. A20).

In May 1994, the AABA withdrew its complaint against the "Howard Stern" Show after Infinity agreed to spend $2.75 million on programs aiding minority businesses in the Washington area. The settlement seemed to have removed the major barrier to FCC approval of Infinity's purchase of WPGC AM-FM in Washington, but the FCC said that it was still considering two anonymous complaints charging indecency on the Stern show.

Howard Stern's off-the-air communications have been as controversial as his radio work. In late 1993, the publication of Stern's book *Private Parts* produced the same kind of public support and official condemnation that his radio show did. *Private Parts* quickly became number one on the *New York Times* nonfiction bestseller list, but the book suffered unique forms of censorship. For example, when the Caldor department-store chain refused to sell the book, it also felt the need to alter the *New York Times* bestseller list posted in its stores. Caldor reprinted the list, deleting Stern's book from the number one spot and moving all other titles up one notch. Only after the *New York Times* legal department complained about the distorted list did Caldor agree to use the complete list, with a notation saying that Caldor would not carry Stern's book.

REFERENCE: Howard Stern, *Private Parts*, New York, Pocket Star Books, 1993.

STROSSEN, NADINE, 1950–   On February 1, 1991, Nadine Strossen became the first woman president of the American Civil Liberties Union (ACLU). At the time she assumed the presidency, Strossen was a forty–year-old professor of constitutional law, federal courts, and human rights at New York Law School. She had previously been an ACLU board member and had served as its general counsel since 1986.

Strossen was born in Jersey City on August 18, 1950. Her maternal grandfather had endured ridicule as a conscientious objector in Europe during World War I. Her father had emigrated to the United States after American troops liberated him from a German labor camp where he had been imprisoned for anti-Hitler activities. Nadine Strossen said, "I had a strong sense of individual rights and sticking one's neck out on behalf of unpopular causes, even at the risk of personal ostracism" (David Gonzalez, "Dynamic Advocate," *New York Times*, January 28, 1991, p. A14).

Strossen attended Radcliffe College and Harvard Law School, where she was editor of the *Harvard Law Review* and graduated magna cum laude in 1975. Despite her legal background, one of her first initiatives as president of the ACLU was to extend the organization's activities beyond litigation to lobbying and public education, areas that had been marginally pursued in earlier years. She lectures around the country and appears regularly on national television, debating and lecturing on civil liberties. She has forcefully opposed antipornography laws and has frequently debated feminists like Catharine MacKinnon, who helped author an antipornography statute. Strossen's 1995 book *Defending Pornography: Free Speech, Sex, and the Fight for Women's Rights* warns against regarding sexually oriented expression as less worthy of constitutional protection than other forms of speech, arguing that there is no evidence that pornography leads to sexual violence or negative attitudes toward women.

Strossen has also led the way in opposing campus speech codes and restrictions on hate speech. Her position was hotly debated within the ACLU, but the organization eventually agreed that such patronizing codes or laws weakened the First Amendment. This position was represented in ACLU lawsuits, resulting in federal court decisions invalidating restrictive speech codes at the Universities of Michigan and Wisconsin and a Supreme Court ruling against a Minnesota ordinance that criminalized hate speech. Strossen explained, "There are many things that are special about the ACLU, but if I had to single out one, I would say it is that we are the only organization that fights for *all* fundamental rights for *all* people" (Lynne Marek, "In Defense," *Chicago Tribune*, January 8, 1995, sec. 6, p. 3).

REFERENCE: Nadine Strossen, *Defending Pornography: Free Speech, Sex, and the Fight for Women's Rights*, New York, Scribner, 1995.

SUSSMAN, PETER, 1941–   In 1986, when Peter Sussman, editor of the *San Francisco Chronicle*'s "Sunday Punch" section, published an article on AIDS submitted by Dannie Martin, an inmate at California's Lompoc Prison, he began an unlikely partnership that would eventually test the First Amendment rights of both prisoners and publishers. Two years later, when Martin wrote and Sussman published an article about prison conditions at Lompoc, Martin was thrown in "the hole." Sussman, learning of the detention of his writer, alerted *Chronicle* reporters and other media, and within twenty-four hours Martin was released from solitary confinement. Sussman then negotiated guarantees for Martin's continued writing and personal safety with the warden of Lompoc, but a week later, Martin was handcuffed and transferred to a remote prison in the Arizona desert. This time the charge against the convict was that he had violated a prison regulation stating: "The inmate may not receive compensation or anything of value for correspondence with the news media. The inmate may not act as a reporter or publish under a byline."

The prison had been aware of Martin's bylined reports for the *Chronicle* for two years, and Sussman maintained that the actions against Martin resulted from the content of his writing, a violation of First Amendment guarantees. Sussman obtained the services of a pro bono attorney who, with the *Chronicle*, filed suit against the Bureau of Prisons, the Lompoc warden, and other prison officials. They demanded, among other things, that the regulation upon which the prison relied in censoring Martin's publications be declared unconstitutional, that Martin not be punished further, and that he be allowed to continue writing for the *Chronicle*.

In consultation with Sussman, the attorneys won a temporary restraining order barring further harassment and then a preliminary injunction granting Martin the right to continue writing without further official retaliation. However, in June 1990, the court vacated the injunction, affirming the appropriateness of prison regulations that prohibit inmates from acting as reporters, from being paid for newspaper articles, or from writing bylined articles.

Sussman never ceased defending Martin's and his newspaper's First Amendment rights, for which he was vilified in court and, occasionally, in the press. He has also been widely praised. In 1988, he was cowinner, along with Dannie Martin, of the prestigious Media Alliance Award for Special Achievement. In 1989, Sussman won a James Madison Freedom of Information Award and an Edward Willis Scripps Award for Service to the First Amendment. In 1990, he won the Society of Professional Journalists' Freedom of Information Award, and in 1992 the Hugh M. Hefner First Amendment Award.

In 1993, Sussman published *Committing Journalism: The Prison Writings of Red Hog*, a book that gathered fifty of Martin's previously published articles along with Sussman's essay on the history of Martin's career. The title of the book comes from one of Martin's pithy observations: "I committed bank robbery and they put me in prison, and that was right. Then I committed journalism and they put me in the hole. And that was wrong" (Dannie M. Martin and Peter Y. Sussman, *Committing Journalism*, New York, Norton, 1993, p. 124).

In 1995, when California officials decided to prohibit all media interviews with state prisoners, Sussman, northern California president of the Society of Professional Journalists, denounced the action in a press release. "Our entire system of government is based on the public's right to know about the operation of public institutions," said Sussman. "Prisons are public institutions . . . and no law or court ruling gives prison officials the right to hog-tie news media reporting for capricious reasons. . . . Freedom of the press was enshrined in our Constitution specifically to guarantee the independence of the news media to report on issues of public concern. . . . Filtering of those reports through the prison bureaucracy is inimical both to the press's constitutional right to report on government affairs and the public's right to know how its government is conducting its business."

REFERENCE: Dannie M. Martin and Peter Y. Sussman, *Committing Journalism: The Prison Writings of Red Hog*, New York, W. W. Norton, 1993.

T

TELEVISION   The broader First Amendment issues associated with television are the same as for radio and the other broadcast media (see BROADCASTING), but television has had its own unique challenges. Because TV is a visual medium and, more important, the nation's preeminent mass medium, it maintains a much more homogeneous and conservative programming image than radio. Award-winning television writer Barbara Hall has said, "To fight the issue of censorship in television is already an absurd project. It is currently the most censored art form in existence. Every week our scripts are scrutinized by a faceless contingent of people who tell us when we've crossed the line. Even so, you won't hear a lot of TV writers railing against Broadcast Standards because we have long ago accepted the obligations of the industry to censor itself" (Barbara Hall, "Death by Prime Time," *LA Weekly*, September 9, 1993, p. 1).

Because of its conservative tradition, television has had nothing comparable to radio's high-profile rows with the FCC over indecent programming, but unlike radio, TV is the perfect medium for America's national vice, violence. In 1989, Senator Paul Simon (D-Ill.) attracted strong support for his Television Violence Act, an attempt to get the major television networks to "voluntarily" meet and reform their propensity toward violence. To Simon's chagrin, Senator Jesse Helms (R-N.C.) tacked on a "sex and drugs" rider expanding the scope of the bill into broader First Amendment territory, but Simon's bill eventually regained its focus on violence and enough bipartisan support to pass Congress.

In December 1990, President Bush signed the Television Violence Act, granting the TV networks, cable operators, and independent stations three years of immunity from antitrust regulations to allow them to establish guidelines for TV violence. Many in the industry feared that the "voluntary" negotiations would be conducted under pressure, producing arbitrary standards that would eventually be used by the FCC as licensing requirements. There were also concerns that the standards would leave the networks open to First Amendment lawsuits. Network officials recalled a 1976 lawsuit by Hollywood guilds that led a federal judge to remove TV's so-called family viewing policy, which had established sex and violence guidelines from 7 to 9 P.M. The court rejected the broadcasters' claim that they had adopted the policy "voluntarily," saying that it had been foisted upon them by the FCC.

Nonetheless, by the end of 1992, the three major TV networks announced a joint plan for limiting violent programming, and Senator Simon expressed satisfaction that his bill had done its job. Still, political pressure continued to build for more direct controls on television violence. In 1993, Attorney General Janet Reno told the television industry to clean up its act, or legislative action would be "imperative." Indeed, Congress was already considering such legislation. Representative Edward Markey (D-Mass.) introduced a bill requiring new TV sets to come equipped with a "V-chip" enabling parents to block violent programming. Representative John Bryant (D-Tex.) offered a bill under which TV stations could lose their licenses and face heavy fines for violating the bill's antiviolence standards. Bryant's bill, regarded by many as unconstitutional, failed, but Markey's V-chip bill was eventually passed as part of the 1996 Telecommunications Act.

That act would not only require all TV sets to contain a computer chip allowing parents to block objectionable programming, but would require the development of a ratings system to guide parents in the use of the V-chip. If the industry did not produce a ratings system acceptable to the FCC within one year, a politically appointed commission would establish rules for rating violence and other objectionable content. Thus the door was left open for controls that went far beyond violent programming.

Just a few weeks after the V-chip legislation was passed, the frightened TV industry announced the outline of its own ratings system. The heads of ABC, CBS, NBC, and Fox, along with cable magnates like Ted Turner and Michael Ovitz, met with President Clinton to promise a ratings system similar to that used by the Motion Picture Association of America (MPAA). At a subsequent press conference, the TV executives were asked whether sports and news shows would be among the programs rated. NBC's chief executive said that all things appearing on television would be considered for ratings, but CBS's chief executive said that he guaranteed that there would be no rating of news.

Jack Valenti, MPAA president, lauded the ratings proposal, but admitted that details, such as who would develop the system, were yet to come. He could not even say whether the MPAA's ratings—G, PG, PG-13, R, and NC-17—would be the exact model for TV shows, though a joint statement had previously committed the TV industry to a "similar" system.

Though the V-chip got its name from the original desire to reduce TV violence, the chip itself was content neutral. It would rely on the associated ratings system to make judgments about program content, and the proposals from the industry were clearly adding "sex" to the list of criteria used to rate objectionable programming. Brandon Tartikoff, former head of programming at NBC and now chairman of New World Entertainment, said, "It may not be Hitler going into Poland, but it's still an invasion. Once you open the door, you're inviting two things to happen: censorship, and the government getting into a business it has no business being in. Where is it going to end? Next, we'll have the S-chip for sexuality, the R-chip for religious beliefs that are controversial, and PIC-chip for politically incorrect material" (Tom Shales, "Chip of Fools," *Washington Post*, March 10, 1996, p. G5).

Cable television has a more recent and somewhat different history of federal control. The Supreme Court first addressed the extent of First Amendment protections for cable television in early 1994 when, in *Turner Broadcasting System v. Federal Communications Commission*, it examined the question of whether Congress could require cable systems to set aside one-third of their channels for local broadcasters, called "must-carry" regulations. The cable companies had appealed a 1993 decision by a district court that found that the regulations did not target programming content and therefore needed to meet only an intermediate standard of review on First Amendment grounds. The cable companies claimed that the government was trying to regulate the content of protected speech. During oral arguments, Justice David H. Souter said that cable television might, for legal purposes, be defined as somewhere between a newspaper and telephone services, both an originator and a carrier.

On June 27, 1994, the Court rendered a unanimous landmark decision that said that cable television was entitled to virtually the same constitutional guarantees of free speech as newspapers and magazines. Though the Court did not strike down the must-carry regulations as the cable companies had sought, it set up new legal ground rules for cable and wire-based communications systems that provide more First Amendment protection from government interference than is available to broadcasters. The Court distinguished cable systems from broadcast systems, whose "spectrum scarcity" has been used to justify heavy regulation. "Cable television does not suffer from the inherent limitations that characterize the broadcast medium," said Justice Anthony Kennedy. "Indeed, given the rapid advances in [technology], soon there may be no practical limitation on the number of speakers who may use the cable medium." Kennedy, joined by all of the other justices, said that a cable regulation should only be upheld if it furthers an "important or substantial" government interest, a standard slightly below the level of protection accorded newspapers, but greater than that for broadcasters.

Even as the Supreme Court was establishing the broad parameters for cable television's First Amendment protection, the medium was struggling with the same kinds of challenges to its programming content that the broadcast media endured. In January 1994, in response to congressional criticism of violent television programming, the cable industry submitted an eleven–point plan for a voluntary rating system and an outside monitor for violent content. Following the lead of broadcast television, the cable rating system would work in consort with the V-chip, the technology that allows viewers to block programs with certain ratings. Congressional critics who had threatened legislative action if the industry did not curb violent programming were very receptive to the new plan.

Cable television also came under federal pressure to curb its sexually explicit programming. In early 1996, in *Denver Area Educational Telecommunications Consortium, Inc. v. Federal Communications Commission*, the Supreme Court heard arguments over the constitutionality of 1992 "indecency" restrictions sponsored by Senator Jesse Helms (R-N.C.). Under that law, a cable company could ban programming that it "reasonably believes describes or depicts sexual or excretory activities or organs in a patently offensive manner as measured by contemporary standards." During arguments before the Court, the government claimed that though the law allowed cable operators to block indecent programs, it did not "significantly encourage" them to do so, and therefore any programming censorship could not be attributed to the government. Justice Ruth Bader Ginsburg said that the provision authorizing cable companies to block indecent programming unless a subscriber made a written request to the contrary made it difficult and uncomfortable for a person to access protected speech.

On June 28, 1996, the Supreme Court voted 5–4 to strike down the section of the law that allowed cable companies to refuse to air indecent material—defined as sexually explicit or "patently offensive"—on "public access" channels, those required by local governments, including educational and governmental programming. The Court also voted 6–3 to strike down the section of the act that required subscribers to "leased access" channels—those paid for by independent programmers—to submit a written request before "indecent" programs could be received. By a 7–2 vote, however, the Court upheld sections of the law allowing cable operators to refuse "indecent" programming on these "leased access" channels. Justice Stephen Breyer wrote that the two provisions struck down by the Court violated the First Amendment, "for they are not tailored to achieve the basic, legitimate objective of protecting children from exposure to patently offensive material." See V-CHIP.

REFERENCES: Colin R. Munro, *Television, Censorship, and the Law*, Hampshire, Eng., Grower, 1983; Murray Schumach, *The Face on the Cutting Room Floor: The Story of Movie and Television Censorship*, New York, Morrow, 1964.

UNCLASSIFIED CONTROLLED NUCLEAR INFORMATION

On April Fools' Day 1983, the Department of Energy, in response to earlier amendments to the Atomic Energy Act of 1954, proposed regulations to prohibit the unauthorized dissemination of what it called unclassified controlled nuclear information (UCNI). Sections 147 and 148 of the Atomic Energy Act had given the Nuclear Regulatory Commission and DOE the authority to prohibit dissemination of certain unclassified information, and now the rules for defining and enforcing these prohibitions were being introduced. The DOE was directed to protect from unauthorized dissemination unclassified information pertaining to (1) the design of nuclear production or utilization facilities, (2) security measures for the protection of such facilities or their nuclear material, or (3) the design, manufacture, or utilization of any nuclear weapon or component.

UCNI was described very broadly, even to the point of allowing that information not specifically described in these regulations could still be treated as UCNI. The justification given for the new restrictions was the government's fear that unauthorized dissemination of such unclassified information could result in significant adverse effect on the health and safety of the public or the common defense and security. Herman E. Roser, then Assistant Secretary for Defense Programs, said that he hoped to achieve a balance between controlling truly sensitive information without abridging the freedoms of the academic community and the public at large.

David Steiner, then vice president and general counsel at Harvard University, complained, "Even read narrowly, the proposed rule would prevent dissemination of extensive nonsecret—indeed, published—information, and would likely chill or thwart academic or public discussion in the nuclear field." Hugh E. DeWitt, a nuclear scientist at the Lawrence Livermore National Laboratory, claimed that the notion of UCNI belonged in the mad world of George Orwell's book *1984* (Herbert N. Foerstel, *Secret Science*, Westport, Praeger, 1993, p. 173).

Librarians around the country were notified that once the proposed regulations were passed, all UCNI documents in their collections would require the same security as classified documents. Access to UCNI documents would be restricted to authorized U.S. citizens with a "need to know" demonstrated. Librarians feared that important unclassified nuclear information would now be denied to their libraries, but they were more concerned about the application of UCNI regulations to their existing collections. The regulations specified that any person found in violation of any provision would be subject to a civil penalty up to $100,000 per violation, in addition to criminal penalties.

After librarians and civil libertarians lobbied intensively against the UCNI regulations, the DOE finally acknowledged the impossibility of controlling or gutting existing unclassified library collections, and it exempted from the regulations any material that the DOE determines to have been widely disseminated in the public domain. UCNI regulations nonetheless continued to deny unclassified materials to universities and institutions around the country. Thus the concept of UCNI has receded from public view and concern, but remains alive and well behind the scenes.

REFERENCE: Herbert N. Foerstel, *Secret Science: Federal Control of American Science and Technology*, Westport, Praeger, 1993.

V

V-CHIP   The V-chip is a microchip designed to be installed in television sets for the specific purpose of allowing parents to screen out undesirable programs. The political argument for the chip began with a concern over violent programming, hence the "V" in V-chip, but opponents of "indecent" programming have supported the new technology as well. First Amendment concerns initially slowed legislation that would require TV sets to be equipped with the chip.

In January 1996, when the Supreme Court accepted the FCC's restrictions on "indecent" programming, FCC Chairman Reed Hundt said that the decision would also reduce legal challenges to legislation requiring the V-chip in TV sets. "The Supreme Court in effect held that a flat prohibition on certain kinds of broadcasts is constitutional if those programs hurt kids," said Hundt. "If a prohibition is constitutional, rules that give parents more power to protect their kids have to be constitutional also" (Paul Farhi, "FCC Chief: Ruling 'Vindicates' Agency's TV Smut Policy," *Washington Post*, January 10, 1996, p. G3).

Just two weeks later, in his State of the Union Address, President Bill Clinton said, "I call on Congress to pass the requirement for a 'V-chip' in TV sets, so parents can screen out programs they believe are inappropriate for their children. When parents control what their young children see, that's not censorship. . . . To make the 'V-chip' work, I challenge the broadcast industry to do what movies have done: identify your programs in ways to help parents protect their children."

One week after President Clinton's address, Congress passed a Telecommunications Act that, in addition to regulating sexual material on the Internet, required TV set manufacturers to install the V-chip in all TV sets with thirteen-inch screens or larger that are sold in the United States. The chip would allow set owners to block any programs that a ratings committee identified as containing violent, sexual, or indecent content. The bill does not mandate that broadcasters tag their shows with signals that the V-chip can block, but the FCC would be required to set up an industry and community advisory committee to rate the programs if the industry fails to do so.

REFERENCE: U.S. Senate, Committee on Commerce, Science, and Transportation, *Television Violence: Hearing*, 104th Cong. 1st sess., July 12, 1995.

VIDEO GAMES   Since their invention in the 1970s, video games have drawn criticism for being trivial, mindlessly addictive, and, more recently, for being excessively violent. As congressional pressure to control video games grew, the industry indicated a willingness to accept a rating system for its games, but an understandable reluctance to accept any control of their content.

The Software Publishers Association advocated an industry coalition that would work with Congress and parents' and teachers' groups to find a system satisfactory to all. The industry council would work with retailers and rental-store owners to publicize the system and ensure that juveniles could not obtain certain games without parental permission. Initially, eighteen game companies signed on to the coalition, along with the Video Software Dealers Association, which represents companies that rent video games. A spokesman for Nintendo of America Inc. claimed that it already had strict guidelines that limit its games to family fare, but Nintendo said that it would nonetheless play an active role in whatever rating system was devised. Sega of America Inc., one of the larger video-game distributors, says that it is already keeping violent games away from children, and it recommends self-regulation rather than government regulation.

In June 1993, Sega created the Video Game Rating Council, made up of Sega-appointed experts in the fields of education, psychology, and sociology. The Sega council established three rating categories: GA for general audiences, MA-13 for "mature audiences," and MA-17 "for adults, not appropriate for minors." These ratings were applied to a few hundred video games produced by Sega and other companies, but Congress felt the need for an independent rating system. Many in the industry also felt uncomfortable with a Sega-appointed rating council, claiming that Sega's ratings might be crafted to serve its individual corporate interests.

In December 1993, video-game executives speaking for 160 companies staged a press conference on Capitol Hill to announce plans for a new, industrywide rating system. Hoping to preempt legislation that would impose a rating system, the coalition of video-game producers and rental stores agreed to create a national system to rate the games for violence, sex, and profanity. Most of the game makers claimed that there was no scientific evidence establishing a causal link between video games and violent behavior, but Senator Joseph Lieberman (D-Conn.), accompanied by Captain Kangaroo and other children's advocates, promptly held his own Capitol Hill news conference to decry the proliferation of violent video games for children. Lieberman claimed that few parents would buy such games for their children if they knew what was in them.

Lieberman said that he would prefer that Congress ban such games, but he felt that they were constitutionally protected speech. Lieberman and Senator Herb Kohl (D-Wis.) then introduced legislation that would give the video-game industry one year to produce a credible, uniform rating system to warn parents. If the industry failed to produce its own rating or labelling system, the bill would create an independent council to impose such a system.

Lieberman and Kohl also called for action from the Federal Trade Commission and state attorneys general to control advertising that they claimed was illegally targeting children, for whom the violent games were rated as inappropriate. They wrote to the FCC urging the commission to take immediate action to halt false and misleading advertising that might induce consumers to purchase violent and inappropriate games for young children. At Senate hearings, a Sega TV ad was shown that depicted a schoolboy winning the respect of his peers by mastering video games. The ad concluded with the boy kicking over a tray of cookies brought to him by two cowering children as he shouted, "I said chocolate chip!"

Claiming that such games contributed to the growing violence in American society, the senators showed reporters segments of two of the more violent games, "Mortal Kombat" and "Night Trap." "Mortal Kombat" pits two martial arts warriors against each other, with the game players given the choices of killing the opponent by ripping his heart out, tearing off his head and spinal column, or other blood-spattering strategies. In "Night Trap," the player fights hooded killers who try to capture sorority sisters and drain their blood. Shortly after the news conference, Toys R Us announced that it would no longer sell "Night Trap."

Subsequent Senate hearings again suggested that the video-game industry might be a contributing cause to the nation's plague of violence. "The rating system must not be a fig leaf for the industry to hide behind," said Senator Lieberman. "They must also accept their responsibility to control themselves and stop producing the worst of this junk." The harshest criticism was aimed at Sega, the company that had produced controversial titles such as "Mortal Kombat," "Night Trap," and "Lethal Enforcer" ("Video Game Firms Yield on Ratings," *Washington Post*, December 10, 1993, p. F1).

The industry claimed that violent or sexually oriented games represent only a small fraction of the $5.5-billion video-game market, and that even those games were legitimate entertainment for adults and older children. Any government action to control the content of video games, said industry spokespersons, would amount to censorship.

When Senator Lieberman asked Sega's William White why "Night Trap" should be sold at all, White said that the game had been developed for an adult audience. He said that if the violent scenes from classic movies were gathered together out of context, they too would seem needlessly violent. Nintendo's executive vice president, Howard Lincoln, attempted to distance his company from Sega, claiming that Nintendo had kept violence to a minimum in its games.

Tom Zito, CEO of Digital Pictures, which created Sega's "Night Trap," chose to respond to congressional attacks in an op-ed article in the *Washington Post*. He complained that "Night Trap" had received the kind of media attention normally reserved for serial killers, natural disasters, and panda births and described the theatrical nature of congressional justice. "[S]ingling out violence on television and rap records, in films and on the pages of newspapers is a great case of political expediency. Politicians would rather spend a dime on a study that claims to link TV violence and crime in the streets than spend a dollar on cleaning up a crack house. Then they can simply point their fingers at the TV industry and ignore the real problem and its fiscal ramifications." Zito challenged the senators' characterization of "Night Trap," saying that it was simply a low-budget parody of a vampire film. He claimed that thirty seconds from PG films like *Jurassic Park* or *Bram Stoker's Dracula* would appear much more provocative or violent, and he concluded that if his name were Steven Spielberg or Francis Coppola, he would be receiving no criticism. Indeed, Zito said that he did not consider Digital Pictures to be a video-game company, but a company that made interactive films. Zito noted that in the first year of its marketing, "Night Trap" sold over 100,000 copies, and almost all of the warranty cards returned were from individuals between the ages of eighteen and twenty-five ("Senate Demagoguery," *Washington Post*, December 17, 1993, p. A25).

The video-game industry was deeply divided over the desirability of ratings. Ken Wasch, executive director of the Software Publishers Association, expressed fear of what he called "the politics of control." Still, under growing political pressure, the association presented a new ratings proposal to a meeting of industry executives in January 1994. The proposal would have video-game makers rate their own products for violence and sex, using a four-category system: suitable for all ages; for children aged six to thirteen; for children aged thirteen to seventeen; and for adults only. Details on the ratings were to be developed by an industry-appointed council that would include psychologists, educators, and parents. Manufacturers who falsely rated their games would be subject to fines imposed by the council.

If the ratings proposal was to be accepted, someone would need to administer it, and the Software Publishers Association seemed the most likely candidate. However, Sega suggested that the New York–based Council of Business Bureaus Inc., which oversees children's advertising, might be a more appropriate organization to administer an industrywide rating system. The Motion Picture Association of America (MPAA), which has been rating movies since 1968, was also considered, since many video games have begun to incorporate movie footage. MPAA President Jack Valenti had originally refused to apply his film-rating system to video games, but after meeting with game-industry executives, he admitted that the film and game industries were becoming virtually indistinguishable.

The assignment of ratings to video games is much more complex than rating a motion picture, since the games have multiple levels or "pathways" that can only be reached by the skillful player. How does one apply a single rating to a game that may have sixty hours of pathways? Some industry executives wanted individual companies to rate their own games, using industrywide guidelines and submitting their rationale to an industry panel that would, among other things, give consumers a chance to appeal the rating. But companies like Sega felt that the possibility of false or inconsistent ratings would be greatly increased if there were hundreds of different raters.

In late July 1994, members of the video-and computer-game industry visited Capitol Hill once more with two new ratings proposals. Congress was more receptive to the Interactive Digital Software Association's proposed five-category rating system: early childhood; age three and older; age six and older; teen, age seventeen and older; and adults only. To receive an IDSA rating, a video-game maker would have to submit a thirty–minute videotape including the most graphic or extreme scenes in the game to the Entertainment Software Ratings Board. Submitting material for review would be voluntary, but it was assumed that political and consumer pressure would force game makers to participate.

Members of Congress were less satisfied with the ratings system proposed by the Software Publishers Association, which rated levels of violence, sex, and profanity on a scale of one to four. Concern was expressed over the SPA's failure to specify appropriate ages for game players as well as SPA's statement that as much as 95 percent of the software industry's games would not trigger a rating. Under the SPA system, a proposed Recreational Software Advisory Council would assign ratings.

In the end, both ratings systems were implemented on a trial basis, and by the end of 1995, Congress joined with the Parent Teacher Association to issue a "report card" on how well the ratings had worked. Senator Lieberman, an early congressional advocate of ratings, announced at a press conference that, overall, the report card was "pretty good . . . , in the sense that more games are being rated and more retailers are requiring them."

Lieberman added, however, that the content of some of the games continued to be too violent.

Lieberman continued to favor the IDSA rating system, and he expressed hope that it would eventually become the universal standard for the industry. Many in the industry, however, maintained doubts about the effectiveness of any rating system. One industry executive said that ratings actually encouraged game makers to insert more violence in their games, because the worse the rating, the more attractive the game was to teenage boys. "I'm still opposed to them as a matter of principle," he said, "though, of course, we will get rated if the retail channels will not accept [the games] without it" ("The Games People Rate," *Washington Post*, December 13, 1995, p. F1).

REFERENCE: U.S. House of Representatives, Committee on Energy and Commerce, Subcommittee on Telecommunications and Finance, *Violence in Video Games: Hearing*, 103rd Cong., 2nd sess., June 30, 1994.

WARREN, EARL, 1891–1974   After receiving his law degree in 1914 from the University of California at Berkeley, Earl Warren worked for a few years for private law firms before enlisting in the Army in 1917. After World War I, Warren became a prosecutor for Alameda County, California, then became county district attorney and eventually California attorney general. In 1942, Warren was elected governor of California on a platform of liberal Republicanism. In 1948, he was chosen as running mate with Thomas E. Dewey in Dewey's unsuccessful challenge to President Truman.

In 1953, President Dwight D. Eisenhower nominated Warren as Chief Justice of the Supreme Court, and the Senate confirmed the nomination unanimously. In Warren's first major decision, *Brown v. Board of Education* (1954), he stated that racially segregated public schools deprived children of equal educational opportunities. Warren called for desegregation to proceed "with all deliberate speed."

By the mid-1950s, Warren had aligned himself with the Court's more libertarian members. Under Warren, the Court significantly broadened the rights of free speech and expression and limited the government's power to punish individuals for their beliefs or associations. On loyalty-security issues, Warren voted consistently with the individual against government control. In 1956, he spoke for the majority in overturning a conviction for sedition, and in 1957, his opinion for the majority reversed the contempt conviction of an individual who had refused to answer questions from the House Un-American Activities Committee.

As the civil rights movement grew, Warren delivered the Court's first ruling on sit-in demonstrations in a 1961 opinion that overturned the breach-of-peace convictions of sixteen black protesters. In 1962 and 1963, Warren spoke again for the Court in voiding the convictions of civil rights demonstrators. He also joined the majority in decisions prohibiting the exclusion of blacks from certain private restaurants.

In cases involving communism, Warren consistently voted against the government's position. He dissented from a 1961 Court decision sustaining provisions of two federal antisubversive laws, and during the same year, he opposed a ruling upholding contempt convictions of individuals who refused to answer questions before the House Un-American Activities Committee. In the next few years, he joined with the majority to overturn similar convictions. During the mid-1960s, the Warren Court restricted government action against members of the Communist Party, and in 1965, Warren wrote an important opinion overturning a federal law barring Party members from serving as union officials. He also spoke for the majority in a 1967 decision nullifying a federal statute that made it a crime for Communists to work at defense facilities. Between 1964 and 1968, the Warren Court also overturned numerous state loyalty-oath laws.

In 1962 and 1963, Warren joined the majority in holding that school prayer was a violation of the First Amendment guarantee of freedom of religion. In 1966, Warren spoke for a unanimous Court in ruling that the Georgia House of Representatives had violated Julian Bond's right of free speech by excluding him from the state legislature on the basis of his opposition to the Vietnam War.

Warren's last opinion for the Court was on June 16, 1969, when he reversed an appeals court decision by Warren Burger that had upheld the exclusion of Adam Clayton Powell from the U.S. House of Representatives. A week later, Chief Justice Earl Warren retired. Most analysts consider him to have been an outstanding Chief Justice whose dedication to the ideal of equal justice for all had an important impact on American law and society. REFERENCES: D. J. Herda, *Earl Warren: Chief Justice for Social Change*, Springfield, Enslow Publishers, 1995; Bernard Schwartz, *Super Chief, Earl Warren and His Supreme Court: Judicial Biography*, New York, New York University Press, 1983.

WHISTLEBLOWING   During the latter half of the twentieth century, as federal officials railed against the danger of leaks from within their agencies, the whistleblower emerged as a prominent challenge to government secrecy. The kinds of secrecy that have been revealed by whistleblowers in recent years cover everything from dangerous conditions at nuclear laboratories and power plants to falsified scientific data on the Strategic Defense Initiative (SDI). But the tradition of whistleblowing and its legislative basis go far back in American history.

In 1863, Abraham Lincoln discovered that the same horses were being sold several times to the Union cavalry and that sawdust was being added to the gunpowder. In response, Congress passed the False Claims Act, designed to encourage people who knew of such fraud to step forward. However, during World War II, military contractors succeeded in amending the law in ways that left it ineffective, and there has been little federal support for whistleblowers since then. President Nixon had a well-known distaste for whistleblowers, and in 1973, he increased and formalized reprisal techniques against them by having his Director of the White House Personnel Office, Fred Malek, issue a secret manual on how to purge whistleblowers without running afoul of the law. Ironically, whistleblowers eventually exposed the Malek manual, and it was published in the Watergate Committee's report.

The Civil Service Reform Act of 1978 created a whistleblowing disclosure channel through the Office of Special Counsel (OSC) that was also designed to protect whistleblowers from harassment. Within a few years of its passage, the Civil Service Reform Act proved to be not only inadequate to protect whistleblowers, but a legal basis for increased harassment. In 1982, Special Counsel Alex Kozinski was forced to resign after he was discovered teaching a course for federal managers on how to fire whistleblowers without OSC interference. Congress later considered a bill to abolish the OSC, which was described as a Trojan horse for whistleblowers—a legalized dirty-tricks unit that identified dissenters seeking help and then teamed up with employers to finish them off.

In 1986, Senator Charles Grassley (R-Iowa) led a successful fight to put teeth back into the False Claims Act, which allows individuals to sue private firms on behalf of the federal government if they believe that fraud has been committed. The False Claims Act protects the whistleblower from reprisal by allowing him to file separate claims against his employer if he has been discharged, demoted, threatened, or discriminated against as the result of his revelations. However, the extremely high cost of litigation has limited the use of the False Claims Act.

The Whistleblower Protection Act (H.R. 25) was proposed in 1986, but the threat of a presidential veto prevented action on the bill. In 1988, the House and Senate unanimously passed an almost identical bill, but President Reagan pocket-vetoed it. Finally, congressional negotiators convinced President Bush to accept the Whistleblower Protection Act of 1989, again passed unanimously. The new law was a strong affirmation of free speech and the right to dissent, but whistleblowers were still not entitled to a jury trial by their peers, but were forced instead to turn to the Special Counsel, whose abuses had led to the passage of this law.

Congress also passed the Military Whistleblower Act, providing military personnel with the same protection from reprisals that is provided to civilian whistleblowers. More important, it protects a whistleblower's right to communicate with Congress, which had previously triggered the most extreme reprisals. Unfortunately, enforcement of the new act is left in the hands of the Inspector General, regarded by military whistleblowers as the hatchet man for military services.

Despite these acts and others intended to protect whistleblowers, conscientious individuals still find themselves charged with "stealing" the evidence necessary to expose fraud or deception. Federal employees or government-contract workers are particularly vulnerable to this approach, which, like the British Official Secrets Act, proclaims that the government owns all the information it creates or maintains.

The distinction between "leaking" government information and blowing the whistle on government deception is tenuous. Sissela Bok, in her book *Secrets*, said that whistleblowers call attention to "negligence, abuses, or dangers that threaten the public interest. They sound an alarm based on their expertise or inside knowledge, often from within the very organization in which they work. With as much resonance as they can muster, they strive to breach secrecy, or else arouse an apathetic public to dangers everyone knows about but does not fully acknowledge." Unlike whistleblowing, said Bok, leaking need not concern danger, negligence, or abuse, though both forms of public revelation "bring something that is secret or unnoticed into the open from within an organization. . . . But when a leak from within does concern misconduct, it is a variant of whistleblowing, undertaken surreptitiously because the revealer cannot or does not want to be known as its source" (Sissela Bok, *Secrets: On the Ethics of Concealment and Revelations*, New York, Pantheon Books, 1982, p. 211). Thus the fundamental distinction between the leaker and the whistleblower is that one discloses information covertly while the other acts in public protest.

In 1988, leaker/whistleblower Samuel Loring Morison was sent to prison in a case establishing the legal precedent that giving classified government information to the press is a criminal act. Morison had been employed as a ship analyst at the Naval Intelligence Support Center (NISC) from 1974 to October 1984, when he was arrested for providing secret photos and technical information on Soviet ships to a conservative British magazine, *Jane's Defence Weekly*. Morison had been working part-time for Jane's Publishing Company, whose various military publications were devoted to magnifying the Soviet threat and advocating the need for a Western military buildup. In June 1984, after reading a classified NISC report, Morison sent a long memo to *Jane's* describing an explosion at the Soviet Severomorsk naval base. *Jane's* soon published a story based on the classified leak, a practice that had been common in the American press for years. In July, Morison mailed three U.S. spy-satellite photos of the Soviet Union's first nuclear-powered aircraft carrier to *Jane's*.

Morison was convicted of violating the Espionage Act of 1917 and an obscure government theft statute. His defense lawyers claimed that the espionage law used in this case was intended to apply to clandestine activities by spies and saboteurs, not public disclosures to the news media. They warned that by defining public communication of government information to be theft, the executive branch would be acquiring absolute control over what American citizens could be told. Part of the odd logic of the government's new interpretation of the Espionage Act was that the press would be criminally liable along with the leaker. *Jane's* could also have been prosecuted, but the cozy relationship between the U.S. Navy and this promilitary publishing house led the two of them to cooperate in convicting Morison.

The Supreme Court's subsequent refusal to hear the Morison case put legal force behind the Justice Department's interpretation of the Espionage Act while leaving dangerous ambiguity in the law. The law criminalizes disclosure of information "relating to the national defense" to those "not entitled to receive it," but it does not make clear whether reporters or even congressmen are "entitled" to access.

Perhaps overlooked in the legal debate on the Morison case was the harmless nature of the classified information that was disclosed to the public. The first count on which Morison was convicted concerned his memo about the Severomorsk explosion, yet reporters from CBS and UPI said that they had received the same information directly from administration sources. The second count concerned satellite photographs that the government admitted were of no consequence. In 1981, *Aviation Week and Space Technology* had actually published a KH-11 photograph of a Russian airstrip, and no one was reprimanded, much less charged with a crime.

Roland S. Inlow, the CIA official who had headed the committee directing the use of spy satellites, admitted that U.S. national security could not be hurt by Morison's disclosure. "The damage in terms of the technical characteristics . . . is zero," he said. "In my opinion the operational detail that is reflected in the fact of the photography is zero . . . and zero plus zero equals zero. That is the simplest way that I can put it; and I say that having deliberated a great deal about it."

When Morison appealed his convicion to the Fourth Circuit Court of Appeals in Richmond, news organizations submitted a friend-of-the-court brief arguing that the Espionage Act was being applied in a way that was unconstitutionally broad and violated the First Amendment rights of the leaker. The brief said that the leaker "is engaged in activity at the core of the First Amendment's protection," and that "the overall effect of public disclosures concerning the affairs of government is to enhance the people's ability to understand their government and to control their own destiny." Though the court of appeals unanimously upheld Morison's conviction, the judges acknowledged the case's substantial First Amendment aspects due to the troubling breadth of the Espionage Act. One judge called on Congress to step in and define the Act, but Congress has shown little inclination to address the subject (Philip Weiss, "The Quiet Coup," *Harper's Magazine*, September 1989, pp. 54–63).

In August 1989, the Bush administration's Justice Department reversed a decade-long policy of not prosecuting whistleblowers for unauthorized disclosure of government information. Attorney General Richard Thornburgh, responding initially to congressional complaints about politically motivated leaks from his own department, announced that he would not only track down all leakers and whistleblowers, but that he would send them to jail. Thornburgh had taken a new look at an old theft statute and decided that unauthorized disclosure of any government information to the press was a crime punishable by up to ten years in prison.

Among the hundreds of major whistleblower incidents during the last twenty years, a surprisingly large number have been in the areas of nuclear power and nuclear weapons. In 1984, a whistleblower at General Electric's nuclear fuels production facility in North Carolina was fired for attempting to enforce the industry's safety requirements. During the same year, engineers at the Diablo Canyon nuclear power plant charged manipulation of the data in the plant's seismic design review. As a result, they were transferred away, and replacement engineers were hired. In 1989, an employee at the Nuclear Regulatory Commission was the subject of retaliatory action after he told Congress of lax NRC regulation of drug and alcohol use at nuclear sites.

In 1990, the U.S. Navy cut the pay of four sailors on the USS *Nimitz* because they publicly questioned the ship's nuclear reactor safety. The Navy also fired an engineer for reporting flaws in the sonar systems on American nuclear submarines. Not only was he unable to get his job back, but private contractors, under orders from the Pentagon, blacklisted him.

In March 1996, *Time* magazine featured a cover story on two whistleblowers at Northeast Utilities, which operates five nuclear power plants in New England. George Galitis and George Betancourt, senior engineers at Northeast, had reported chronic safety problems in 1992, but they were ignored by plant officials. Two years later, Galitis reported the matter to the Nuclear Regulatory Commission. Again, there was no action, but by now Galitis was experiencing harassment, retaliation, and intimidation. Betancourt, who had given testimony to the NRC in support of Galitis's safety allegations, was threatened with termination and eventually transferred. A series of NRC investigations eventually confirmed the whistleblowers' charges, but their vindication came at heavy cost to their careers. Dozens of other employees at their plant suffered similar punishment, and workers were well aware of the dangers of speaking out. A 1996 Northeast internal document reported that 38 percent of employees "do not trust their management enough to willingly raise concerns [because of] a 'shoot the messenger' attitude" at the company (Eric Pooley, "Nuclear Warriors," *Time*, March 4, 1996, p. 46).

One of the more dramatic and ultimately unsuccessful whistleblowing incidents concerned the tragic *Challenger* space-shuttle mission. At 11:38 A.M. on January 28, 1986, on an unseasonably cold day, the space shuttle *Challenger* lifted off its Cape Canaveral launch pad. Just one minute and thirteen seconds into its journey, it exploded into an inferno before millions of horrified television viewers.

Six months before the *Challenger* launch, Roger Boisjoly, a structural engineer for Morton Thiokol, the company contracted by NASA to supply its booster rockets, had written a memo informing his supervisors that the booster rockets' crucial O-ring seals were dangerously flawed. At a management caucus shortly before the launch, Boisjoly used photographs of previously damaged O-rings in an unsuccessful attempt to convince the managers to cancel the launch. Within seconds after lift-off, the *Challenger* exploded before Boisjoly and the shocked engineers, who sat in stunned silence. Boisjoly said, "The beginning of hell started from that time on." Nearly a month after the *Challenger* explosion, Boisjoly was unhospitably treated as a messenger of unwelcome news during his testimony revealing the sorry history of the *Challenger* launch before the Rogers Commission investigating the disaster. The pressure within NASA to silence whistleblowers like Boisjoly was intense, but it may have been even more repressive within Morton Thiokol. Boisjoly's conscientiousness and candor were treated hostilely back in Utah, where Thiokol officials felt that his testimony had jeopardized the company's billion-dollar contract. Colleagues who had met with him on a daily basis would now turn away when they saw him coming. Even his neighbors in his home town of Willard, Utah, turned against him. Soon the strain was more than Boisjoly could handle. His doctor diagnosed him as having post traumatic stress disorder, and in January 1987, he went on disability leave from Morton Thiokol. The company quickly fired him. "I have never regretted what I have done," Boisjoly said, "and I would do it exactly the same way. I think the lesson that needs to be learned is that people have to stand up and have enough courage to stand by their convictions" ("Story behind the Story," NBC-TV special, November 3, 1990).

Another area in which whistleblowing has played a dramatic role is the Strategic Defense Initiative (SDI), popularly called "Star Wars." Roy Woodruff is a scientist who has spent his entire career working on weapons systems, yet he is best known as a whistleblower on Star Wars disinformation. In 1968, Woodruff joined the University of California's prestigious weapons lab, the Lawrence Livermore National Laboratory (LLNL), as a research physicist on projects in advanced nuclear explosive design, and he was subsequently named associate director for defense systems, the second-highest position at the lab.

From the beginning, Woodruff was a strong advocate of Ronald Reagan's Strategic Defense Initiative, but he soon became uneasy with politically slanted reports of SDI progress by LLNL physicists Edward Teller and Lowell Wood. Even the Pentagon was skeptical about Teller's claims, but because of President Reagan's unquestioning support for anything related to Star Wars, officials at LLNL continued to feed inaccurate and rosy reports to the White House.

As punishment for his complaints, Woodruff was banished to a window-less cubicle, and his salary was frozen. Woodruff's account of events at Livermore was subsquently confirmed by the finding of an in-house panel authorized to investigate his grievance. The panel concluded that he had suffered administrative reprisals simply because he expressed disagree-ment with Teller. A General Accounting Office investigation in December 1987 concluded that Batzel and other lab administrators had prevented Woodruff from correcting the one-sided reports from Teller and Wood. None of this vindication made life easier for Woodruff at LLNL. In 1990, under continuing pressure, Woodruff transferred to the lab in Los Alamos, New Mexico.

A more recent but similar story involves Aldric Saucier, the Strategic Defense Command's chief scientist for advanced technologies and archi-tectures. In 1991, after more than twenty-five years of government service, Saucier was ostracized, browbeaten, cursed, and physically abused by military supervisors after he spoke out within the Pentagon about gross waste and mismanagement in the Star Wars program. As a whistleblower, he submitted an affidavit to the Government Accountability Project (GAP) in April 1991, noting that he had an unblemished record until he began challenging Star Wars abuses. When Saucier was threatened with dismissal, lawyers from GAP contested the action as a violation of the Whistleblower Protection Act.

In addition to his charges of Pentagon fraud and abuse, Saucier echoed Roy Woodruff's conclusion that despite rosy public reports, the Pentagon never really believed that it could field a functioning Star Wars system. Saucier had first expressed his concerns about understated costs and in-flated claims for SDI in 1989, and despite his continuing warnings, he was ignored and isolated. A senior SDI engineer who worked with Saucier said,"He's a classic whistleblower type. He has high moral ideals. When he sees things are wrong, he is willing to fight."

On February 14, 1992, Saucier was fired. Representative John Conyers (D-Mich.), then chairman of the House Government Operations Commit-tee, charged that the firing had every appearance of retaliation. In a letter to Army Secretary Michael Stone, Conyers said that Saucier's dismissal raised "serious questions . . . of violations of the Whistleblower Protection Act, of personal grudges by military superiors, and even of deliberate falsification of documents by Saucier's supervisor" ("Army to Review Scientist's Firing," *Washington Post*, February 23, 1992, p. A12).

As criticism of Saucier's firing grew, Army Secretary Michael Stone suspended the dismissal and ordered a review of the case. Then, after the government's Office of Special Counsel found a "substantial likelihood" that Saucier's allegations of Pentagon fraud were well founded, Defense Secretary Richard Cheney was ordered to investigate those charges. At this point, the Special Counsel conferred official "whistleblower" status on Saucier.

Thomas Devine, legal director for the Government Accountability Project, called the case the first major test of the Whistleblower Protection Act because of the high political stakes and billions of dollars of contracts at risk. Unfortunately, the law failed the test when the Office of Special Counsel closed its investigation of Saucier's firing. Though many of Saucier's complaints were verified, an agency official said that there was no evidence of a prohibited personnel practice that would require corrective action. The separate Pentagon probe of Saucier's charges of waste and corruption resulted in a similar judgment, as the DOD's Office of Inspector General concluded that there was no violation of law, rule, or regulation within the Star Wars program. As a result of the two judgments, another whistleblower was removed from government employment, and the Star Wars program maintained its privileged political position and massive funding.

The painful experiences of whistleblowers like Boisjoly, Woodruff, and Saucier remain all too common. In late 1993, a General Accounting Office (GAO) survey of federal employees who sought protection under whistleblower laws found overwhelming dissatisfaction with the Office of Special Counsel (OSC), the government agency authorized to investigate whistleblowers' allegations. The GAO survey found that 81 percent of respondents gave the OSC low marks for fairness, efficiency, competency, and responsiveness. Seventy-eight percent of respondents did not believe that OSC investigations obtained the information necessary to properly examine their claims, and 88 percent said that reprisals had taken place after they complained of waste, fraud, or abuse. About 76 percent said that the OSC generally or primarily acted in the interests of the agency, not the whistleblower.

Evidence like the 1993 GAO survey convinced many in Congress that whistleblower laws needed revision, and toward that end other studies were conducted. A 1996 survey by the Department of Health and Human Services once more found that the majority of people who reported scientific misconduct faced some form of retaliation, but there was an encouraging aspect to the HHS survey as well. It turned out that a substantial majority of whistleblowers were eventually able to go on with their careers with no lasting damage. "On the one hand, these findings refute the notion that every whistleblower suffers substantial negative consequences," said the HHS report. "On the other, they confirm that whistleblowers frequently face the prospect of significant hardship for their efforts" (Justin Gillis, "Whistleblowing: What Price among Scientists?" *Washington Post*, December 28, 1995, p. A21).

Whistleblowing and leaking are citizen responses to widespread governmental secrecy and the official inclination to extend property rights to government information. In her book *Secrets*, Sissela Bok stated: "The alarms of whistleblowers would be unnecessary were it not for the many threats to the public interest shielded by practices of secrecy in such domains as law, medicine, commerce, industry, science, and government. Given these practices, whistleblowers perform an indispensable public service; but they do so at great human cost, and without any assurance that they uncover most, or even the worst, abuses. While they deserve strong support in their endeavors, every effort should therefore be made to combat the problems they signal by other means." Bok concluded: "The most important task is to reduce the various practices of collective secrecy in order to permit the normal channels of public inquiry to take the place of whistleblowing and of leaking. The more encrusted a society becomes with unnecessary secrecy, confidential procedures, systems of classification, and means of corporate, professional, and administrative self-protection, the harder it is for the public to learn in time about risks and wrongdoing" (Sissela Bok, *Secrets: On the Ethics of Concealment and Revelations*, New York, Pantheon Books, 1982, pp. 211, 228).

REFERENCES: Myron Glazer, *The Whistleblowers: Exposing Corruption in Government and Industry*, New York, Basic Books, 1989; Gerald Vinten, ed., *Whistleblowing: Subversion or Corporate Citizenship?*, New York, St. Martin's Press, 1994.

WILDMON, DONALD E., 1938– Donald Wildmon is a conservative minister best known for his efforts to reduce sex and violence on television. He founded the Coalition for Better Television in 1981 to organize advertiser boycotts against networks whose programming was not sufficiently "wholesome." Wildmon is also president of the American Family Association, an organization that has conducted challenges to films and TV shows, including *The Last Temptation of Christ* and the cartoon *Mighty Mouse*. Wildmon is the author of several religious books, including *Stand Up to Life: A Man's Reflection on Living*.

REFERENCE: Donald E. Wildmon, *Don Wildmon: The Man the Networks Love to Hate*, Wilmore, Bristol Books, 1989.

WOMEN AGAINST PORNOGRAPHY Women against Pornography (WAP) was founded in 1979 by a group of antipornography feminists, including Susan Brownmiller, author of *Against Our Will*. The organization attempts to educate the public about the degrading and brutalizing effects of pornography on women. It provides tours, programs, and multimedia materials showing the dangers of pornography, and it offers a referral service to victims of pornography and sexual abuse.

The organization's newsletter, *Women against Pornography—Newsreport*, is published two to four times per year, providing information on WAP's activities and the feminist antipornography movement. It also analyzes current trends and legislation related to pornography and sexual violence.

Women against Pornography is located at P.O. Box 845, Times Square Station, New York, NY 10108–0845. Dorchen Leidholdt is its contact person.

REFERENCE: Jonathon Green, New York, Facts on File, *The Encyclopedia of Censorship*, 1990.

ZAPPA, FRANK, 1940–1993   Frank Zappa was ten years old when his family moved from Maryland to California, where his romance with avant-garde music and rock and roll began. He made more than sixty albums, most of them with his group, the Mothers of Invention. His heroes were composers like Stravinsky, Webern, and Varese, and there was no place on rock-and-roll radio for most of his unique and provocative music. He nonetheless became an influential figure in modern popular music, with a wide following that remained loyal even as musical fashions changed.

Zappa opposed the drug culture even as he encouraged the young to rebel against the corruption of government. His opposition to censorship led him into frequent confrontation with powerful institutions, governmental and private. In September 1985, Zappa appeared before the Senate Commerce Committee hearing testimony on proposals to establish a rating system for records and tapes to warn the buyers of potentially offensive lyrics. A group called the Parents' Music Resource Center (PMRC) demanded R and X ratings on records, and Tipper Gore, wife of then Senator Al Gore (D-Tenn.), spoke in favor of similar restrictions on lyrics and album covers.

Frank Zappa testified that the federal government had no business censoring or otherwise calling attention to controversial lyrics. He was challenged by Senator Paula Hawkins (R-Fla.), who said that Zappa's children required the same protection from bad records as they did from bad toys. When Zappa expressed some doubt about the need for ratings on toys, Hawkins sarcastically said that she would be interested in seeing what toys his children owned. Zappa invited her to come on over to his house so he could show them to her.

At the conclusion of the five-hour hearings, there was general agreement that Congress would be ill advised to involve itself in legislative action to cleanse the record industry of offensive music, but the question of how to protect American youth from the dangers of rock and roll continued to bedevil American society. In 1990, a *USA Today* editorial asked musicians, record producers, and retailers to develop a set of "voluntary" labels, comparable to those used by the movie industry, to help parents learn what musical messages kids were receiving about sex and drugs. In an opposing view shown next to the editorial, Frank Zappa warned against "voluntary" labelling. Zappa described the labelling plan proposed by the Parents' Music Resource Center as a "Twilight Zone" scenario in which the Recording Industry Association of America, which represents the record companies, signs away the First Amendment rights of all recording artists and music retailers to a tax-exempt organization representing the lunatic fringe of Christendom. Zappa concluded by stating that the censor's belief in bad words was a religious concept. "Those who choose to believe this voodoo are welcome to it—the First Amendment guarantees that freedom. But it also guarantees everyone else that these 'no choice people' may not impose their beliefs on others through laws" (Frank Zappa, "Protect Us from 'Voluntary' Labels," *USA Today*, January 10, 1990, p. A8).

On December 4, 1993, Frank Zappa died of prostate cancer at the age of fifty-two. After his death, his family designated the American Library Association's Office for Intellectual Freedom and the Freedom to Read Foundation to receive memorial donations. The Freedom to Read Foundation then established the Frank Zappa Memorial Fund to receive such contributions.

REFERENCES: Ben Watson, *Zappa: The Negative Dialectics of Poodle Play*, New York, St. Martin's Press, 1995; Frank Zappa, *Them or Us*, New York, Barking Pumpkin Press, 1984.

ZENGER, JOHN PETER, ca. 1697–1746   John Peter Zenger was a German emigrant to colonial America who became the focus of one of America's earliest and most important newspaper-censorship cases. As printer of the *New York Weekly Journal*, he frequently spoke in opposition to the policies of the British colonial government, as represented in the government paper, the *Weekly Gazette*. In 1734, an official committee was appointed to investigate Zenger and his paper on charges of seditious libel, and his articles on the liberty of the press were specifically found to be libelous as charged. Zenger's articles were ordered to be burned, and he was arrested and jailed pending trial.

Andrew Hamilton, then a distinguished Philadelphia lawyer, and James Alexander, a founder of the American Philosophical Society, formed

Zenger's defense team. The basis of the argument for the defense was that the truth cannot be libelous. When the court rejected this argument, the defense successfully argued that juries, not judges, should determine the law and the facts in such cases. The jury returned a verdict of not guilty, setting an informal precedent used in many subsequent free-speech trials. The details of the case were documented in *A Brief Narrative of the Case and Tryal of John Peter Zenger*, published in 1736.

REFERENCES: Livingston Rutherfurd, *John Peter Zenger: His Press, His Trial, and a Bibliography of Zenger Imprints*, New York, Arno, 1970 [c.1904]; John Peter Zenger, *A Brief Narrative of the Case and Trial of John Peter Zenger, Printer of the New York Weekly Journal*, by James Alexander. Edited by Stanley Nider Katz, 1989 [c.1963].

SELECTED BIBLIOGRAPHY

Baker, C. Edwin. *Human Liberty and Freedom of Speech*. New York: Oxford University Press, 1989.

Black, Gregory D. *Hollywood Censored: Morality Codes, Catholics, and the Movies*. New York: Cambridge University Press, 1994.

Black, Hugo. *A Constitutional Faith*. New York: Alfred A. Knopf, 1969.

Blanchard, Margaret. *Revolutionary Sparks: Freedom of Expression in Modern America*. New York: Oxford University Press, 1992.

Chafee, Zechariah, Jr. *Free Speech in the United States*. Cambridge: Harvard University Press, 1941.

Curry, Richard O., ed. *Freedom at Risk*. Philadelphia: Temple University Press, 1988.

Demac, Donna A. *Keeping America Uninformed: Government Secrecy in the 1980's*. New York: Pilgrim Press, 1984.

Dick, Bernard F. *Radical Innocence: A Critical Study of the Hollywood Ten*. Lexington: University Press of Kentucky, 1989.

Dorsen, Norman, ed. *The Evolving Constitution*. Middletown, Conn.: Wesleyan University Press, 1987.

Dorsen, Norman, and Gillers, Stephen, eds. *None of Your Business: Government Secrecy in America*. New York: Viking Press, 1974.

Dycus, Stephen, Berney, Arthur L., Banks, William C., and Raven-Hansen, Peter. *National Security Law*. Boston: Little, Brown and Co., 1990.

Emerson, Thomas I. *The System of Freedom of Expression*. New York: Vintage Books, 1971.

Halperin, Morton, and Hoffman, Daniel. *Top Secret: National Security and the Right to Know*. Washington, D.C.: New Republic Books, 1977.

Jensen, Carl. *Censored: The News That Didn't Make the News—and Why: The 1996 Project Censored Yearbook.* New York: Seven Stories Press, 1996.

Levy, Leonard, ed. *Freedom of the Press from Zenger to Jefferson.* Indianapolis: Bobbs-Merrill, 1966.

Lofton, John. *The Press as Guardian of the First Amendment.* Columbia: University of South Carolina Press, 1980.

Martin, Shannon E. *Bits, Bytes, and Big Brother: Federal Information Control in the Technological Age.* Westport, Conn.: Praeger, 1995.

Navasky, Victor S. *Naming Names.* New York: Penguin, 1981.

O'Brien, David M. *The Public's Right to Know: The Supreme Court and the First Amendment.* New York: Praeger, 1981.

Relyea, Harold. *Silencing Science: National Security Controls and Scientific Communication.* Norwood, N.J.: Ablex Pub., 1994.

Sharkey, Jacqueline E. *Under Fire: U.S. Military Restrictions on the Media from Grenada to the Persian Gulf.* Washingtion, D.C.: Center for Public Integrity, 1991.

Spitzer, Matthew L. *Seven Dirty Words and Six Other Stories: Controlling the Content of Print and Broadcast.* New Haven: Yale University Press, 1986.

Wise, David. *The Politics of Lying: Government Deception, Secrecy, and Power.* New York: Random House, 1973.

TABLE OF CASES

INDEX

Page numbers for main entries appear in **boldface** type.

About the Author

HERBERT N. FOERSTEL is the former Head of Branch Libraries at the University of Maryland, College Park, and currently serves on the Board of the National Security Archive, located at George Washington University. His previous books include: *Surveillance in the Stacks* (Greenwood, 1991), *Secret Science* (Praeger, 1993), *Banned in the USA* (Greenwood, 1994), and with Karen Foerstel, *Climbing the Hill* (Praeger, 1996).